# Thought Patterns for a Successful Career®
## PX2® Higher Education

THE PACIFIC
INSTITUTE®

7600-500-0810

Book

Tice, L. and Pace, J. (2010). *Thought Patterns for a Successful Career*. italics

Seattle, WA: The Pacific Institute, Inc.

Copyright MMX, The Pacific Institute, Inc.
1709 Harbor Avenue SW • Seattle, WA  98126-2049
(206) 628-4800  • (800) 426-3660 • Fax (206) 587-6007
www.thepacificinstitute.com
7600-500-0510

# About Thought Patterns for a Successful Career® / PX2® Higher Education

The foundation of all human action is human thought. Our thought process forms the foundation upon which we build every facet of our lives. Therefore, it is important for each of us to understand how our minds work – how we got the habits and attitudes, the beliefs that may stand in the way of releasing our vast inner potential and leading fulfilling and purposeful lives. Our beliefs and expectations about ourselves, our families, our organizations – indeed, our world – are directly reflected in our "performance reality."

*Thought Patterns for a Successful Career / PX2 Higher Education* is designed to build your understanding, with a structured process, of how your mind works, and how you can control the way you think to achieve success – in any part of your life that you desire. Based on decades of research in the fields of cognitive psychology and social learning theory, the education presented here stands at the forefront, reflecting the qualities and characteristics of high-performance individuals and organizations.

Vividly presenting the concepts and education on video, Lou Tice provides revealing and productive insights into how you think and how your thoughts affect how you act. This information unlocks a toolbox of skills and applications that unleashes your potential in ways you never before thought possible. These tools and techniques can be applied immediately, to help you reach your goals easily and enjoyably. Life is propelled out of the ordinary and into an exciting adventure.

By your participation in this program, you join millions upon millions of people around the world who have discovered that the path to true success lies in their own thinking. From small business proprietors to Fortune 1000 executives; from clergy to the military; from educators to political leaders, the economically disadvantaged and prison inmates; from students to bureaucrats, athletes, healthcare professionals and high-tech industries – all are using this information, this education, to make a positive difference in the world around them.

# About The Pacific Institute®, Inc.

The Pacific Institute was founded by Lou and Diane Tice, in 1971. Since then, the company has expanded onto six continents and into over 60 countries, and its programs have been translated into a multitude of languages. It has developed a reputation for offering the most practical and enlightening programs ever to come out of the fields of cognitive and self-image psychology and high-achiever research. International headquarters for The Pacific Institute is in Seattle, Washington.

The guiding principle of The Pacific Institute is that individuals have a virtually unlimited capacity for growth, change and creativity, and can adapt readily to the tremendous changes taking place in this fast-paced, technological age. Central to this is that individuals are responsible for their own actions, and can regulate their behavior through a structured process that includes goal-setting, self-reflection and self-evaluation, among other things.

By applying The Pacific Institute's education, people are able to develop their potential by changing their habits, attitudes, beliefs and expectations. This, in turn, allows individuals in an organizational setting to achieve higher levels of growth and productivity, as well as shifting the collective behavior. This shift leads to more constructive organizational cultures, and healthier, higher performing workplaces.

Solidly grounded in the latest research coming out of the fields of cognitive psychology and social learning theory, documented results clearly show measurable increases in organizational effectiveness and productivity after applying The Pacific Institute concepts.

# About Lou Tice

He may have started out as a high school teacher and football coach, but a belief in "no limits" has led Lou Tice to become one of the most highly respected educators in the world today. His singular style of teaching – taking the complex concepts and current research results from the fields of cognitive psychology and social learning theory, and making them easy to understand and even easier to use – has brought him students from all over the globe.

Lou Tice believes that excellence is a process – an achievable, continuous process that inevitably results when we learn to control how we think, what we expect and what we believe. International business, political and military leaders consult with him on how to do more with less and bring out the best in those with whom they work. Top athletes come to him for help with mastering the psychological aspects of peak performance. He works with educators on strategies that motivate both staff and students to set and achieve meaningful goals.

Lou's experience in working with Fortune 1000 companies spans over 35 years. When working with organizations, Lou translates his message into practical applications that impact corporate culture and group performance.

Lou's ability as a consummate teacher and mentor has brought him to some of the world's hot spots: to the leaders of Northern Ireland, where he has worked since the mid-80's; to Guatemala, where he has worked since the signing of the Peace Accords in 1995; and to South Africa, from before the end of the era of apartheid to this very day. In 2004, he brought his considerable talents to bear in an on-going partnership with then—University of California head football coach, Pete Carroll, to make a positive difference in South Los Angeles.

Born and raised in Seattle, Washington where he and Diane, his wife, still make their home, Lou received his bachelor's degree from Seattle University. He went on to earn an MA in Education from the University of Washington, with a major focus in the mental health sciences. Lou is the internationally recognized author of the popular books, *Smart Talk for Achieving Your Potential* and *Personal Coaching for Results.* He is also co-editor, with Dr. Glenn Terrell, of the *Cultures of Excellence* book series.

In the final analysis, Lou Tice is a masterful teacher and educator who is remarkably successful at empowering individuals to achieve their full potential.

# About Dr. Joe Pace

Dr. Joe Pace is a nationally known speaker who conducts seminars and workshops in areas of school management, faculty development, student retention, psychology, and motivation. He has instructed thousands of college-level students in the areas of psychology, personal development, and business administration.

He has earned a Doctorate in Education, a Masters degree in psychological counseling, and a Bachelors degree in business administration. His doctoral dissertation and over 30 years of research, concerning success concepts and innovative student retention and persistence techniques, have been the sources for his authoring numerous articles and lecturing internationally.

Dr. Pace, psychologist and former college president, currently serves as the Managing Partner of the Education Initiative for The Pacific Institute. He is the creator of the *Success Strategies for Effective Colleges and Schools* program, which has been implemented internationally by The Pacific Institute. He is also an educational and psychological consultant for various schools, colleges and organizations throughout the United States and Canada.

From 1974 to 1988, Dr. Pace was Chairman of the Board and President of Prospect Hall College in Hollywood, Florida. Before joining Prospect Hall College, he was the Director at Fort Lauderdale University; prior to relocating to Florida, he served as the Director of Jamestown Business College in Jamestown, New York.

Dr. Pace was appointed, by the Governor of Florida, to the Florida State Department of Education's nine-member licensing commission for private schools, serving on the commission for ten years, and elected chairman twice. Additionally, he is a former president of the Florida Association of Postsecondary Schools and Colleges.

On a national level, Dr. Pace served as Commissioner of the Accrediting Council for Independent Colleges and Schools in Washington, DC. He served on the Executive Committee of the Council and also on the Board of Directors of the Association of Independent Colleges and Schools, currently known as the Career College Association CCA).

# Using this Manual

This book is designed and written to supplement the video and audio programs. This investment is in yourself, and the manual is designed to enhance and expand those excellent qualities you already possess. Your active participation will cause a wealth of effective, practical, self-educating concepts to come alive for you.

The reflective questions in each unit are designed for just that – reflection. As the Greek philosopher Plato once said, "The unexamined life is not worth living." This course gives you time to think about what you think about – something most of us do not take the time to do. The reflective questions will help you see how the concepts can apply immediately to your quest for education, and to the way you run your life, your family, your team or organization.

In this process, you are the co-author with Lou. Thus, you are urged to not view this manual as a work designed for passive reading. It is a guide for your personal fulfillment and future purpose. Like you, it is a work in progress.

## Introduction to Journal Writing

You are encouraged to keep a personal journal. A journal is similar to a diary. Here are some examples of the type of information you record in your journal:

- Successes
- Setbacks – particularly how you overcome them
- "Ah-ha's" (major learning moments)
- Life events
- Your beliefs
- Information from your classes, good books you read or wise people you meet
- Your feelings about situations, both past and present
- Information to identify where you are getting in your own way
- Your goals and affirmations
- Dialogues with yourself, so that you encourage you with positive self-talk when you feel discouraged
- Etc., etc., etc.

Keep your journal. Always date your journal entries. Review it often. You will be amazed at how much you discover about you. You may more easily recognize behavior patterns that are getting in your way, beliefs that no longer serve you well, scotomas to problems or solutions. Once you recognize a problem, you can overcome it by writing an affirmation.

For more information about The Pacific Institute's products and services, please call 1-800-426-3660 (U.S. and Canada) or visit our website at www.thepacificinstitute.com.

# A Note from Lou

We are going to deal with some very powerful material in this course. I am going to show you how to turn yourself loose in a way you have never been turned loose before. Do not think of this text as a workbook. Rather, think of it as an affirmative guide we are co-authoring. Think of this text as being your book, your chart, your guideline to personal growth and excellence – the kind of growth you never believed possible.

What I intend to help you do is to throw away many invalid, conditioned beliefs you now have. As we work together in this book, you will see how practical this information can be. A whole planned, positive way to enhance your life is open to you. You will not only grow yourself, but you will also show the people around you how they can grow too. You will learn how to achieve goals you never thought possible before – personal, family, spiritual, organizational, whatever you choose. There is no limit, I assure you. You will learn how to increase your self-efficacy – your ability to make things happen – both personally and professionally.

In this course, we will compare restrictive, negative ways of thinking with constructive, positive concepts we have always had at our disposal. These are live, vibrant concepts that will help you break out of old traps. I will show you that we have unlimited potential for growth and creativity.

By applying yourself to this program, by giving it your own reflective input, you will see that most barriers to personal growth and development are self-imposed. You will see that we live and work on partial beliefs, partial truths, and that sometimes we function with false beliefs. A wealth of sound psychological material has been condensed here. I have presented it in practical, easy-to-understand concepts. Our basic premise is this: we act, we work, we produce, we behave, not in accordance with the truth, but only with the truth as we perceive it to be. You will see throughout this curriculum and exercises it asks of you, that if we change the way we think, we can change the way we act.

So, let us now get on with your life. What you are about to learn is as practical as balancing your checkbook. Once you have learned these principles, you will be amazed at what you can really do and become.

Let us begin to open doors together.

*Lou Tice*

# Acknowledgements

## Program Development

Lou Tice, M.A. Education

Joe Pace, Ph.D. Education

## Curriculum Advisors

Diane Tice, B.A. Education

Glenn Terrell, Ph.D. Psychology

## Video and Audio Production and Editing

Christy A. Watson, B. A.

Chris Christmas

## Written Text and Editing

Joe Pace, Ph.D.

Scott Fitzgibbon, Ph.D.

Christy A. Watson, B.A.

Ali Klister

## Layout and Design

Courtney Cook Hopp

## Other Contributors

Our thanks to The Pacific Institute staff, project directors and many interested facilitators and seminar participants. A special "thank you" to our studio audience.

# Table of Contents

## My Thought Patterns for a Successful Career

## COURSE OVERVIEW
# Looking Forward Safely

## Unit Overview

Up until today, many of us have let a fear of new things, new places or new people keep us from moving toward the futures we want for ourselves and our families. No more. Throughout this course, we will gain the knowledge, and learn the tools and techniques that will help us attain our best futures.

## Unit Objectives

*By the end of this unit, I will:*

- understand how to begin helping myself get ready for my future, in my imagination.

- know that this course will teach me what I need to know to be successful.

- know the importance of comfort zones.

## WHO IS IN CHARGE?

## COURSE OVERVIEW
# Looking Forward Safely

## Key Concepts

- Comfort Zones

- Visualization

- Anxiety

- Tension

- Fear

- Subconscious

- Potential

- Self-Concept

- Self-Talk

- Locus of Control

## Notes

## COURSE OVERVIEW
# Looking Forward Safely

**Notes**

## Reflective Questions

What are some of the reasons I am going to school?

What do I want my life to look like when I finish school?

## COURSE OVERVIEW
# Looking Forward Safely

## Personal Beliefs Inventory

Please read each statement and place a check in the box that most accurately describes your beliefs and/or feelings.

| | | Strongly Agree | Agree | Mildly Agree | No Opinion | Mildly Disagree | Disagree | Strongly Disagree |
|---|---|---|---|---|---|---|---|---|
| 1 | When I enter a new situation, I typically see others as smarter than me. | | X | | | | | |
| 2 | My past successes are due to luck. | | | | | | X | X |
| 3 | I expect to be successful in life. | | | | | | X | |
| 4 | When life events are difficult, I can adapt. | | X | | | | | |
| 5 | I have complete control of my attitude. | | X | | | | | |
| 6 | I have virtually no alternatives in my life. | | | | | | X | |
| 7 | Outside events have a great impact on my life. | | X | | | | | |
| 8 | When my mind is made up, there is no changing it. | | | X | | | X | |
| 9 | My past successes are because of me. | | X | | | | | |
| 10 | I can change if I want to change. | | X | | | | | |
| 11 | I know how my self-talk impacts my attitude. | | X | | | | | |
| 12 | I am responsible for my own happiness. | | X | | | | | |
| 13 | My happiness is increased when my goals are met. | | X | | | | | |
| 14 | Goal setting is worthwhile. | | | | | | X | |
| 15 | I like me. | | X | | X | | | |
| 16 | I know how to set goals. | | X | | | | | |
| 17 | I am satisfied with my current situation. | | | X | X | | | |
| 18 | I rarely miss a day of work or school due to illness. | | X | | | | | |
| 19 | I rely on others to motivate me. | | | | | | X | |
| 20 | Good things happen because I cause them to happen. | | X | | | | | |
| 21 | I am capable of making changes in my personal life. | | X | | | | | |

## COURSE OVERVIEW
# Looking Forward Safely

| | | Strongly Agree | Agree | Mildly Agree | No Opinion | Mildly Disagree | Disagree | Strongly Disagree |
|---|---|---|---|---|---|---|---|---|
| 22 | I make friends easily. | | X | | | | | |
| 23 | I typically solve my own problems. | | X | | | | | |
| 24 | Despite the attitudes of others around me, I decide my own attitude. | | X | | | | | |
| 25 | I know how my self-talk impacts my feelings. | | X | | | | | |
| 26 | I am proud of who I am. | | X | | | | | |
| 27 | I know the feeling of wanting something so bad that I can "taste" it. | X | | | | | | |
| 28 | It is my choice to be whatever I want to be in life. | | X | | | | | |
| 29 | I know how to set goals so that they will come true. | | X | | | | | |
| 30 | When I believe I can do something, I do it. | | X | | | | | |
| 31 | I need support from others to succeed. | | | | | | X | |
| 32 | I can be my own worst enemy. | | X | | | | | |
| 33 | Getting the right job is up to me. | | X | | | | | |
| 34 | Self-talk has an impact on my behavior. | | X | | | | | |
| 35 | I am open to new ideas. | | X | | | | | |
| 36 | I typically picture what it is I want before I get it. | | X | | | | | |
| 37 | When I set my mind to it, I make things happen. | | X | | | | | |
| 38 | I have support from home. | | | | | | | X |
| 39 | I am satisfied with my personal life. | | X | | | | | |
| 40 | There are at least 3 things about me that I would like to change. | X | | | | | | |
| 41 | Attitude and success are directly related. | | X | | | | | |

*Assessment developed by Dr. Scott Fitzgibbon and Dr. Joe Pace*
*Licensed exclusively to The Pacific Institute, Inc. No part of this assessment may be reproduced, in any form,*
*without express written permission of The Pacific Institute.*

# COURSE OVERVIEW
# Looking Forward Safely

## Balance Wheel

Instructions:

1. Please consider the Balance Wheel below as a visual representation of the most important corporation in the world to you, Me Inc. In each of the slotted spokes, please identify the key functional areas of your life that are most important to you. If the sample works, please use it. If not, replace some of the suggestions with key functional areas more appropriate to you.

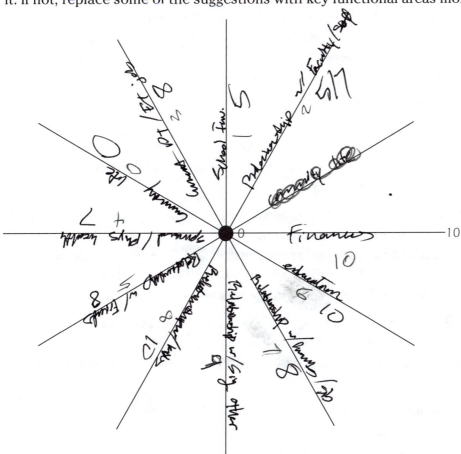

- Education
- Finances
- Relationship with Parents/Siblings
- Relationship with Significant Other
- Relationship with Kids
- Relationship with Friends
- Spiritual Life, Physical Health
- Community Life
- Current PT or FT Job
- School Involvement
- Relationship with Faculty/Staff

2. Next, please reflect on your personal satisfaction that you feel currently in your life with regard to each functional area. On a scale of 1 (lowest) to 10 (highest), please place a dot within each key functional area that represents your current satisfaction within that area of your life.

3. Next, please connect the dots to your wheel.

   • Does it give you any insights?

   • Are there any areas that you would like to change/grow?

## COURSE OVERVIEW
# Looking Forward Safely

## Summary

Let's say you have this little kid, five years old I suppose, about right for kindergarten. If the kid's mother or father wanted school to be the surprise of their life, do you know what to do? Don't talk about school. Surprise the kid on that first day. Load 'em up in the car and drive 'em to this building. The kid doesn't know what it is. Then say, "Have a nice day. I'll be back to get you about 4 o'clock." What would the kid do? Right, freak out.

Parents who do it right would probably play school at home, or they talk about school, or maybe even go to school and let the kid sit in the desk. Do you see the difference? What I'm leading you to is this: You need to prepare for your future in your mind, whether you're five years old, 20 or 30 years old. It doesn't matter. If you are surprised with something new, what goes on inside of you is anxiety and tension. That anxiety, subconsciously, causes you to want to go back to what's familiar, to what you know.

The principles that you're going to learn will show you how to get yourself ready for your future, so you can be at your best. Instead of running away from your future, you will run toward it. Some of you can look forward and scare yourself.

Let's take that five year old again. The parents could say, "Honey, you're going to school, and that teacher, I'm telling you, is she mean. If you get out of line, she's going to slap you silly. Have a nice day!" Wow. So, you can look forward and scare yourself with fear, or you can look forward with safety and security. You can look forward and see the benefit of being there. It's all going to be how you control the way you talk to yourself and the way you think in your mind.

You're also going to see that others around you, who've been there and got scared, will tell you, "Oh, that teacher is terrible," or, "That school is awful." What you need to learn to do is to control not only what you think, but you need to be able to block out information that might scare you or make you quit.

Have you ever been to a ball game, theater or school, and needed to use a rest room? Have you ever gone into the wrong rest room? You have in your mind where you belong. If you're a woman you belong in "Ladies," and if you're a man, you belong in the "Men's" room. Now, think about this. You actually have the potential to use either one, right? But the way your mind works, if you accidentally find yourself in the wrong one, what happened? Have you ever done that? What happens when you find yourself in the wrong one? Do you get really nervous about someone seeing you in the wrong restroom? Do you stay? No, you get out of there!

So, even though you need to use it, and even though you have the potential, you have the know-how, isn't it hard to use your potential when you're in the wrong rest room? That's my whole point to you. You need to learn how to prepare yourself in your mind. The whole idea is this: The image in your mind (this is what we're going to talk about) is what you've assimilated into

# COURSE OVERVIEW
## Looking Forward Safely

your mind about the way your world looks, what your friends are like, and where you belong. You got that from your mothers and fathers, and where you grew up. This image can become a trap, a kind of a restriction on where you let yourself go or the kind of business you have. A lot of people, they won't go more than just a few miles away from where they grew up. It's not because they don't have the potential, but because, in their mind, everything is so different.

If you came to the United States from the Philippines or Africa or Asia, there would be a lot of differences. How would you feel? At first, you feel like you don't fit. If you didn't have some reason to stay, or you couldn't go back, you probably would have found lots of reasons to go back to the familiar. Your job will be to make the new business, the new career, or your new relationships more familiar, in your mind, than what is in there now. Most of you didn't deliberately put in what's in your mind. It was what your brothers and sisters knew, or where you were raised, the religion you were brought up in, or whether you were brought up in wealth or poverty.

In your mind, this is called your self-concept. That self-concept creates a comfort zone, as long as your senses tell you everything looks about right. When it doesn't look right, it's like being in the wrong rest room. It's like a little kid going to school without being briefed ahead of time, in their mind.

I work with some of the best athletes in the world, Olympic swimmers, etc. Now, I can't even swim from here to the camera. Why would they come to me? Because I know how to help them be their best in competition. If you left your own local swimming pool, in your own country, and traveled to someplace like China or London or Germany, wow, it's like the wrong rest room. What happens, you're going to see later on, is you tighten up physically. You don't think correctly. Even though you have the knowledge and the skill or the potential, you can't use it.

What an advantage you're going to have when you learn this information! You're going to keep yourself from rationalizing, or making excuses like, "I'm going to stay with my friends, in my neighborhood." "I'm going to do what my dad did." "I'm going to do what my mother did." You're going to allow yourself to really grow, to get way, way past where you are, if you want to. That's what I'm going to teach you.

When you're out of your comfort zone, the anxiety and tension inside you increases. It squeezes off recall. It squeezes off your memory. If you were taking a test, and you knew the answers the night before, as you go and take the test, you just can't remember the answers. Have you ever had that happen? Probably. So, what you tell yourself is, "I'm stupid. I can't remember. I must not be good at this." Wrong reasons. You didn't practice in your mind, like the five year old about to go to school. You need to learn to make yourself feel safe and comfortable in a test setting, or an interview, or wherever you're going to go. You don't force yourself into it, or push yourself into it. I'm going to show you how to visualize, like astronauts do. They practice in their mind. Great

# COURSE OVERVIEW
# Looking Forward Safely

athletes practice in their mind. They visualize what the environment will look like. They talk about what they want.

I'm also going to teach you about self-talk. How you talk to yourself is going to be important, and who you listen to is going to be important. You must stop listening to people who try to scare you, or tell you what's stupid. You're going to learn to make up your own mind. I want you to become skeptical, not cynical, but skeptical, because there are going to be a lot of people who will try to talk you out of your future.

I'm going to show you what high performance people in the world actually think and how they think. Now, it's up to you to do it. I'm going to teach you how to change your mind. I'm going to teach you why you should change your mind. Just like that five year old, if they don't expand their mind, safely, into the first grade or second grade or third grade, they will be frightened all the time and act like they're dumb or stupid. They aren't stupid, they're just out of place. When you're out of place, you can't think. You can't remember. You block information. There are so many things that happen. The tendency is to think, "Well, I don't have the aptitude. I'm not smart enough," or so on. There probably are some classes or situations you've been in where you told yourself, "I just can't do that," like talking in front of people. You can do it. You can do it very well, but not if you don't practice in your mind.

For astronauts, simulators are built for them, so they can rehearse in their mind, safely, what they need. I'm going to teach you how to do all this, but whether you do it or not, that's all up to you. I'm not going to make you do anything. I'm just going to show you what to do. Now, it isn't enough to understand it. You want to practice it. Practice it socially, or when you're taking a test. Practice it when you're going for an interview. Practice it when you're going to meet new friends. Let yourself expand.

That's what this course is all about. There's one very important principle: It's called the locus of control. Now, I had to look that up myself. It just means, "Who's in charge?" Is it in the stars, is it in my horoscope? Is it outside of me that's controlling my life, or is it inside of me? Got it? Now, there's always going to be some stuff outside, but most of it is inside. I want to show you, if you change your mind and can improve the way your reality looks in your mind, I swear to you, the world around you will respond similarly.

The whole idea is this: How do I change my mind? Why do I change my mind? I'm not going to tell you what to change to. That's your business. That's what you want to do. But I'm going to show you why you change your mind, how to change your mind, and I'll give you some suggestions on what others have done that make them successful.

That's what the course is all about. Are you interested? Okay, stay tuned. There's more to come.

# UNIT 1
# What's Holding Me Back?

## Unit Overview

The question we must all ask ourselves is, "Am I seeing all there is to see?" Most of us don't realize that we don't see everything because of the way we were raised, where we were raised and how we were taught. The good news is that we can see more than we've seen in the past, and this will open up a new future for each of us.

## Unit Objectives

*By the end of this unit, I will:*

- know that I have real potential.

- understand scotomas.

- realize that everybody has scotomas, we just don't know where they are.

- know that I am smart and capable, and that scotomas are caused by my past conditioning.

# WE BEHAVE AND ACT NOT IN ACCORDANCE WITH THE TRUTH OF OUR REAL POTENTIAL, BUT ACCORDING TO THE TRUTH AS WE BELIEVE IT TO BE.

# UNIT 1
# What's Holding Me Back?

## Key Concepts

- Beliefs

- Conditioning

- Potential

- Skeptical

- Perception

- Scotoma

- Reality

## Notes

# UNIT 1
# What's Holding Me Back?

**Notes**

# UNIT 1
# What's Holding Me Back?

## Reflective Questions

- What are the benefits of knowing I have scotomas?

- What beliefs or thoughts do I have that might be limiting me in completing my education?

# UNIT 1
# What's Holding Me Back?

## Reflective Questions

- Where am I stuck? Why? (The way I was raised, culture, parents or other?)

- If I could make one change in my life, what would it be?

## UNIT 1
# What's Holding Me Back?

## Exercise: Attitudes

| | | | |
|---|---|---|---|
| SAND (box) **1** | MAN BOARD **2** | STAND I **3** | R E A D I N G **4** |
| WEAR LONG **5** | R ROAD A D **6** | T O W N V **7** | CYCLE CYCLE CYCLE **8** |
| LE VEL **9** | 0 / M.D. B.A. PH.D. **10** | KNEE / LIGHT **11** | ii O O O O O O O O **12** |
| CHAIR **13** | (dice) **14** | T O U C H V **15** | GROUND (feet) **16** |
| MIND MATTER **17** | HE'S/HIMSELF **18** | ECNALG **19** | DEATH LIFE **20** |

# UNIT 1
# What's Holding Me Back?

## Summary

Do you remember in the third grade, or the second, or the first grade, when kids already knew who was smart and who wasn't? You knew who was the fastest, who was the best reader. How did you rank? Some of you were pretty average, some good in music or art, but not good at math. Some of you may have had trouble with science.

Years ago, when I was a teacher, we used to give IQ tests. They still do that today, but the tests are called something different. Have you ever taken an IQ test or an aptitude test? Do you know what's wrong with those tests? You start to believe you're only so smart. You start to believe that, "This is as good as I am." The tests try to tell you, "This is where you will belong in your future. This is the career you should take; forget about everything else."

What happens if a teacher knows your IQ score? They teach you like they see you, don't they? I believe that IQ tests and aptitude tests are one of the greatest injustices ever perpetrated upon human beings. As a teacher, if I already know you are stupid, I don't need to teach you. If I know you can't do it, why should I care? You have enormous potential inside you, but there are some things getting in the way. There are some constraints, some things that block you. What blocks you are your beliefs about yourself. What else blocks you is how you've been conditioned as a child and how you've been taught. What you've learned to believe about yourself is holding you back.

Just like in the "Finished Files" card exercise, the way you were taught to read kept you from seeing the F's in the word "of." How may F's did you count? 2, 3, 4, 5 or did you get all 6? For some of you, your belief about your ability to read got in the way. Just like some of our audience members on the video, even knowing there were six F's in the sentence, you still only saw three. And yet, when I asked you to count the number of times you saw the word "of," then you saw all six F's!

Now, let me tell you why. When you were taught to read English, for most of you, you were taught to read phonetically. You sounded out your words. When you sound out an F in a word, oftentimes the F sounds like a V as in the word "of." O-V, got it? Not an O-F. Once you get your mind set that "of" sounds like O-V, it affects your perception. You can look right at a sentence like this, and you can't see the Fs. You can't see them.

It has all to do with how you were conditioned by your mothers, fathers, brothers, sisters, culture, other teachers, friends in the school and so on – or how you conditioned yourself. Now, once you get your mind made up and set, you build what is called a "scotoma." I want you to remember that word, because you are going to love it.

"Scotoma" is Greek for blindness. It's a sensory, in this case the visual sense, blocking out of reality. Again, how can you look right at something and not see it? It's not because you're stupid and not because of your IQ. It's because of the way you were taught or what you believe. You have thousands, if not millions, of scotomas.

# UNIT 1
# What's Holding Me Back?

As you build your future, build your life, if you don't know about scotomas, you give up quickly. You take the wrong solution. You think, "I can't get it through my thick head. Everybody else seems to get it. I just don't get it. I must be stupid." Now, you don't want to do that, because then you start acting like you're stupid.

There's a principle I want you to remember: We behave and act, not in accordance with the truth, but the truth as we believe it to be. You're going to see that the beliefs we hold won't let us see more than the Fs. It won't let us see people, business opportunities, answers or solutions. Honest to goodness, our beliefs just don't let us see all there is to see. Now, I can show you visually, but you do the same thing with hearing, smelling, tasting, feeling. All of your senses block out information.

Have you ever known anybody to say, "Well, I'm a sensible person. All you need to do is show me. You can't show me, can you?" Most people don't know they have scotomas. You'd be surprised how many people in business, how many teachers don't even know. And if teachers don't know about scotomas, let me show you how they behave – which gives you opinions of yourself. They think, "I know my subject very well, and this person just can't get it." So they flunk the person and keep the teacher. Wrong. Think of the students as smart enough, if you're good enough. Everybody could see if you could teach them, if you could show them. Get a new appreciation for yourself, that's what I want for you. You're full of scotomas, full of blind spots.

When you're stuck and you can't see the answers – to building your business, creating your future or you can't see the answer and can't hear what somebody is saying – don't give up. It may be that you're stupid, okay, but probably not. You're probably just full of scotomas.

Now, when I found this sentence, I only got three. I remember what I felt like. I thought, "Gosh, how could I miss it?" Then when I found out why I could miss it, you know what I said? I want you to think this same way. "What else am I leaving out? I'm smarter than I thought." Yeah, I'm smarter than I thought. Whenever I'm stuck and I want to build my business, or I want to grow and I don't know how, I don't care if I don't know how. I'll find the way. I persist. I know the answers exist. I do know the answers exist. Somebody can see them. What am I doing? Why am I trapped?

The most important thing is to know that you're so smart, you're so capable. You can build your future. You don't need to know where the answers are coming from. Does that make sense? I want to encourage you that as you approach your careers and approach school, don't be intimidated. Many of you didn't do well in grade school. Maybe you didn't do well in junior high or high school. Maybe it was because of the way the teachers were teaching. Remember, if you get your mind made up to, "I can't do this. I'm not good at that," you start behaving like it. Then, you won't let yourself get the information. I just wanted to give you that, because we have a lot more to go.

# UNIT 2
# Who Am I Listening To?

## Unit Overview

Most of us have spent our lives listening to others tell us "the way it is," and we believed them. What we didn't do was question if what they said was the truth or an opinion. We must learn to become skeptical listeners.

## Unit Objectives

*By the end of this unit, I will:*

- be careful about who I listen to in the future.

- know that my past conditioning affects what I see.

- understand that I can look right at something and not see it.

- tell myself what I want, and not what I don't want.

## YOU ARE VERY
## CAPABLE AND VERY SMART.

## UNIT 2
# Who Am I Listening To?

## Key Concepts

- Ah-ha

- Scotoma

- Insight

- Conditioning

- Truth

- Skeptical

## Notes

# UNIT 2
# Who Am I Listening To?

**Notes**

# UNIT 2
# Who Am I Listening To?

## Reflective Questions

- Where have I discovered my perception of the truth was actually quite different from the real truth?

- What others say about me can affect my perception of myself and my abilities. How can being a "skeptical listener" help me achieve more in school and life?

- Where have I been "conditioned" to think something about myself and how am I allowing it to affect my actions today?

## UNIT 2
# Who Am I Listening To?

## Reflective Questions

- What kind of conversations do I listen to, and join in, at home or at school?

- Where might I be building scotomas to my classes, my instructors, taking tests, giving presentations? How is this affecting my behavior toward these things?

# UNIT 2
# Who Am I Listening To?

## Exercises: What Else is There to See?

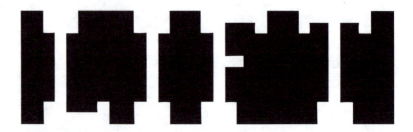

# UNIT 2
# Who Am I Listening To?

Please count the number of triangles
in the diagram. Count carefully!

# UNIT 2
# Who Am I Listening To?

## Summary

So, what did you think about missing the Fs? Eye-opening, wasn't it? Now remember, that's called an "ah-ha" experience. When you break through a scotoma, that's called an insight. When you open your businesses and you are looking for solutions to problems and so on, you're looking for insights. It's an emotional, intellectual, "I'll be darned! Wow, look at that." People sometimes say, "Well, I had one, once." You want them all the time.

You need to be careful about who you listen to. Another way of getting conditioned is when people give you opinions and you agree with them – whether it's true or not. There is a difference between opinion and the truth. Unfortunately, most people talk about opinions like they are true, and they come on strong. "This is the way it is." You need to ask, "Where did you get your facts? Where did you get your information?"

If you accept their opinion and it's wrong, you can't see the Fs. Bam! It just blocks your mind. It blocks your mind, and then you behave in accordance with the truth as you've come to believe it. You are so full of opinions. You will get them from the radio, music or television, or sometimes your teachers who mean well. You will get opinions from your parents, brothers and sisters. Go out today and just see how many opinions people give to you, as though they are a fact. Once you get these opinions in your mind, your mind is set and you can't see another way. Isn't that amazing? Then you act like, "This is it. No other way." I want you to remember that.

In this video segment, I gave you a card. I told you about some of the objects on the card. The easiest to see was an arrow. Others included a silhouette of a cigar store Indian head with a feather and one that looked like a log cabin. I told you that one was very hard, and that it looked like the top view of an architectural blueprint. I knew that some of you are pretty good in art and stuff like that, so you'd get it right away. I told you that there were several other objects, with greater and lesser difficulty. Some of you would get them right away because you are very smart. I can tell. Some of you would take a lot longer; I could tell by looking.

Then, I told you that if you didn't see everything on the card once you looked at it, you wouldn't see it for two days, per our studies. The bad part? You wouldn't sleep until you found everything. Did you want to try? Did you find all of the objects? How long did it take you to find the word FLY? I admit, I gave everyone a pretty hard time, and even suggested that I wasn't telling the truth. When I suggested that you look at the negative space, did it make it easier to find FLY?

Remember, scotomas, stuck, unstuck. You need to change your mind. Why should you change your mind? It helps you see the world differently. It helps you see solutions. It helps you see the way. If you don't change your mind, you are just living in a reality that the rest of the people hang out in. There's nothing wrong with them, but you're going to be much better.

# UNIT 2
# Who Am I Listening To?

Now, why was it hard to see? You were focusing on the black images. Why would you do that? You were listening to me. I misled you on purpose, didn't I? There is another reason why immediately you go to the black. Every time you go to read something, it's black lettering on white paper. That's kind of a conditioning, isn't it? You have been conditioned, in your past, to look for black letters on white paper.

You have been conditioned by your religions, by your educational systems, your parents and grandparents, older brothers and sisters, by the neighbors, and anyone who influenced you as you grew up. You've been conditioned. Everyone comes with different blind spots, but we don't know that, because everybody thinks they see the truth. If I am your boss, and I can see the word "FLY" and you can't, what do I do? I say, "My goodness, how stupid. I wish I had smarter people." But what if you can see and the boss can't? That happens, too. The boss may still think you're stupid. "You're telling me something that doesn't exist."

Nations go to war over scotomas. "Can't they just see?" Marriages and relationships break up over scotomas. "I'm trying to tell you something, and you aren't even listening." "Well, you're being pushy." Most people that you are going to come up against haven't the slightest idea how their mind works. So, you need to be careful who you listen to. With the FLY exercise, I was changing your mind. I am an authority, right? Of course I am! You listened to me.

You should be skeptical of me, and skeptical of people. I didn't say "cynical." Cynical is when somebody has had their big dreams smashed, and now they try to rip your dreams away. They try to talk you out of stuff, tell you it's stupid, how ignorant you are. "I'm smarter than you and if you only listened to me you would be better off." But skeptical is questioning. Is that the truth? What is he trying to tell me? Is he trying to mess up my mind? Sometimes it's intentional, sometimes it's not. I was trying to do it intentionally. You have so many people around you who aren't trying to do it intentionally, they just do it.

Here you are, going to school or going to university. What are your parents, who have never gone to university, telling you? "Why waste your time?" Has anybody ever told you that? "Why waste your time?" Your friends might say, "What are you doing that for? Look at all the money you're wasting. You're going into debt. You're working yourself to death. You could just get a job someplace." "Don't go into the music business, look at the competition." And, and, and, and. Am I right? If you fall for that, you can't see the Fs, can't see the word "FLY." And do you know something else? You prove them right. So, from now on, be careful who you listen to, including me.

## UNIT 2
# Who Am I Listening To?

# UNIT 3
# Lock-On / Lock-Out

## Unit Overview

Each of us has tremendous potential, and no one can know its limits. For the most part, we are only limited by our beliefs, our truth; and sometimes, the absence of the truth will set us free.

## Unit Objectives

*By the end of this unit, I will:*

- understand that I act according to the beliefs I hold about myself.

- learn that, as a human being, I cannot hold two opposing thoughts/beliefs at the same time.

- know that my job is to keep improving my beliefs.

- know that by locking on to my goals, I am locking out the things that would interfere.

# THE ABSENCE OF THE TRUTH
# WILL SET YOU FREE.

## UNIT 3
# Lock-On / Lock-Out

## Key Concepts

- Behavior

- Truth

- Cognitive Dissonance

- Beliefs

- Scotomas

- Lock-on / Lock-out

- Goal

## Notes

# UNIT 3
# Lock-On / Lock-Out

**Notes**

## UNIT 3
# Lock-On / Lock-Out

## Reflective Questions

- What are my academic strengths?

- What are my academic weaknesses?

- What beliefs have I "locked-on" to about myself that may hinder my academic performance or success in school?

# UNIT 3
# Lock-On / Lock-Out

## Reflective Questions

- What positive beliefs have I "locked-on" to about myself that will help me achieve academic success?

- What factors outside of school may have an impact on completing my education (family, friends, transportation, work, children)?

## UNIT 3
# Lock-On / Lock-Out

## Exercise: Opinions, Beliefs and the Truth

For each of your current beliefs in column 1, fill in what others have said to you in column 2, and then whether those opinions have shaped your belief in a positive or negative manner.

| 1 | 2 | 3 |
|---|---|---|
| **What are some of my current beliefs with regard to...** | **What are some of the opinions that others have shared with me regarding their view of my potential?** | **How have the opinions of others shaped my belief: Positively or Negatively?** |
| Completing my Education | | |
| Starting the career I want | | |
| Getting the salary I want | | |
| Setting Goals | | |
| Creating the future I want | | |
| | | |
| | | |
| | | |

## UNIT 3
# Lock-On / Lock-Out

## Exercise: 9 Dots

Connect the nine dots using ONLY 4 straight lines, WITHOUT lifting your pen.

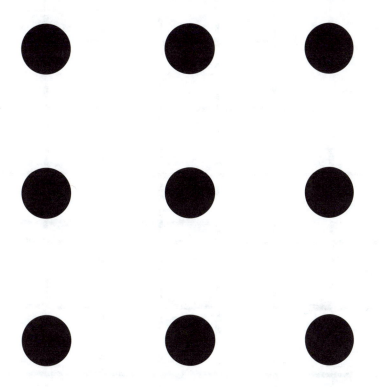

## UNIT 3
# Lock-On / Lock-Out

## Exercise: Maze

The object is to get from gate A to gate B, without crossing any lines, in the quickest time.

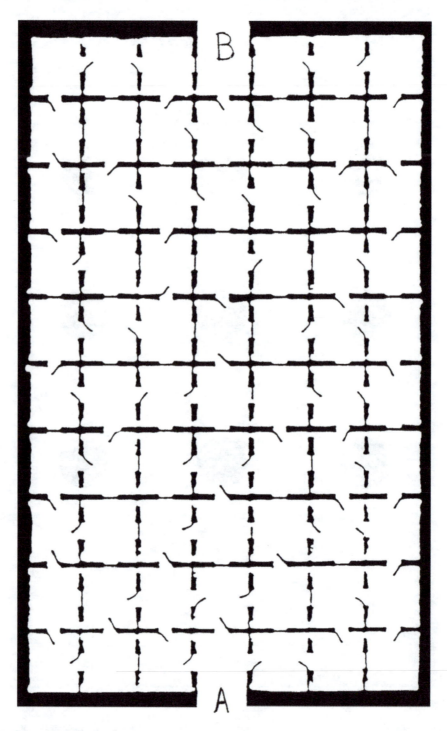

# UNIT 3
# Lock-On / Lock-Out

## Summary

Remember the principle, because it will be a thread that runs through the whole course: We behave and act not in accordance with the truth, but the truth as we believe it to be. This is so important to remember. We don't act in accordance with the truth, but we act in accordance with the way our mind is made up. I'll show you this in a moment. What is even more important is that you don't let yourself see things when your mind is made up. I want to come back and say, be careful what counselors tell you. They mean well, but they may not know anything about how the mind works. Be careful what teachers tell you, what your friends tell you, what you see on television, or what you hear from well-intentioned people. Most people aren't trying to screw you up, they just do with incorrect information. They say, "This is the way it is. That's the way it is."

Let's go back to we behave and act in accordance with the truth as we believe it. When you were a child, did you believe in something like Santa Claus? Now, when you thought there was Santa Claus, how did you behave? Were you really excited? Did you listen for him on your roof? Did you leave milk and cookies, or fruit for him? See, you behaved in accordance with the truth as you believed it. Now, how did you feel when you found out there wasn't a Santa Claus? Were you disappointed, or upset? That's what is called "cognitive dissonance." It's almost like somebody died on you. Now, a lot of kids don't want to let go of that, so they keep believing until they're nine or ten or twelve that there's still a Santa Claus. So we behave and act in accordance with the truth as we believe it – very important to remember.

Here is another example. There was a time in history when people believed the earth was flat. They would sail their boats out only so far, knowing if they went any further. they would fall off the edge. They acted in accordance with the truth as they believed it. Once they figured the earth was round, they sailed a little bit differently. Where are people, where are you, telling you the "earth is flat"? Where do you say, "This is as good as I can do. This is as far as I can go. This is where I belong." We are full of constraints, but most of them are mental.

We have a company in Australia, and one time when Diane and I were there 20-odd years ago, there was a race between the cities of Sydney and Melbourne. Entered into this race was a person by the name of Cliff Young. Now, this race is about 600 miles long. That's a long race. So, Cliff Young showed up for the race, at the age of 62. Nobody had ever seen him before, and he showed up in overalls and galoshes. No professional running gear. The media interviewed the guy, because he looked like he was lost and got into the wrong food line. He didn't look like he could run against the best in the world.

Well, not only did he enter the race, but this guy, Cliff Young, won the race. The first time he ever raced, and he ran against the best in the world. Now, how in the dickens could he do that? That's an interesting question, because he not only won the race, but he beat them by a day and a half. Now, think about that; a day and a half. Not just by minutes or seconds, he cut a day and a half off the race. How? Because he didn't know the truth. Remember, sometimes the truth will set you free. Sometimes, the absence of the truth allows you to do well. Something doesn't need to be true for you to believe it. You can believe it, and call it true. See, these runners got together all over the world. They knew that if you're going to run 600 miles, you run 18 hours a day and you sleep for six. That was what the best in the world believed. If you told me you run for six and sleep 18, I'd believe that!

Cliff Young had no horses, so he got himself in shape by chasing his cows. He didn't have television or radio to listen to. He never hung around people who knew "the truth." It wasn't that he was faster. He didn't know you were supposed to sleep. Everybody else thought you were supposed to sleep. "It's not humanly possible. You can't run that far, or run that long without collapsing." He was too far ahead for anybody to tell him. So in this case, the beliefs that the experts were holding constricted what they allowed themselves to do. They acted in accordance with the truth as they believed it to be.

You need to keep that in mind. What's stopping most of us isn't outside of us as much as it is inside of us. The beliefs we've been told, by people who really cared about us and loved us – coaches, teachers, friends – who do you believe now? Who do you listen to now? What kind of people are you hanging around? Are you hanging around people are doing and creating and becoming, or are you hanging around people who are afraid, small, negative, devaluative, always finding fault with the world? No more. No more. No more. Got it? Once you take in that kind of information, Boom, you're stuck with it.

Now, when I gave you this next test, did you listen to me when I said it was going to be harder than the other two? Stop listening! You almost bought into it! In fact, it was pretty easy. You probably got it right away. Did you get the card with the young lady, or the old lady? This test was another way to build scotomas. This is called the "Lock on/Lock out" principle. Just remember that. It's really the LO/LO principle. You could name the lady "Lolo" if you want. The way your mind works, if you lock on to the old lady, you immediately lock out the young lady. If you locked on to the young lady, then what would happen? You'd lock out the old lady. You can't hold those two beliefs in your mind at the same time. You switch back and forth, really fast, but you can't hold them both, at the same time.

Now, you need to be careful of whose opinions you lock on to, and who you're listening to. You need to be careful about all the information other people are telling you, about what you lock on to, what is right, what is true, what isn't, what you can do, what you can't do. Why? Because if the information is wrong, then what? You won't see the truth. You don't see the other way. You just don't see it. The problem is, you don't know you don't see it.

# UNIT 3
# Lock-On / Lock-Out

You also need to be careful of your own strong opinions, your own beliefs about yourself. "I've always been this way. I was slow as a child, and I'm still slow, and I don't mean running. I was in the dumb class, that must prove it." "I can't get that; it's hard for me."

I was so opinionated when I was a teacher, so strongly opinionated, that I could tell whether you were going to be good or not, the first day you came into my class. That first day, I could see, "You're a trouble maker; I can tell by your hair." "Get your hat off." "You, you have too much makeup on." "You, you're wonderful. I had your sister and she was lovely." "I know your mother, hmm." Do you realize that once I get my opinion made up, I can't see? Now, how many people make up their minds about you because of the color of your skin or your backgrounds or the way you look?

Here's what I want you to lock on to: I want you to lock on to your future, the way you want it to be. I want you to lock on to your goal. I want you to lock on to the business you want. I want you to lock on. Now what happens if you lock on to, "This is the way I'm going to do it," and then it doesn't work? What would happen? You wouldn't see another way. You see, this is a way, and here's another way and another way and another way. I want you to lock on to your goals, not necessarily the way. If "the way" isn't working, let go, and find another way. Find another way. Never give up on your goal. That's what you want to lock on to.

# UNIT 3
# Lock-On / Lock-Out

# UNIT 4
# My Brain's Filter System

## Unit Overview

The human brain has a formation in the central cortex, the Reticular Activating System (RAS), which filters all the information that is bombarding our senses. It only lets through that which is important to us right now. We can put the RAS to work for us, by setting clear, concise goals, so that the right information gets through to us.

## Unit Objectives

*By the end of this unit, I will:*

*   understand the Reticular Activating System.

*   know how to energize my RAS by clearly defining what I want.

*   learn that I am accountable for achieving the future I want.

*   be accountable.

# THE GOAL COMES FIRST
# AND THEN YOU SEE.
# YOU DON'T SEE FIRST.

# UNIT 4
# My Brain's Filter System

## Key Concepts

- Lock-on / Lock-out

- Scotomas

- Reticular Activating System (RAS)

- Significant

- Goals

- Awareness

- Accountability

## Notes

# UNIT 4
# My Brain's Filter System

**Notes**

## UNIT 4
# My Brain's Filter System

## Reflective Questions

- Where have I discovered my perception of the truth was actually quite different from the real truth?

- What are my career goals? How can my RAS help me achieve them?

# UNIT 4
# My Brain's Filter System

## Reflective Questions

- My RAS does a better job of providing clues when the goal is clear. Write some words to describe what I want my life to look like and be like when I graduate.

- I have a clear picture of the results I want from each class I am taking. (List each class and the results you want.)

# UNIT 4
# My Brain's Filter System

## Exercise: Stuck in Traffic

Have you ever been stuck in traffic on a freeway or turnpike?

Suppose you are on a crowded expressway on your way to meet with your boss and your most important client to close a big deal. It's 10:45 AM, and you're one hour away from the restaurant meeting place. It's raining, and the sky is dark.

All of a sudden the traffic gridlocks.

There's been an accident. Up ahead a tanker lies on its side across three lanes. From the ruptured tank, oil gushes all over the pavement.

In the middle lane where you are, you're surrounded by idling cars and trucks. There's a divider wall on the left, and the shoulder on the right is crammed with emergency vehicles.

Would you make it to your appointment?

Now we'll alter the scenario somewhat.

What if I told you that at that meeting your boss had a cashier's check for one million dollars, in your name, provided you arrive in time for the meeting. The check will be torn up at noon, so you have one hour and 15 minutes to get there. Can you do it?

Can you? How might you do it?

The point of all this is that when a desired goal is of sufficient personal value, the resources and action required to reach that goal tend to show up.

## UNIT 4
# My Brain's Filter System

## Exercise: RAS Activity

Choose one item from the list below, and make it significant to find by the next session of this class. Do not actively look for it, but rather allow your R.A.S. to find it.

- Bassett Hound

- Yellow pickup truck

- Black and white cow

- Balloons

- Ballet dancer

- Umbrella

- Picket Fence

- Indian restaurant

- Vehicle just like yours

- Airfare special to Australia


Circle your choice.


Where did you see it? _____


When (date and time) did you see it? _____


What were the conditions? _____

# UNIT 4
# My Brain's Filter System

## Summary

What I'm going to tell you now is so much fun, and it's so important, because it's going to give you a whole new appreciation for how you're going to live your life. First of all, we need to know that human beings are physically limited with our senses: vision, sound, smell or touch. Have you ever seen anybody with a dog whistle? They'll blow the whistle, you don't hear anything, but the dog hears it. Do you know why? Dogs hear at about 30,000 vibrations per second. Human beings hear at about 20,000 at the high end. Our range of hearing is about 50 to 20,000 vibrations per second. What a dog hears is above what you can hear. If you can't hear it, what would you conclude? There is no sound.

Bats hear at about 80,000 vibrations per second, and they use sonar to catch bugs. They send out sound and zip, got one. The bottle nose porpoise, out in the ocean, hears at about 120,000 vibrations per second. See, there's sound outside of what you and I can hear. But because we can't hear it, people say it doesn't exist. Keep in mind that there's information beyond your human sense.

Now for the sense of sight, human beings see between red and violet. If you use infrared or ultraviolet, or X-ray, or telescopes, you see more. Starlight scopes show you the energy that everybody casts off, in near total darkness. Starlight scopes are built like binoculars and you can see a green aura around living beings. Because you can't see it and because you can't hear it, be careful you don't lock on and build scotomas: "It doesn't exist. There is no way. It's impossible." Being open-minded is what I'm trying to encourage you to be.

Let's take the sense of smell. Animals have a very keen sense of smell. They can detect food, they track, detect danger, and so on, far beyond the human range. Now, I know you'll want this piece of information. The world record holder for the sense of smell is a species of the silk worm moth, who can detect the odor of a female moth 6.2 miles away. Now, that's really being aware of your environment!

Now, even within your human range, there's too much information bombarding the central cortex of your brain. You couldn't concentrate, read a book, hold a conversation, or drive. You would be too distracted. So, located from the base of your brain to the central cortex is a filter system called the Reticular Activating System. You don't have to remember the whole name; just remember "RAS." RAS, the Reticular Activating System. The RAS has the job of screening out junk mail. It's like a good executive secretary who screens out that which would disrupt your attention.

The Reticular Activating System builds scotomas. It locks out the old lady or the young lady. It locks out the word "FLY". It locks out all information except what's important to you. Only significant information gets through to your brain. Only information that you say is of value to you gets through to your brain. If you thought you weren't good at reading or math as a child ("I'm not good at this. I don't care anymore."), whatever the teacher would say from then on didn't get through. It's not because you're stupid. You saw it as unimportant. Only important information gets through. Everything else, just like the word "FLY" is locked out.

# UNIT 4
# My Brain's Filter System

That's why a mother can be sound asleep at night, with a baby close by. Airplanes can fly over at very high decibel levels and the mother will sleep through it. But if that baby wakes up in the middle of the night, with the slightest cry, Bam, that mother is wide awake. Even though she was sound asleep, she hears the baby's cry. So, it isn't the loudness of the information, it's the importance. If your class isn't important to you, it won't get through. You must set goals for what you want. Have you ever read a book twice and have nothing get through your thick head? You didn't know what you were looking for, that's all. You're not stupid. "No value, no get through." Once I learned this, Wow! Instead of Fs, or old lady/young lady, instead of FLY, it is anything that isn't significant to me doesn't get through to my brain.

This is why goals are so important. When you set a goal, you're declaring that something is significant. You set the goal. In the music business, you start hearing information and you think you're lucky. You think it's just a coincidence. There's probably information that will help you fulfill your goals all over the place, but you don't hear it, see it, smell it, or feel it, because that's the way your mind works. It blocks out everything that is not important to you. Got it?

Before you go to class, know what you're looking for. Before you read the book, know what you're looking for, because otherwise you don't see it. If you want to buy a cell phone or you want to buy a new computer, and you get in your mind what you're looking for, do you ever go through the paper or go online, and, "There's one. There's one. There's one!" You drive downtown and you see them on sale. Have you ever done that? If you go back and look at the paper or look someplace from two weeks ago, it was advertised then. But you don't see the ad for the cell phone until you want a cell phone. There's too much information.

Let's suppose that you say, "I wasn't good at reading," or "I wasn't good at literature." "I wasn't good at art." "When I was in the third grade, or the fifth grade, I was dumb at it." You are building your future based upon what you think you used to be good at. But if it wasn't important to you when you were in the sixth grade, or in high school, it still didn't get through. It doesn't mean you're stupid! If you set the goal, then the information gets through. Information doesn't come through first. You need to give yourself another chance.

I tell teachers this. "Teachers, come on. Help people create goals that are important to them, and then you can't keep your information out. If you can tell them why your subject matter ties to their goal, like the baby's cry, you couldn't keep it out." Otherwise, teachers use grades. They use grades, because they can't tell you why what they're teaching is important. "I'll flunk you if you don't get it. If I flunk you, you won't graduate. If you don't graduate, you won't get the job you want. So, do you want to study?" "Yeah." "Do you like the subject?" "Hate it." Then why are you studying? "Because I don't want to flunk and go through this class again." It's like the baby's cry. You set the goal, and then the information gets through. I want you to be able to set goals far beyond your present awareness. You don't need to know where things are coming from. You set the goal and you find what you need.

# UNIT 4
# My Brain's Filter System

Now, if all this works, then how come the father doesn't wake up when the baby cries? Because he knows the mom will wake up. It's not his department. He is giving up accountability. You need to remain accountable for your own future. You need to remain accountable for your own goals, for your own business. Otherwise, you will be passing by opportunities, and all kinds of things that would make you successful. You won't see, and it doesn't even exist to you. You want to become accountable. What does "accountable" mean? It's your goal. It's your life. It's my career. It's my wealth. It's my future I'm building. When you become that way, look out – you will find what you need.

Word to the wise: Opportunities need to be seen to be seized. Start with the premise what I need exists. I just don't see it, yet.

Have you ever shopped for something, maybe a birthday present or a holiday present of some kind, and you say, "I'm going to go look for something for my friend." "I'm going to go buy something, a gift for my friend." You look all day and come home with nothing. Have you ever done that? I have. It's like there's nothing out there! You mean there's nothing in all of New York? There's nothing in Chicago? Nothing in San Francisco? Nothing in Seattle? "Nothing and I looked all over." What was wrong with my thinking? I didn't know what I was looking for. If you identify exactly what you're looking for, you'll see it all over the place. There's one. There's one. There's another one. You can even tell yourself what price you want.

A fun thing to try, if you're looking for a parking spot in a busy part of town, is tell yourself exactly where you want to park. Watch: as you drive down the street, your Reticular Activating System is looking for information. It sees heads in cars two blocks away. It sees people approaching cars. It sees red lights flashing. Those aren't parking spots. Those are clues that lead you to your goal. You set your mind for what's important to you, and now you're scanning. But instead of looking for parking spots, I want you to look for opportunity, for education or information, or for jobs. You can even look for a spouse. That would be all right. You need to be clear, in your mind, what you're looking for, or anything will do. And you don't want just anything.

I'm just giving you the principles, and we'll put them all together before we are finished. But, you can see now how important it is to change your mind. You can see how important changing your mind is, because if you don't change your mind, you only let the stuff that's important to you now get through. Set new goals, and "Wow! Where did that come from?"

On the way home today, try this: When you're driving home, tell yourself you want to see every green car with license plates that have a 4 and an H on the plate. You can be going 60 miles an hour, and "There's one, there's one, there's one!" That's how smart you are. And then you take that skill and go after what you want in your life. I'm going to teach you how to set goals. I'm going to teach you why it's important. I'm going to teach you why you can't be waiting for the teacher to teach you. It's not the teacher. The teacher is as good as the teacher can be. If you need the information, you go get it, because you have your own future to build.

# UNIT 5
# How My Mind Works

## Unit Overview

As scientists unravel the mysteries of the human brain – the magnificent complexity of its structure – we have discovered the levels of the mind involved in the thought process. Our conscious, subconscious and creative subconscious work together to perceive the world around us, store our reality and make sure that each of us acts like the person we know ourselves to be.

## Unit Objectives

*By the end of this unit, I will:*

- have a full understanding of the three parts involved in the thought process – conscious, subconscious and creative subconscious.

- know that if the outside world does not match my inner idea of who I am, I subconsciously make the outside match the inside picture.

- understand that I guide my life at my belief level, not my potential level.

## WE SELF-REGULATE
## AT OUR BELIEF LEVEL.

# UNIT 5
# How My Mind Works

## Key Concepts

- Scotomas

- Reticular Activating System (RAS)

- Potential

- Conscious

- Subconscious

- Creative Subconscious

- Perception

- Truth

- Reality

- Sanity

- Self-Concept

- Self-Image

- Free-Flow

- Belief/Believe

- Self-Regulate

- Behavior

- Assimilation

## Notes

## UNIT 5
# How My Mind Works

**Notes**

# The Thought Process

Perceives
Evaluates

**Conscious**

Associates
Decides

**Subconscious**

**Creative Subconscious**

Stores
Truths

Resolves
Conflict

Stores
Habits
Attitudes

Maintains
Sanity

Creates
Drive and
Energy

# UNIT 5
# How My Mind Works

## Reflective Questions

- What are some beliefs I hold about myself?

- How did I come to form these beliefs about myself?

# UNIT 5
# How My Mind Works

## Reflective Questions

- What are my expectations of myself?

- How did a great experience I have had on the job or in school affect my self-image?

# UNIT 5
# How My Mind Works

## Exercise: Maintaining Sanity

In the table below, the left-hand column lists some perceptions of our abilities to perform certain tasks. In the column on the right, list what your Creative Subconscious does to maintain your sanity, and prove that you are always right.

| My Perceptions | What my Creative Subconscious does to Maintain my Sanity |
|---|---|
| Can't speak in front of others | Gives me a million reasons not to make the presentation. Makes sure I forget what I want to say when I do get up. |
| Not good at math | |
| Can't draw | |
| Can't ski | |
| Can't learn a foreign language | |
| Can't sing | |
| Can't play a musical instrument | |
| Don't interview well, at all | |
| Don't like an instructor | |
| Don't test well | |

## UNIT 5
# How My Mind Works

## Exercise: Black Box

In the graphic below, pick a black box and stare at it. Really concentrate your vision on that one box. After a few moments, do you see anything else?

## UNIT 5
# How My Mind Works

## Summary

Now you don't have distinct compartments like these, but in order for me to make sense of how your mind works, I want to break it into three parts: Conscious, Subconscious, and Creative Subconscious. The problem with most of us is we don't respect our subconscious enough. We think our conscious is very smart, and it is; but your subconscious is the genius. When you activate that, it's amazing what happens.

The conscious process has four functions. One function is what we call "perception" through our senses. Before birth, some your senses are activated. Balance, sound and temperature are activated. Then after birth, more are added. You take the information that you are perceiving – have been and still are – and you store that information on the subconscious level. Now we might call this memory.

We don't know for certain how memory actually works yet. We do know that there is a chemical change that takes place in the neuron structure of the brain. All the information that we have learned in books, experienced in our life, conversations, all of that information is stored in the neuron of your brain – never to be lost, never to be forgotten. That stored information most of you call the "truth." Another word for it is "reality," but your reality or your truth is incomplete.

Now, the second function is that of "association." An association just means as you perceive a person or a situation at work, you're asking yourself the question, "Have I seen anything like this before?" If you have something stored in experience, it becomes meaningful. If you don't have anything stored, the information you're looking at is meaningless. You have an emotional stored history. Sometimes, from an embarrassment, or ridicule, sometimes through being scolded, hurt, ashamed, it is there, never to be lost – unless you fix it. You are constantly bouncing your perceptions off of that stored emotional history.

Then, the third function of the conscious is that of "evaluation." Evaluation is asking yourself the question, "What is this, that I am looking at or experiencing, probably leading me toward? What is this probably leading me to?" Is it something good or something harmful? Something positive or something negative? You are evaluating the probabilities of what you're experiencing.

The accuracy of your judgment has a lot to do with your stored reality. You make a lot of decisions about your future, not based on what can be, but what has been. Most of the results you get will be based, not upon what can be, but what has been. With the process of visualization and affirmation, you'll be able to improve your stored reality, so that the decisions you make will be releasing and helping you with your future. It won't inhibit you or hold you back.

Now, I'm going to come over to the creative subconscious. The creative subconscious has four functions. I'm going to give you just the first one for now. The first one is to "maintain sanity," or what you and I refer to as "reality." In other words, whenever you get something stuck in the neu-

## UNIT 5
# How My Mind Works

ron structure of your brain like, "This is the way it is," the creative subconscious needs to make sure you behave consistently with what you know to be true. Not consciously, subconsciously. When you activate that creative subconscious, it's amazing what happens.

If you play soccer, you must play as good as you think you are. If you know you're stupid, you must act stupid. If you know you're forgetful, you must forget. Even though you have the potential to do better, it doesn't matter. So, whenever you perceive your behavior, the world around you, people or your actions, and that doesn't match your idea of how good you know you are, or what's normal for you, this creative subconscious corrects for the mistake. The creative subconscious corrects for mistakes in your life.

Now, what is a mistake? Watch, when a poor person wins the lottery, they just win a lot of money. I perceive, "Wow, I've won millions, but I'm a poor person." Subconsciously now, not consciously, what are they going to do? They're going to spend it all right now. They'll give it away. They'll blow it. And people will say, "Why did you spend all that money?" Do you know what they're going to say? "I don't know." They got rid of it because it was a mistake to have money, so they don't save.

You correct for mistakes based upon not your potential, but the reality you have stored. What kind of a student are you? "I'm a C student," or "I'm a C plus student," or "I'm an A student," or "I'm a D student." How are you at this subject? "I'm average or I'm a C, whatever." What happens to a person who knows they're a C student and for some reason they get an A in a test. If what I'm saying is true, the A is a mistake. Do you know what you tell yourself? "Now I don't need to study for two tests and I can still get my C." Am I right? You can't make yourself study. Why? Because you're a C student. Now, if you're a C student and get an F on a test, provided that's how you grade, and you know you're a C student, if somebody says, "Let's go out this weekend," what do you say? You're going to say, "I can't go out. I've got to study all weekend so I can pass my test and get an A." How come? "So I can get my C." Now, why don't you get an A all the time? "Because I'm a C student." You don't do it consciously. You do it subconsciously.

Once you establish what's normal for you, once you establish how you are, that process in the creative subconscious makes sure you stay pretty close to behaving like yourself. If you do worse, you correct up. But if you do better than you think you are, you correct down. You correct for the mistake inside yourself. You check and balance your actions, your behavior, your life, not at your potential level, but at your belief level. Now, how did you get your beliefs? What do you believe to be true? What you believe may be true, but it may not be true. Remember, it doesn't matter. If you don't change your belief, which is changing your mind to a higher level that you expect, you will always self-regulate at that level. You are a self-regulating mechanism.

Now, years ago my wife Diane and I adopted a lot of children. Some of the children we adopted had been taken away from their parents. We got two who were just babies, but most of them

# UNIT 5
# How My Mind Works

then were older. We got these three half brothers; same mother, different fathers. They were five, six, and seven at the time we got them. They had been shot at, run over; they had been abused. The picture in their minds, by the time they're five or six, would be what? What would the reality be? "The world is not very good. The world beats me up."

We didn't know much about the psychology when we were adopting our children years ago, so Diane and I were going to be the best mother and most positive father anybody could be. Every time these kids did something good, and it didn't have to be much of anything, we would praise them and tell them how good they were and say, "Wow, you're special." Now, perception from the outside world, "You are wonderful." But inside they say, "Oh, no, I'm not." Do you know what the creative subconscious would make them do? Act worse. They'd start a fire in the closet, or behind the couch. They'd steal the neighbor's mail, or bust a kid's tooth out in school. The sheriff brought my six year old home, the first day he went to school, arrested for shoplifting. He left St. Francis and went down to Burien and was shoplifting – at six! These two big cops bring him home. "Is this your kid?" I said, "I guess so." I'd ask, "Now why did you start the fire or why did you steal?" Do you know what the kid would say? "I don't know." Now, wouldn't that make a parent mad? "What do you mean you don't know? You just started the fire. Get in your room until you can figure it out." Do you know, the kid would say, "Good." They were setting us up to punish them. It is the quality of your reality, in your mind, that you are recreating in your life all the time.

You want to change your mind about how good you are. You want to change your mind about what you deserve. If you don't, then you will push away good jobs. You'll push away good relationships. Somebody comes to you that you can create a wonderful future with. "Well, that's too good to me," and you do something to sabotage your chance of success. You should be asking yourself the question, "What is too good for me?" Who said so? You may have been told that, but who is saying so now is you. You either change your mind or you keep behaving and acting, playing, athletically, just like you know you are. I'm going to show you, if you want, how to raise your self-image.

You will need to do all the work, because it isn't just, "I wish, I hope." There's a lot of work to it, but you can do it, and it is well worth it. You can change your mind once, and then again, and then again, and then again, and then again, and then again.

How many of you came from wealth? If you did, then you probably assimilated in your mind how to deal with money and how to live. But if you came from poor parents, then what's too good for you in your future? You may not want to be better than your mother and father. You might not want to be better than your brothers and sisters, or your uncle or aunt. "Nobody went to college in my family, so therefore… " "Nobody really held a professional job. Nobody became a doctor." "This is good enough for us." You learned what was "good enough," and that's all you get. And not because you don't have the potential to do more, but because of your belief.

# UNIT 5
# How My Mind Works

Remember, we act in accordance, we behave in accordance, with the truth as we've come to believe it. Most of you did not put your reality in on purpose. Most of you just allowed it to happen by the way you were raised and who was around you. I'm going to show you, if you choose, how to deliberately change it to a level of excellence where you want to live. You are going to need to study. You are going to need to work. You are going to need to develop. As you change your mind, you will find yourself thirsty for knowledge, thirsty to grow. "I gotta do this." How come? "I don't know why. I've just got to do it." When you change your mind, you behave differently.

# UNIT 5
# How My Mind Works

# UNIT 6
# Free-Flowing at a New Level

## Unit Overview

As we go deeper into our understanding of the thought process, we see that we are constantly taking our perceptions of current reality and checking them against our past stored reality in our subconscious. We need to remember that this stored reality isn't just a memory of what has happened, but also our feelings about what has happened to us.

## Unit Objectives

*By the end of this unit, I will:*

- understand the decision-making process of perception, association and evaluation, all leading to making a decision.

- know that my stored reality may not be "the truth" because of the emotions that are tied to my memories of a situation.

- have learned that sanity is more important than success, to my mind.

## THERE IS A DIRECT RELATIONSHIP BETWEEN THE QUALITY OF EXCELLENCE IN YOUR MIND AND THE WAY YOUR LIFE GOES.

## UNIT 6
# Free-Flowing at a New Level

## Key Concepts

- Conscious

- Perception

- Association

- Evaluation

- Decision-Making

- Emotional History

- GI/GO – Garbage In / Garbage Out

- Potential

- Scotomas

- Reality

- Intelligence

- Subconscious

- Creative Subconscious

- Self-Concept

- Self-Image

- Sanity

- Truth

## Notes

# UNIT 6
# Free-Flowing at a New Level

**Notes**

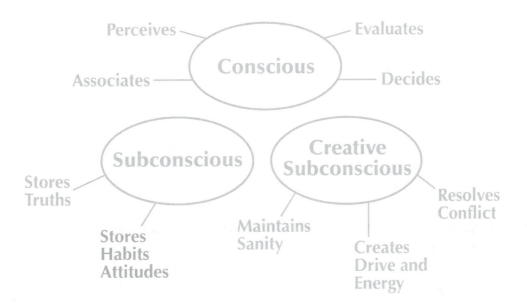

**The Thought Process**

Perceives — Conscious — Evaluates

Associates — Decides

Subconscious    Creative Subconscious

Stores Truths

Stores Habits Attitudes

Maintains Sanity

Creates Drive and Energy

Resolves Conflict

# UNIT 6
# Free-Flowing at a New Level

## Reflective Questions

- How can changing my beliefs about my myself and my abilities actually change my performance or my success at school? In what way?

- What do I believe to be true about myself as a student, friend or co-worker?

- Why is it important to understand how the thought process forms my beliefs about myself and the world around me?

# UNIT 6
# Free-Flowing at a New Level

## Reflective Questions

- How might I be letting others sabotage my opportunities?

- During the next week, I will list here 5 things I hear myself say or that I overhear others say that sabotage my success.

## UNIT 6
# Free-Flowing at a New Level

## Exercise: What Is It?

Study the picture, and answer the questions below:

Individually:

1. Perception – What is it that I think I see?

2. Association – Is there only one possibility, or many?


Working with a partner or with a group, record the possibilities of what others might think they see.

3. As a Team, Evaluate the possibilities.

4. As a Team, make a Decision about what you see.


## Up For Discussion . . .

Let's reverse the scenario Lou presented. What if the easel actually weighed 500 pounds, but you were hypnotized to "believe" that it only weighed 10 pounds. Would you be able to lift it?

# UNIT 6
# Free-Flowing at a New Level

## Summary

Let's go a little bit deeper into how the mind works. Once you have this understanding, it isn't just think good thoughts. It isn't just try hard, because you're going to see that trying hard doesn't do it. You need to change your mind, and then your life changes.

Norbert Weiner, the founding father of the computer, had a saying called the GI/GO principle. Have you heard about that? What do you think "GI" stands for? Garbage in. "GO" stands for? Garbage out. If you put misinformation into a computer, I don't think the right answer will come out. If you have misinformation, erroneous beliefs, bad ideas, poor emotional history, don't expect the right decisions to come out. You keep making the same mistakes. You keep not letting yourself go, being afraid of the same things. You won't let yourself go places, do things, create things. Not because you don't have the potential, but because of the stored reality in your subconscious. It is the job of this creative subconscious to make sure you stay like yourself.

Remember scotomas? The quality of the reality you have stored on the subconscious doesn't even let you see something different. "This is the way I am." No, this is not true. This isn't who I am. You just block out reality. Give yourself another chance. I'm going to show you how to change the quality of the information in your subconscious so that your decisions get better.

I have a friend out of the United Kingdom who is supposed to be the best in the world at perception and how the mind works. He has a wonderful definition of intelligence that I want you to remember and think about yourself. He said, "Intelligence is just the art of guessing correctly." Anything you can do to improve your guesswork is going to make you more intelligent about the job, about people, your investments, about what you want to do with your life. It may even help about what horse to bet on if you go to the races, or which way you drive to work. It's the art of guessing correctly, and what interferes with your guesswork is your history.

So, it is the quality and quantity of reality stored in your subconscious that your creative subconscious makes happen in your life, all the time. Change the quality and quantity here, and your life gets better all the time. Again the question becomes, is it outside me or is it inside me? Is it outside me or is it inside me? If you don't know how your mind works, do you know what you do? You keep waiting to win the lottery. You keep waiting for something outside of you to happen that will change your life for the better.

If you knew that if you changed the quality in your subconscious, your life gets better, that's good news. You can control that. You can't control whether the world outside is going to discover you and make you a superstar. Because you're going to change your mind, you will become a superstar. There is a direct relationship between the quality of the picture in your mind and the way life goes outside. Believe me, that is so.

# UNIT 6
# Free-Flowing at a New Level

Remember, I told you we had some children that we had adopted. This one son we adopted, when he's in grade school, the kids picked on him. Then he went to junior high school. Darn the bad luck, kids picked on him. Now, he's big, strong, and he could beat people up if he wanted to, but people picked on him. Then he went to a new high school, where nobody knew him. Guess what? People picked on him. Then he went in the Army, and the sergeant picked on him. Got out of the Army, and his first job was fast food place, and the boss picked on him. Can you imagine the bad luck?

We got him a tow truck business, and I hired the guy that formerly owned the tow truck business to mentor and take care of him, to make sure he did all right. It was about six weeks into the business, and my son comes home and says, "I quit." I said, "What do you mean you're quitting?" He says, "Bill is picking on me." I said, "Man, you can't quit. You own the business!" Now, do you think it was a string of bad luck? Could've been. But you know, he was so abused as a child, fiercely abused as a child, that he keeps letting people do that to him. Your body language – how you stand, how you talk, how you hold yourself—gives you away, and it's all subconscious. It's all subconscious. If you don't change your mind, your life keeps repeating itself.

People act towards you as they see you. If you look like and think you're shy, they treat you like you're shy. People do respond to you based upon how they perceive you. Your body language is constantly telling others how to treat you. If you change this inside, you'll be surprised how the people out here change. The world changes. So there's so much more to this, but I want you to get the whole idea.

One last piece: You know how important the self-concept is, the self-image is. I'm going to show you how it's created, and then I'm going to keep showing you how to change it. Have you ever seen anybody under hypnosis, watch it on TV or anything like that? Under hypnosis you go right past the conscious right into the subconscious. I would just tell you that this chart right here weighed 500 pounds. So, under hypnosis you'd probably believe that. Once I get you convinced it's the truth, that it weighs 500 pounds, I'd say "I'll give you a thousand dollars if you just come over and pick it up." It would be worth a try, wouldn't it, for a thousand dollars? So, you come, and you try to lift this with your arms, and it won't come up. Now, why won't it come up? It doesn't weigh more than about 4 or 5 pounds.

If we attached electrodes to your biceps, we might show that you're lifting with 75 pounds of energy up, and this only weighs 5 pounds, and it won't come up. Tell me, why is it staying down? Now watch, sanity is more important than being successful, having a good relationship, having a good future, having people treat you well. Sanity is more important. Sanity means what I know to be true needs to happen in my life all the time. If it doesn't, my creative subconscious corrects for mistakes. Got it?

Now, I know I'd get a thousand dollars if I lift this, but I believe it weighs 500 pounds. I'm lifting

# UNIT 6
# Free-Flowing at a New Level

and we're measuring 75 pounds of energy. It still stays down. Here's why: My brain, my creative subconscious, sends a message to the muscles at the back of my arm called my triceps that I use for pushing. So, while I'm lifting with my biceps for a thousand dollars, without knowing it (I have a scotoma) I'm pushing with the muscles at the back of my arm. I'm pushing with at least 75 pounds of energy down. I'm doing what's called an isometric contraction. I'm lifting and pushing at the same time. But I don't know I'm pushing. All I know is how hard I'm working.

If you ever work "real hard" at something with no results, change your mind about how good you are, whether it's hard, or of what you're capable. Because what you'll do is you'll try hard, try hard, try hard, with no success. The process between the subconscious and the creative subconscious always tries to make this truth happen.

Your job is to do what? Change the truth. Change the truth, that's right. For the most part you didn't put the truth in there in the first place. You allowed it to happen. Teachers, parents, being teased, being told who you were, what you are – you didn't know any better. You wanted to resist it, but you didn't resist it. You just accepted it, and now you act like it. You act like the person – we do, I do – that we know ourselves to be. If you never saved money, you never had enough money. You keep telling yourself you don't have enough money. It doesn't matter if you make a lot of money, you'll still get rid of it. If you have trouble making friends, you don't need to have trouble making friends. If you change your mind, it's easy to make friends. You follow what I'm talking about? Change your mind over and over and over and over. You can be successful.

# UNIT 6
# Free-Flowing at a New Level

## UNIT 7
# Leaning in the Right Direction

## Unit Overview

There is a great advantage to being able to rely on our habits. We don't need to stop and think about how to do many routine things. However, when those habits keep us stuck in a rut, under-living our potential, we need to see about changing them. In the same manner, our attitudes can limit our achievements. The good news is that habits and attitudes can be changed.

## Unit Objectives

*By the end of this unit, I will:*

• understand that my subconscious holds my habits and attitudes.

• know that habits are good, if I have the right habits.

• understand that attitudes are neither good or bad; they just cause me to either lean toward or lean away from whatever is before me.

• know that by setting goals, I can uncover attitudes I may not know I have.

# HABITS ARE A LEARNED BEHAVIOR
# AND CAN BE UNLEARNED.

## UNIT 7
# Leaning in the Right Direction

## Key Concepts

- Conscious

- Subconscious

- Reality

- Habit

- Mindless Efficiency

- Mindful Efficiency

- Attitude

- Perception – Association – Evaluation – Decision-Making

- Procrastination

- Creative Avoidance

- Emotional History

- Goal

## Notes

# UNIT 7
# Leaning in the Right Direction

**Notes**

# UNIT 7
# Leaning in the Right Direction

## Reflective Questions

• What are my attitudes about myself? How smart am I, how capable, and do I see myself being successful in life?

• How am I letting my past habits control my present and future?

# UNIT 7
# Leaning in the Right Direction

## Reflective Questions

- What habits or attitudes do I have that have prevented me from being as successful as I know I could be?

- What are some habits or attitudes I would like to change so I can be more successful in life and in school?

# UNIT 7
# Leaning in the Right Direction

## Exercise: Lifeboat

Imagine that the cruise liner, on which you have been having the holiday of a lifetime, has just sunk, following a devastating explosion in her boilers. With very little time available to save yourself, you now find yourself adrift in a lifeboat with other survivors, miles from the nearest land and without the means of contacting the outside world to summon help.

Your lifeboat is totally alone and contains other survivors like yourself. The lifeboat, however, is not quite full and has the capacity to take four more survivors and no more. As time goes by, the lifeboat comes across the following survivors in the water:

- Mother & Child (count as one)
- Liner's First Mate
- 16 year old boy (High dependency drug user)
- 86 year old woman
- Winner of a reality TV show
- Nurse
- 80 year old survivor of the Asian Tsunami disaster
- Secondary school teacher
- Lone parent
- Foreign National
- Prostitute
- Head of an organized drug consortium

In pairs, your task is to decide which four survivors in the water you wish to save. Be prepared to justify your decision afterwards to the group as a whole.

You have 10 minutes to complete the exercise.

# UNIT 7
# Leaning in the Right Direction

## Exercise: Habits

Here are some of my HABITS that help me do things well:

_____

_____

_____

_____

_____

_____

These are some of my HABITS that make it difficult for me to do well:

_____

_____

_____

_____

_____

_____

Now, which of the above HABITS do I want to change?

_____

_____

_____

_____

_____

_____

# UNIT 7
# Leaning in the Right Direction

## Summary

Do you know that shoe manufacturer's ad, "Just do it"? It doesn't work. I mean you can just do it, but you only do it once. There's a reason for that. Remember when we talked about the subconscious stored reality? There are two other functions of the subconscious. One is to handle everything that is a habit, a routine. Driving a car starts off on the conscious level, and then through repetition and repetition, you turn it over to your subconscious. You don't even think about what you're doing. When you first started driving, probably in the parking lot, you were frozen.

As you learned, everything was sequenced. The right skills, repeated over and over again, allowed you to flow. Even though you couldn't get out of the parking lot, now you can drive down the road, one hand on the wheel, the other one around a girlfriend, looking for people on both sides of the street and looking for cops out of the rearview mirror. You are listening to the radio, you can do it all. There was a time when you couldn't do it all. That's what habits are good for, they let you free flow.

If I said, "Two times two is?" you would respond, "Four" right away. There was a time you couldn't do that. But if I said, "87 times 96, how much would that be?" you would probably have to work that out. Do you know, there are people in Las Vegas that could just tell you, just like that. These are the ones who compute the odds. Now, once you get it down, it just flows. If you are a musician, you start practicing, practicing, practicing. You turn small things, little steps and knowledge, sequenced together, over to your subconscious and it flows. See, you could have learned two times two equals seven. That would be wrong. So practice doesn't make perfect. Only practice of perfection makes perfect.

Not just anybody should teach you your skills. Not just anybody should give you information about your profession. You're spending all the time to get that education in. Then, when you let go of the conscious level, you just let it flow. You just let it flow. You are at your best when you flow.

Have you ever said, "What's that person's name?" It's blocked and you can't get it out. If you just tell yourself, "Forget it for a moment. By the time I walk out the door, it'll come to me." And, it does. Your subconscious, when you bring it to the conscious level, it blocks it. "How do you spell that word?" Do you ever do that, and trap yourself? If you give me a pen, I go right back to the subconscious, and it comes out.

You are at your best at the subconscious level. Sometimes, when you're in the subconscious level, the flow is called "mindless efficiency." It's called mindless efficiency, because you don't need to think about it. When you're in a state of mindless efficiency, with the way you run your day, or what you do with your life now, you reject new information. You reject new ways. It's all subconscious. New information screws up, interferes with, my mindless efficiency. What you need to do is recognize that, in order to improve your income, your life, the way you're going to do things, you need to shift gears to a mindful efficiency. You need to get new skills, new knowledge. You're

# UNIT 7
# Leaning in the Right Direction

going to the right schools, but you need to get the right people teaching you, because you're going to habituate what you learn.

The second thing that is important on the subconscious level has to do with your attitude. I've been meaning to talk to all of you about your attitudes. "You have a bad attitude, and I can tell, just by looking." Have you ever been told you had a bad attitude? Yes? Now, do you know what an attitude is? An attitude is just your emotional history. Remember that perception, association, evaluation and decision making I told you about the conscious level? You see something, and you have a negative attitude. Now, negative doesn't mean bad or wrong; negative means avoidant. Positive doesn't mean good. Positive means you seek out, and try to possess.

The best definition of an attitude I ever found was airplane terminology, like pilots use. If my arms were the wings of an airplane, stretching out to my sides, the attitude of an airplane is just the direction in which the airplane is leaning in relationship to a fixed point like the horizon. So if you just remember, an attitude is just the direction in which you lean.

It all has a lot to do with the emotion that's inside of you. You picked up some emotions when you were three, seven, or 17. You are picking up emotion about what you like and what you don't like about food, about people, about work. With your mind, you're going to perceive something. You associate, "Have I seen anything like this before," and how did I feel about it? Then you say to yourself, evaluative, "What is this probably leading me to?" If it's hurtful, going to embarrass you or make a fool of you, you subconsciously engage in avoidant behavior.

A negative attitude just means moving away. It doesn't mean you're wrong or bad, it just means you move away. If you have a negative attitude about talking in front of people, about certain kinds of classes, or a negative attitude about certain kinds of work or jobs, when you perceive the opportunity to engage in it, you subconsciously figure out why you don't like it. You subconsciously tell yourself why you can't do it. You start to procrastinate, putting it off. When you have a negative attitude, it just makes you take longer to do your homework or do your work. If you have a negative attitude, you even get yourself sick. You'll want to avoid, subconsciously. You don't do this consciously. It is that emotional history. When it comes up and it's negative, you get procrastination. Or, you get creative avoidance, and find stuff to do that doesn't need to be done. Instead of doing the stuff you need to do, you find stuff that doesn't need to be done. Why? Because you don't want to do what you're supposed to do. It's procrastination, creative avoidance, and you just can't get yourself to do it.

Do you know what most people do? They give up on their goal, because they can't get themselves to do the schoolwork or do what's necessary – talk to the people, whatever it might be. You just can't get yourself to do it, and you can't understand why. You might say to yourself, "I was born this way." Well, you may have been born this way, but I doubt it.

# UNIT 7
# Leaning in the Right Direction

Don't give up on what you want you want. Change your attitude. I'm going to show you how to do that. You need to change your attitude from avoidance and negativity – where you see doubt and fear, or something that would be embarrassing or hurtful, or cause you to look stupid or feel foolish. That's from the time you were a little kid, perhaps, but it still comes up on you, even now that you're in your 20s or in your 30s. It doesn't matter, it still comes. If you don't change the emotional history, you'll be tied to that forever. When we talk about changing an attitude, just watch. Can you get yourself to do the things that need to be done to build the career, to get the kind of social life, to live the kind of life you want? If you can't get yourself to do it, it's an attitude. It's emotional. You can fix that. All you need to do is learn what I'm going to teach you about changing that emotional history.

What do you love doing? What are some of the fun things you like to do? Write them down. Do you have to beat yourself into doing them? You don't need discipline to do the things you want to do. What you think you need is discipline to do the things you don't want to do. You don't need discipline. You need to change your attitude. You want to see the emotional value. Why? You need to change that emotional history, because a lot of the things that you are able to do you won't let yourself do. Does that make sense?

I needed to change hundreds of attitudes on myself. I'll just give you a sample. How many of you girls or ladies, maybe over the last year or so, put on a sweatshirt and a pair of jeans or pants to go out or go shopping? You know, that used to be considered men's clothing. See, it's an attitude about masculinity and femininity. You don't even know you have it until I ask the guys a question – and don't raise your hands. How many of you have put on a skirt and a blouse to go downtown shopping? For me, no thank you! Now, why is it all right for ladies to put on men's clothing, but it's not all right for men to put on women's clothing? When did you get that attitude? I don't know, but I have it. You get all kinds of attitudes about what's acceptable and what isn't acceptable, what I can do and can't do. Where did you get them? Some of them are holding us back – attitudes about colors of people, attitudes about what women can do and can't do.

You need to change your attitudes. Remember, attitudes are not positive or negative until you set a goal. Then, once you set a new goal, will your attitudes let you seek it, or do they cause you to avoid doing the things you need to do, in order to achieve your goal? Does that make sense? Again, I come back, don't give up on your goal. Learn to change an attitude. That's what I'm going to teach you.

You want to change the routines in your mind. Learn to practice in your mind. Get the right skills, then you rehearse in your mind. You have rehearsed your work. You can rehearse where you're going to go. You can rehearse an interview. You can rehearse your social life. You can rehearse sports in your mind. That's what the great swimmers we work with do. Olympics-class swimmers, they practice in their mind. Once they get the skill, the goal causes them to rehearse

# UNIT 7
# Leaning in the Right Direction

and rehearse and rehearse. Astronauts do it. Martial artists do it. It's all practice in your mind. I'm going to show you how to do that. What to do with the skill is your own business.

One more thing: It needs to be my idea. Nobody is going to tell me to do it. I'm going to do it because I want new goals. I want a new life. I want to earn more money. I want my life to be better and bigger. So do you, don't you? I'll show you how.

## UNIT 7
# Leaning in the Right Direction

# UNIT 8
# How My Beliefs are Formed

## Unit Overview

Our thoughts accumulate to become beliefs, so it is important to control our thoughts. We do this by controlling our self-talk, that constant conversation that goes on in our minds. This self-talk is vitally important in forming our self-image, and can either build us up or tear us down. In fact, understanding the power of self-talk may be the most important thing we can ever learn.

## Unit Objectives

*By the end of this unit, I will:*

- know that self-talk is a three-dimensional form of thought: words trigger pictures, which then trigger emotions.

- understand the importance of self-talk in my daily life.

- realize that I need to clear away all the negative, destructive self-talk from my life.

# THOUGHTS ACCUMULATE
# TO BECOME BELIEFS.

# UNIT 8
# How My Beliefs are Formed

## Key Concepts

- Self-Image

- Attitude

- Words – Pictures – Emotions

- Self-Talk

- Belief

- Self-Regulate

- Potential

- Sanction

- Subconscious

- Perception

## Notes

# UNIT 8
# How My Beliefs are Formed

## Notes

# UNIT 8
# How My Beliefs are Formed

## Reflective Questions

- Where in my life did I believe in myself and it helped me to succeed?

- What am I dissatisfied with, and what would the new picture look like?

## UNIT 8
# How My Beliefs are Formed

## Reflective Questions

- Where have I let my self-talk keep me from succeeding?

- What are some examples of positive self-talk that I have used to help me succeed?

# UNIT 8
# How My Beliefs are Formed

## Exercise: Record your own evidence

- When in your life, whether you were 6, 12, or 18 did you want something so badly that it was all you could focus on? Describe it fully below.

- Did you get it or at least come close? Describe the outcome below.

- Was the picture in your mind so vivid that you didn't give yourself the option to fail? What did it look like?

- Did you have to block the negativity of others around who that tried to take your goal away from you? How did you shut out others' comments?

- Did your self-talk continually take you toward your goal or away from it?

# UNIT 8
# How My Beliefs are Formed

## Exercise: Fact or Opinion

For the list of sources in the middle of the table below, check whether you think information coming from these sources is "Fact" or "Opinion." Prepare to defend your choices.

| Fact | Sources | Opinion |
|------|---------|---------|
| | Newspapers | |
| | Television News | |
| | Social Networking Websites | |
| | Weekly Newsmagazine | |
| | Dictionary | |
| | Your Instructor | |
| | Blogosphere | |
| | Tweets | |
| | Electric Service Invoice | |
| | History Text | |
| | Religious Text | |
| | Doctor's Prognosis | |
| | Math Text | |
| | Astronomy Picture of the Day | |
| | Wikipedia | |
| | | |
| | | |
| | | |

# UNIT 8
# How My Beliefs are Formed

## Summary

What I'm going to present to you now is a way to begin changing your self-image. It's also a way to begin changing your attitudes. It's a way of changing your moods. It's a way of changing your mind. What I am about to teach you is essential to everything else I'm going to teach you. Actually, it's more important than that. It's essential to being successful. Do you realize that you talk to yourself, in your own mind? Are you aware? It's very important to know you're not crazy. Everybody talks to themselves in their own mind. It is how you talk to yourself in your own mind that makes the difference.

How are beliefs formed? Why should we know that? Well, somewhere it was written years ago, "As a man thinketh in his heart, so is he." What they were talking about is this: What you know to be true about yourself is the way you act. You act like the person you believe yourself to be. They couldn't talk about the brain and the neurons in your brain in those days, so they used "As a man thinketh in his heart," the thought you have, "So are you." So, if you change the way you think-eth, you change the way you is-eth. That's a key. Stop waiting for the changes to come from the outside. Change the inside, and the outside changes, believe it or not. It's amazing.

What I need to teach you is how your mind works and how you think. You think in three dimensions. We think with language or words. And what does the language or words do? It triggers the second dimension, pictures. When you get an idea, you get a picture in your mind. It is words and pictures. The third dimension, and very powerful dimension, is how you feel about it. So it's words, pictures and emotion. Those are the three dimensions.

If you hear a language that you don't speak, do you understand the words? If you don't understand the words, then you don't get the second dimension, pictures. If you hear Japanese, or Chinese, Mandarin or something like Spanish, all you hear is noise, and it doesn't give you the images or the pictures. Someone from Japan, they hear those words and get the pictures, just as surely as English gives you a picture. Then, of course, your emotion – how you feel about it – is very important.

Every thought you have accumulates, builds on another to become a belief. It's hard to build a belief with just one thought. The way you speak to yourself about how you are, who you are, is being recorded in the neuron of your brain. This three dimensional form of thought, I want you to remember, we'll call self-talk. Self-talk is the conversation that you carry on in your own mind all the time. While I'm speaking to you, you speak to yourself three times as fast. If I stop talking, you go about six times faster. It is estimated you have about 50,000 thoughts go through your mind a day. (No, I don't know who counted them.) These thoughts don't just disappear into thin air. They cause change in the neuron of your brain, a chemical change. These thoughts, that you give yourself, build on one another. They stack up, accumulate, to become a belief.

# UNIT 8
# How My Beliefs are Formed

It is important for you to know that you self-regulate your life at your belief level, not your potential level. The ceiling on the use of your potential isn't the sky. It is your belief that you have about yourself – what you look like, how you act, how smart you are, what you think about your memory, all those beliefs that you have accumulated since childhood – that you are accumulating. The reason this so important to remember, is that your beliefs control how much you're going to do. They control what you're going to let yourself do.

Now, how do the beliefs get in your mind? Did you zap them in? Did your teachers zap them in? Did your parents zap them in? No. Everybody builds their own self-image with their own thoughts. You just didn't know this when you were growing up. You would accept what a teacher would say. You would accept what a big kid would say. Many of you were taught to respect authority – but who is an "authority"? Parents, family members, coaches – lots of people had opinions that came your way.

Now, these opinions don't become a part of your image until you agree with them. You must give sanction to the opinion of another before it becomes a part of you. If you didn't know this, then you let other people describe you, for you. There are so many people who try to tell you what you should look like, be like, how good you're going to be, what your future's going to be, whether you're loveable, not loveable, whether you're acceptable, not acceptable. So many people are describing you. Just remember, it won't become a part of you until you accept what they say. The comments may be hurtful, but they can't affect you as long as you reject them. You need to reject the negative, destructive self-talk.

Have you ever gotten mad at yourself and started running yourself down? Does it go on for longer than an hour sometimes? Perhaps for a day, maybe even a week? What you're doing, every time you're destructive to yourself, telling yourself what's wrong with you, is building a belief. Remember your subconscious doesn't argue. It accepts, literally, what you tell it. "Literal" means it doesn't argue. It doesn't question. If you say you're stupid, it says, "Okay." If you say you're ugly, it says, "Okay." If you say, "This is hard for me," it says, "Okay." Your subconscious doesn't reject, it accepts literally what you tell it. The important key to remember is you build your own beliefs with your own thoughts.

This process is called self-talk. The key, for people who want to grow, is to control their self-talk. How would I control it? What do I mean when I say, "Control it"? Eliminate the negative, sarcastic, belittling, devaluative, self-talk that goes on in your own mind. Stop putting yourself down. Stop belittling yourself. Stop telling yourself what's wrong with you. Stop the negative self-talk.

So, what do I do? You're going to learn to put a quantity of positive self-talk into your mind. You can change your belief. You can change your belief by telling yourself more truthful information about yourself. You can change your belief by telling yourself what's right with you instead of what's wrong with you. You probably have made mistakes along the way, everyone does. Did you

# UNIT 8
# How My Beliefs are Formed

ask yourself the question, "What's matter with me anyway?" Ever do that? You did something wrong, and asked yourself, "How could I have been so stupid?" The problem is you go on to answer the question! With your self-talk, you start telling yourself what's wrong with you. Every time you do that, you lower your image. "So what?" you say. As you lower your image, your performance lowers. If you can be constructive and positive, you raise your image, and your performance raises.

In every part of your life, whether you're an artist, a musician, a dancer, whether you think you are capable, incapable, every belief was built with your own thoughts. Isn't that amazing? Now, if you had a friend that would talk to you the way you sometimes talk to yourself, would you still go around with them? Probably not. I think you can see how negative, in your mind, you can be. That does affect who you are. It does affect your belief in yourself. It does affect your life; the money you're going to earn, who you have around you, the kind of jobs you're going to have, where you take yourself in your future. Your self-talk does affects you. It is a causative factor on the quality and the quantity of your life, happiness, moods, and your energy. If you tell yourself what you don't want, you will create that. If you run yourself down after making a mistake, you create it.

Some of you have participated in sports. Can you remember the coaches you have had? Did they video your games and then show you your mistakes? Over and over and over and over and over until you got it down good in your mind? They were coaching backwards. The more I tell you what's wrong with you, and the more you accept it, then the more you play like it, the more you act like it. You are going to run into coaches and teachers and bosses, other adults in your world, who are constantly giving you their view of you. It doesn't matter. I want you to become a disputer. I want you to dispute – not out loud, just in your mind – and say, "Who are you to tell me that? You don't look so good yourself." You must be able to dispute, to reject the negative.

For some of you, you need to be able to accept compliments, too. You need to be able to tell yourself you're good. I'll show you later on how to go about doing that. Right now, I just wanted to get across to you that you build your own self-image with your own thoughts. Once you lower your image and give yourself the beliefs, you can't see the Fs in the word "OF", and you can't see the word "FLY". You can't see the old lady or young lady, because your perception is affected by your beliefs.

Now, what would be the most important thing you can do with the new discipline? Stop telling yourself what's wrong with you. Stop being negative to yourself. It won't happen right away. In fact, it might be pretty hard at first. But you're going to get better and better at it, better and better at it. Your life, I promise you, will change. Now, there's a lot more to give you, but that's the important piece right now.

# UNIT 9
# Building My Self-Image

## Unit Overview

The subconscious mind is a literal mechanism – it does what you tell it. If, with your self-talk, you are dwelling on the negative, that is what gets assimilated into your version of "reality" in the subconscious. Since thoughts accumulate to become beliefs, all of your beliefs become negative, and reaching your potential will not be possible. Now, if your self-talk dwells on the positive possibilities of life, what will happen to your beliefs and your behavior?

## Unit Objectives

*By the end of this unit, I will:*

- understand how IxV=R reinforces my beliefs and actions.

- remember to give credit where credit is due, including to myself, for a job well done.

- be mindful of how I teach the young people in my life, so that I am coaching them forward into positive achievements.

# YOU BUILD YOUR OWN
# SELF-IMAGE WITH
# YOUR OWN THOUGHTS.

# UNIT 9
# Building My Self-Image

## Key Concepts

- I x V = R

- Subconscious

- Sarcasm

- Hostility

- Devaluation

- Self-Esteem

- Humble/Humility

- Self-Image

- Self-Regulate

- Belief

- Potential

- Performance

- Attitude

- Attitudinal Balance Scale

## Notes

# UNIT 9
# Building My Self-Image

**Notes**

## UNIT 9
# Building My Self-Image

## Reflective Questions

- What are ten things I have done well in my life?

- What is the self-image I have about myself right now?

# UNIT 9
# Building My Self-Image

## Reflective Questions

- What would I like my new self-image to be?

- What are some self-talk statements I could start practicing to create a better self-image?

## Exercise: Building My Self-Image

On the lines below, list 10 things that you have done well in your life, to date:

- graduated
- all A's honor roll Junior-Senior high
- I draw well
- im still in school
- i've been employed since i was 16
- dose well, balancing school, work, + social life
- I make my own car payment
- I am a good writer
- make friends easily
- I don't have too much drama w/ people

These people have been mentors to me in my life:

- Mr. Ferguson
- Mrs. Reeves
- Fatemah M.
- Mrs. Holder

Why do I think of them as mentors?

They were there for me when I needed them.
I liked them they were positive. They were always happy.

Do I see each of them as like me?

not really. I just liked how they were always positive

Do I see each of them as experts in the areas in which they mentor to me?

yes

Have they mentored others, like me, to achieve goals similar to mine?

Yes

Who do I mentor?

I don't know. Friends ask me for help or vent to me, so
I listen.

# UNIT 9
# Building My Self Image

## Summary

Let's back up a little bit and then go forward. The key is to control how you talk to yourself in your mind. Sometimes, you immerse yourself with a negative boyfriend. Your parents were negative, or your teachers might have been negative. Your coaches might have been negative, and even the bosses around you might be negative. It makes it pretty hard. You listen to negative music. You read the paper. You watch television. You are getting all kinds of opportunities to talk to yourself about the way the world is, aren't you?

It was not long ago, when I was in London, I was standing on the street. This mother had about a four year old in her hand, and she had about a ten year old little daughter, quite a ways behind her. The mother was screaming at her daughter, "Get away from me. I don't love you anymore. You're not my daughter." Then, the mother went across the busy street and left her daughter on the side. Now, this only happened one time. Do you suppose that little girl thought about it that night? I bet tomorrow, the next day, and the next day. I will bet she grows up feeling rejected. I will bet she grows up behaving like she's not worthy. See, it doesn't matter about how often the event occurs. It's how often you think about the event that makes the difference. Something bad could have happened to you once, but you think about it while you can't sleep or it comes to mind the next day, and it's as good as if it's happening to you again.

Remember the formula, because this is so important, I x V = R. "I" stands for imagination. "V" stands for vividness. By vividness, we mean every time, in your mind, you get a clear picture, with emotion, and have the picture repeated, it becomes "R" or reality on the subconscious level. And why is this important? Because then you behave like the person you know yourself to be. You are acting in accordance with the truth you believe about yourself.

What I'm telling you is this: You could have been scolded by a teacher or a boss. You could have been embarrassed by a boyfriend or someone else. That happened once. But if you remember it, or reiterate it (which means repeat it in your mind), it is as good as if it is happening again. Do you see the discipline? The discipline is to control how you think. Stop thinking about what's wrong with you. Stop letting people tell you what's wrong with you. If you make a mistake, or do something that was stupid or hurtful or whatever, the more you dwell on it, the more it pulls you backwards.

Remember, sometimes coaches are coaching backwards, too. If you make a mistake, they play it over in your mind. It's all about the movie in your mind, and your movie is controlled by the conversation you have with yourself. That conversation is controlled if you randomly let people around you describe you for you. What you need to do is eliminate the negative and accentuate the positive.

Do you know what "sarcasm" is? It's hostility being released. When people are hostile, they're sarcastic. They may not be hostile toward you, they're just sarcastic to you because they're mad

# UNIT 9
# Building My Self-Image

at somebody else. Do you know what "devaluation" is? Devaluation is making you think you are littler than you are, taking your value away from you, finding something wrong with your race, your color, with whoever you are. Do you know why people do that? When their own self-esteem is low, they try to pull you down to make themselves look better. Rather than grow, if I can say what's wrong with you, it makes me feel better.

What I'm going to ask you to do, now, is reflect back. Were you ever taught to be humble? Were you taught to be a humble person? What we really mean by "humility" is giving credit where credit is due. You can remember that rule: Give credit where credit is due. If you do something well in your life, give credit to God, if you believe there's a God. Give credit to your parents if they've helped you. Give credit to your classmates or your teammates if they've helped you. Give credit to people that have associated with you and made your life better. You understand that part.

However, the most important part is you need to give credit to yourself. You must give credit to yourself. Now, not out loud. You need to do it quietly. If somebody says, "Wow, you really did well!" you say, "Yeah, I really am great at that, aren't I!?!" They are going to say, "Yeah, and you make me throw up, too." So, it is out loud to others and quiet to yourself. You see, you can't push away that you're good, because if you push it away, you don't record it in your brain. You want to tell yourself. When somebody compliments you, give credit where credit is due, but inside, I want you to say, "Yes! Yes! Darn I'm good." Yes! That's the way people grow.

Dr. Albert Bandura, at Stanford University, is someone we study and work with a lot. He uncovered during his research that most people pass through their accomplishments too quickly and too lightly. "Oh, it was nothing." "I had nothing to do with that." We pass through too quickly and too lightly to have these moments assimilated in our brain. We push it away. What difference does that make? You don't grow. The way you grow is by elevating your self-image. The way you elevate your self-image is by telling yourself when you're doing something well. Remember, with the combination of I x V = R, you can go back and remember the things you've done well, and repeat them to yourself, and you grow again. You don't need the experiences over and over. All you need to do is experience them in your mind, in areas where you want to grow. Every time you do, you raise your self-image.

I would like to have you write down 10 things that you did well in your life. "I can't think of any." Yes, you can, even if you need to go back to the third grade or the sixth grade. It doesn't matter. Then, what I want you to do, after you write that list of 10 successes, at least two times a day, take each one and remember how you felt. Go to the next one, remember how you felt. Go to the next one, remember how you felt. Go to the next one, and so on. Each time you do that, you're developing inside yourself and raising a stronger and higher self-concept. Why is that important? Because you self-regulate at the level of your belief, not at your potential. If you lower your belief, you lower your performance. Your income, your social ability, the way you live, is all con-

# UNIT 9
# Building My Self-Image

nected at that level. You are going to reject the negative and escalate the positive.

Now, you have good friends. You can become a very, very good friend to others. You can become somebody they always want to be around. What you're going to do is you're going to catch them in the act of doing things very well, and you're going to tell them so. "I've been meaning to tell you how proud I am of you," and then you are going to tell them why. "Wow! Really?" "I wanted to tell you how you well you looked." Some of you [audience] are going to be in the spa business or the salon business. You can be the best help for the mental health of anybody, because some people come in with this terrible image of themselves. You are going to be able to affirm how good they are, not just in how they look, but as a person. You find what they're good at, and you tell them how proud you are of them, how much you think of them. Start doing that.

If you have brothers and sisters, try it with them and see what happens. You can do it with your mother and father. You can do it to the people at work. Catch people in the act of doing things well and tell them so. Then watch how they change. Some of them will just push you away, "Oh, no, no, no. My hair is a mess, I'm. . ." If you have low self-image, you push away compliments. You push them away.

See, you can't wait for somebody else to come along and build your self-image. You won't live long enough. I learned that a long time ago. I do it myself, I raise my self-image. Why? Because my life gets better. My earning power increases. The places I let myself go expand, places I would never let myself go before.

Let me give you an idea that you can remember, forever. Remember, we talked about positive and negative attitudes. One bucket will be positive, and the other will be negative. One more thing to remember, an attitude is just the direction in which you lean. It isn't good, and it isn't bad. That is about as simple as it gets – I can, I can't. I'm no good, I'm good.

Now, every time you think about yourself in a certain area of your life and it's positive, instead of putting water in this bucket, what we're going to do is put a positive rock or a positive weight in it. If you get a whole quantity of positive thoughts about yourself in an area, you'll start to lean in a positive direction. If you have a whole quantity of negative weights in your attitudinal balance scale, then naturally you will lean in a negative direction. Again, you build your own self-image with your own thoughts. People can tell you what's wrong with you. It doesn't matter until you to do what? Accept it.

Suppose you were about four years old and you colored your first painting. You loved it. You thought it was good. You ran up to your sister who is six. "Look!" Sister says, "What is it? You didn't even color inside the lines. That's ugly. You can't draw." What she did was hand you a big old negative weight to put on your attitudinal balance scale, and you start to lean in a negative direction. "I can't draw; sister said so." Now, sister didn't need to keep telling you. All you need-ed to do was remember what sister said. Every time you thought about it, you put another negative weight in the bucket, and another one, and down you go. Remember, you build your own self-image with your own thoughts. (By the way, sister's an expert because she has her artwork on the refrigerator.)

Now you have colored another picture. You're going to go to your older brother. Your older brother doesn't want you hanging around, because he's going on a bike trip around the world with his three friends – at least that's your perspective when you're about four and a half or five. So you run up, "Look, look, look!" He says, "Get out of here. You can't draw. Whoever saw a green man? You know, you can't draw." He handed you a negative weight. Now, you need to put it on your own scale, and it causes you to lean a little bit more in the negative direction. You build your own self-image with your own thoughts. Brother doesn't have to keep telling you. You remember, Sister, and you remember Brother, and down you go.

The next time, you are not going to mess around with brother or sister. You spend all morning coloring on this one, and you go to get Mom. Mom is the expert, the authority. You run downstairs, and grab your mother by the hand. "Come see. Come see." Mother is busy, but she walks up into the room. "What have you done? That's nasty! That's sinful!" and she hits you across the head. See, you put your drawing in the wrong place, and you shocked mother with what you drew. So she says, "Get that off the wall, right now." And you are thinking, "Wow, I sure can't draw, can I? In fact," you're thinking, "it's downright darn dangerous to draw sometimes."

You now have an attitude about yourself as an artist, or at least, at drawing. You go to kindergarten, and the teacher says, "Okay, class, I have something really exciting for you to do today. I was saving it. It's a surprise. We are going to pass out the crayons, and we are all going to draw." What do you think this kid is going to think? "Oh, no, we're not. I can't draw. And the last time I drew, I got my head knocked off. No!"

Every attitude you have, every belief you have, has been formed this way. Others keep evaluating you and telling you, but you need to accept it to have it become a part of you. This is just normal stuff. You have more potential. In areas where you put negative weights on your attitudinal balance scale, you're just not living up to it. Does that make sense? It's a do-it-yourself project. From now on, you need a whole quantity of positive weights to override what you've already built in your mind.

## UNIT 10
# My Future is Up to Me

## Unit Overview

We have already discovered that human beings are picture oriented. What we dwell on in our minds tends to come about in our lives. So, it is important to dwell on what we do want, and use our self-talk to see ourselves into the future – the future we want.

## Unit Objectives

*By the end of this unit, I will:*

- know the four levels of self-talk.

- understand that I move toward what I think about.

- use my self-talk to change my beliefs, working toward what I want.

# WE MOVE TOWARD, AND BECOME LIKE, THAT WHICH WE THINK ABOUT.

# OUR PRESENT THOUGHTS DETERMINE OUR FUTURE.

# UNIT 10
# My Future is Up to Me

## Key Concepts

- Self-Talk

- Subconscious

- Teleological

- Visualize

- Goals / Goal-Setting

- Four Levels of Self-Talk

  - Negative Resignation

  - Recognition

  - Vow

  - Replacement Picture

- Three Time Frames

  - Past – Present – Future

- Self-Image

- Mentor

## Notes

# UNIT 10
# My Future is Up to Me

**Notes**

## UNIT 10
# My Future is Up to Me

## Reflective Questions

- When have I told myself "I can't" or "It won't work" and stopped myself from moving forward?

- When have I told myself that I "should" do something, like quitting smoking or going on a diet, and then didn't do anything?

# UNIT 10
# My Future is Up to Me

## Reflective Questions

- When have I told myself "I quit" or "No more" but didn't give myself anything else to do?

- For the three previous questions, what would have/could have happened if I had given myself a replacement picture to follow?

# UNIT 10
# My Future is Up to Me

## Exercise: Balance Wheel Drill Down

Take a look at your Balance Wheel areas, and focus down a little further on what is important to you, for your life.

| Balance Wheel Areas | What did it look like in the past? | What is my replacement picture? | What do I intend for the future? |
|---|---|---|---|
| | | | |
| | | | |
| | | | |
| | | | |
| | | | |
| | | | |
| | | | |
| | | | |

# UNIT 10
# My Future is Up to Me

## Summary

I want you to know that there are at least four levels of self-talk. What I want you to do is to practice listening to your teachers, your friends, to television, and listen for the level. The first level is called **Negative Resignation.** You know what that means? "No way. No way." People resign themselves, negatively, to impossibility, to no way. People who are really losers in life are at that level, particularly in the area of their lives where they feel that way. So listen; listen and watch what their life is like. It won't be much.

The second level is **Recognition** that you have a problem and you should change, but you have no intention of changing. Do you have any friends that say, "I should save money, I should study"? It is, "I should, I should, but I'm not going to." Recognizing you have potential, that you have a problem, but you have no intention of changing the problem. "I should . . ." and you go on, "But I'm not going to." Another one you watch for is, "I could. I could save money, I could study, but I'm not going to." Another one is, "I ought to study. I ought to save money. I ought to be nice. I'm just not going to." Then there is, "I wish I could study. I wish I could save money. I wish I could be nice. I'm just not going to."

The third level is like a **Vow.** Have you ever made a vow? A vow is like, "I'll never eat that stuff," said when you were a kid, and you never eat it. In fact, you don't even see it on your plate until 10 years later. But you knew you didn't eat it, so as soon as it showed up 10 years later, "Nope, I don't eat that."

The problem is, you still need a replacement picture, and here's why: You, as a human being, need pictures to seek. I'm going to come in more depth; you are teleological. If you don't give yourself a picture or a new goal, you die. Your subconscious knows death occurs without a picture, without a goal. So, if you don't give yourself a new picture, all you do is what you did yesterday. Whatever is in your mind, you just repeat. You intuitively know that. You do what's already in your mind, in your subconscious, in the neuron of your brain. This is why yesterday looks like today. You have the same friends, go to the same show or to the same theater, go to the same hang out, and you go home the same way.

The fourth level is all about **Replacement Pictures.** The key phrase for you will be what you're going to do "the next time." "The next time." The next time gives you a picture of who you're going to socialize with. Otherwise, you're going to socialize with the same level of people you've always socialized with. You say, "I should change friends." Your subconscious needs a picture. If you get rid of the old ones, you don't have anything to do. It's all about a replacement picture.

This is where your goals are going to come in. This is the way you're going to change your life, the way you change your mind. You will see, it isn't just telling yourself once. You need to make it dominant in your brain. I'll show you a process of affirmation to do so, but that comes in a little while. You get the idea now. It's all about replacement pictures.

# UNIT 10
# My Future is Up to Me

I'm going to give you a rule or a principle. You move toward and you become like what you think about. Your present thoughts determine your future. Whether it's good for you or not doesn't matter. I repeat: Whether it's good for you or not doesn't matter. What do you think you might be doing when you're worrying? Building negative pictures, and you're seeking them unconsciously. When you're trying to get away from something, you actually are seeking it.

Have you ever known anybody who was accident prone? What do you think accident prone people might think about? Accidents. All the time. Before you leave the house, if your family knows that you are accident prone, what might they do? They remind you of your problem, because they love you. "My dear, I love you, so be careful. You know how you are." I almost forgot. Thank you. "Well, don't forget." The more we think about what we don't want, the more we're drawn to it. When I work with world class hockey players or soccer players, they are so skilled and so good, that if they look at the goalie, when they kick it, they'll hit the goalie. Same with the hockey players. They're so good, so accurate, they can't look at what they don't want. They need to look at what they do want.

I'm giving you these illustrations because some of you dwell on what you don't want, for your life, your business or your relationships. All this does is draw you to what you don't want. It doesn't change you.

Watch a little kid learning to ride a bicycle. They don't know any better, and don't know that the bike goes where they're looking. So, they see a rock or big hole in front of them. They don't want to hit the rock, but what do they do? Hit the rock. Why? Because they keep staring at the rock. You look at the rock, BAM, and then you get mad at the rock. You look where you want to go, and you automatically, free flowingly, habitually, with your skills, guide your path the way you want to go. It's the same whether it's athletics or whether it's driving a car.

Formula 1 race car drivers are taught, if their car is going out of control and heading to the wall, to immediately focus on the recovery point, where you want your car to go. If they look at the wall, they will steer to the wall. Watch yourself when you're driving. You don't know you're doing it, but wherever you're looking, you adjust the gas or the brake. You adjust the wheel based upon the pattern that you're looking at in front of you. I'm giving you examples you can remember, because this is true of your future, your career, your relationships, everything you're doing. When you dwell on what you don't want with your self-talk, which triggers the picture – words – pictures – emotion – that's what you get.

There are three time frames to remember: the past, the present, and the future. If you're thinking about the good old days, what do you become dissatisfied with? The present, and all you want to do is go back. Listen to your friends. Listen to the people you're working with, not just for now, but when you're running your businesses in the future. You don't want to be talking about history. Astronauts, who have accomplished magnificent things with great courage and skill, if you

# UNIT 10
# My Future is Up to Me

ran into one in the supermarket and you wanted an autograph, what are you going to ask him? "Give me your autograph." Why? "Wow, for having been on the moon!" If an astronaut is asked to give a speech someplace, what are they going to talk about? What they did in the past, not what they are going to do in the future. You can get trapped in history by who you hang around. Be careful how you talk, because that's where your life is going – backwards. It's so subtle, isn't it? But it's all in your self-talk.

Now, what about if you only focus on the way things are? You don't go anywhere. How many people say, "I'm a realist; this is the way it is"? "I am a mess; this is a problem. I don't have any money." You keep dwelling on the reality of the present moment. What will tomorrow look like if you move toward what you think about? Same as today. Life doesn't change much. Listen to your friends. Listen to yourself. Where are you constantly reaffirming the problems you have and the way things are now?

What I'm leading you to is how to start changing by visualizing the future. People who are really making successful strides talk about the future as though it has already occurred. They don't just talk about the future. That's the key. Listen, because I say this so you understand it completely; whether you use it or not is your own deal. They don't just talk about the future. They talk about the future as though it's already done. I have my job. I have my business. I have my career. I have the relationship. I have what I want. It's done. (I'm going to show you later on why that works when we get into Gestalt psychology.)

The important thing is for high performance people, like you, to speak as though you already have the career. You already have the degree. You already have the job. You already have what you are seeking. You write your goals the same way. Great leaders always speak of the future as though it's already accomplished. So will you. You are going to learn how to write your goals, but that's not enough. You're going to learn to visualize that way. "Visualize" just means to imagine correctly; imagine your goals correctly. It's the future the way you want it. That's the key.

There's so much more to this, but I'm giving you the fundamentals. I've already talked to you about your beliefs and self-talk. I've talked to you about the power of self-talk in forming your self-image. It is all about your daily self-talk – the way you want your business to go, your life to go, or the way you want the day to go. You'll be surprised at first. "Wow, how come it happened that way?" That's how your mind works. How you going to speak to yourself? How you going to speak to others?

Have you ever had a good mentor? Do you know what a mentor is? A good mentor always sees more in you than you see in yourself. In fact, they always see more in you than you are actually using right now, doing or being right now. It wasn't just that you didn't know. You are not doing/being/acting now. They saw more of you in the future, and they talked to you with words to describe you as they saw you, as though you already were. "I see you as being..." Me? Me? You're

# UNIT 10
# My Future is Up to Me

going to learn to do that to yourself. You're going to learn to mentor yourself with your goals. If you sit around and wait for a mentor, you may not live long enough. So you want to be able to do it yourself.

# UNIT 11
# I'm Worth It!

## Unit Overview

Giving sanction, or agreeing with, what others say to us, about ourselves, is a risky business. What we are really agreeing with are the opinions of others, and they may not be "the truth." Then, we use our self-talk to reinforce a bad opinion, and before we know it, we tear down our sense of self-esteem. We need to remember our successes, and assimilate them fully, so that we escalate our self-worth, our self-esteem.

## Unit Objectives

*By the end of this unit, I will:*

- understand that self-esteem is my estimate of my self-worth.

- build my own self-esteem with my own thoughts.

- take the time to assimilate my successes into my sense of self-esteem.

- be aware of those around me who may want to pull me back, and make a special effort to build up others around me.

# MOST PEOPLE PASS THROUGH
# THEIR ACCOMPLISHMENTS
# TOO QUICKLY AND TOO LIGHTLY
# TO ASSIMILATE THEM.

# UNIT 11
# I'm Worth It!

## Key Concepts

- Self-Esteem

- Self-Image

- Subconscious

- Self-Talk

- Attitudinal Balance Scale

- Performance

- Perception

## Notes

# UNIT 11
# I'm Worth It!

**Notes**

## UNIT 11
# I'm Worth It!

## Reflective Questions

- What are three academic skill areas where I have high self-esteem?

- What are some academic areas where my self-esteem could be improved?

- How can I help others develop their self-esteem?

## UNIT 11
# I'm Worth It!

## Exercise: Too Good for Me

Place a check (✓) next to those things you believe are "too good" for you. Then, explain why you think each is out of reach.

| What is too good for me? | ✓ | Why? |
|---|---|---|
| Dinner and a movie | | |
| Used car | | |
| Scholarship to school | | |
| Vacation to Europe | | |
| Studio apartment | | |
| Career | | |
| Art collection | | |
| New car | | |
| Designer clothes | | |
| Big house | | |
| Safari to Africa | | |
| HD Television | | |
| Significant Other | | |
| A pet | | |
| Positive Future | | |
| | | |
| | | |

## UNIT 11
# I'm Worth It!

## Summary

What is your estimate of your own worth? What do you think? Good question, isn't it? Why would it be important to know your own worth? So you can do better in life? So you are able to offer others more? OK, your sense of self-worth is called "self-esteem." Now, what does that mean? It is your estimate of yourself. It is your estimate of what you're worth as a human being.

Have you ever watched people around a newborn baby, how they just love it and adore it? They talk about how wonderful it is, and ooh and ah. When the kid gets to be three, the perception changes a little bit. When the kid gets to be 20, the perception isn't so good. Same at 25. You know, that baby can't even change its own pants, can't feed itself, can't do anything. And yet, we hold it in high esteem and regard and love it. Somehow, as we grow older, we start judging each other. We can tell you what you're worth in the second grade or the third grade. "He's dumb, he's smart. She's dumb, she's smart. She can sing, he can't sing," and so on. Once you get your mind made up of how good you are, your estimate of yourself, you act like it, you behave like it, even though it's not true.

When you have a low estimate of self, you'll find yourself not wanting to be around people who you perceive as better than you. "They are too good for me." You seek relationships with people, and you want to go places, where you can naturally be yourself. You don't have to fake it. "I can just be myself, and I'm accepted." If you have a low self-image and you're around people who feel very high about themselves, you pretend like you love being there. Do you ever do that? "I love it!" Yes, and you can hardly wait to get out and go back and have a beer with your friends, right? "Let me out of here."

For somebody who has very high self-esteem, who happens to be hanging around bad mouthing and guys talking with low self-esteem, in a tavern, they can hardly wait to get out of there. They may pretend like they like being in that situation, but they can hardly wait until they can go back and be with people where they don't need to fake it and can naturally be themselves.

You have created your estimate with your own mind. If you are raised in a low self-esteem, bullying environment or negative, destructive environment, then it would be very unlikely that you would have high self-esteem. If your self-talk is negative and destructive, and you beat yourself up, you are lowering your self-esteem. So what? Well, you are looking for super jobs and careers, I know you are. You will draw to yourself the kind of job and career you feel worthy of receiving. If a career comes your way that you see as too big for you, you will subconsciously do something to push it away. Not consciously, but subconsciously. When good relationships come your way, you say, "Oh, she's too good for me." "Oh, he's too good for me." You unconsciously do something, even though you'd like to be with them, to push it away.

If you raise your self-image, you allow better opportunities to come to you. You let better relationships come to you. You let better friends come to you. Now, how do you raise your self-esteem? By eliminating the negative, destructive, devaluative self-talk; by not accepting the degrading opinions of others; by being careful about what you pull in off television or off your music.

# UNIT 11
# I'm Worth It!

You want to eliminate that for one reason: You are going to go into the job of putting positive weights on your attitudinal balance scale. You are going to elevate yourself.

When you do something well, you are going to tell yourself you're doing it well. You are going to catch yourself in the act of doing things right, and you are going to tell yourself. Every time you do, it's like putting a positive weight on your attitudinal balance scale. You raise your self-image, and you raise your self-esteem. Why is that important? Because as you raise your self-image, your performance raises. This is scientifically proven.

Remember when I said I wanted you to write down about 10 things you did well. I want you to go back over this list, because every time you remember the success—remember, you don't have to do it again – you remember how you felt. What you are doing every time you remember, is you are putting a positive weight on your attitudinal balance scale. You are raising your self-esteem. If you do that over and over and over for three weeks or four weeks, wow. You can't imagine how you'll carry yourself. Your mind changes and your opportunities change and the people around you change. It's amazing. It's all on the inside, and that is because of the way you're talking to yourself, and what you accept. That's how valuable self-esteem is.

If you were going to sell your car, would you just sell it without finding out what it was worth? Do you ask the first person you see, "Tell me what my car is worth"? "I don't know what it's worth." "Okay, you can have it." I think you'd rather get a better estimate, wouldn't you? But some of you, getting ready to go out, you ask somebody, "What do I look like?" "Oh, you look terrible." "Oh, I'm glad I asked. I almost went out looking like this." We ask others, "What do you think my chance of a future?" "What do you think my chance of getting a job?" "What do you think my chance of. . .?" "Well, I've known you for years, and it's stupid of you to think that way." You ask others' opinions too much about your future and about who you can be.

If your self-esteem is low, you think others' opinions are better than your own. You need to be careful and not allow yourself to be trapped in the negative, destructive world of others who are willing to give you an opinion of who you are. This won't be easy to do, to start with, but it's very important. Do you understand the importance of it?

One time, I was at a prison for young offenders. There was this young guy, about 20 years old, about to get out of prison. He'd been in for maybe four years. In prison, you're not treated very well and your opinion of yourself isn't very high. As he was going out of prison I said to him, "Well, you're going to be looking for a job, won't you?" He said, "Yeah." What kind of a job are you looking for? "Whatever." If your self-esteem is low, then any kind of a job is okay. I don't want you to be that way. I want you to make your self-esteem high so you can select the kind of jobs you want, who you're going to work with and what kind of environment you want. "Anything" isn't going to be good enough for you.

The next thing I asked him was, "What do you think you ought to get paid?" His reply was, honest to goodness, "Whatever." When your self-esteem is low, then it's, "I don't care. I'm not worth much, just pay me what you think I'm worth." If you raise your self-esteem, you'll be given a just

# UNIT 11
# I'm Worth It!

wage. You'll be able to earn a living that you deserve. And, you need to understand, if you keep raising your self-image, you're going to earn more.

So then I said, "You'll probably be looking for a car, won't you? He said, "Yeah." "What kind of car you looking for?" And his reply was, "Just some wheels." If you have high self-esteem, you want to pick a car you want, don't you? You want a better car. Now get this. (I don't make these up.) I said to him, "You're probably going to be out looking for a girl to get married to, won't you?" He says, "Yeah." Honest to God, I said, "And what kind of a girl you looking for?" Do you know what he said? Yep, he said, "Whatever. Anything." And he'll find one who is looking for "whatever and anything," too. See, you attract each other. We attract the kind of relationships, the kind of jobs, the kind of opportunities. Make sense? It's not luck "out there," it's in your mind.

Remember when we started, I asked why should you change your mind? Isn't this a good reason? Your self-esteem not only affects your perception, it affects what you draw to yourself. Your self-esteem affects whether you think you deserve this class and this kind of a grade, or what kind of relationship you deserve.

One more piece. Children of royalty are treated royally, because some day they'll be king. What if you beat them up, run them down, tell them they're no good, and then tell them to go out and be a king? It probably won't work all that well. The military used to do that. They used to run people down, then tell them go out and be brave. They've changed their mind about that. Coaches used to beat you up, run you down, tell you you're no good, and then all of a sudden you are supposed to go out and play like a hero. Doesn't make a lot of sense.

You can't run yourself down and perform high. If you start devaluing your children, those children will be shy, scared, and will not do well in school. You need to treat your children with dignity and with respect. That does not mean you aren't going to discipline them. It just means that you're not going to put them down. You're not going to bully them or intimidate them. You are going to elevate them. You are going to tell them how much you love them, how good they are.

People with low self-esteem are intimidated by people they perceive as having high self-esteem. If you work for somebody and they have low self-esteem, you'll never do anything right. They'll always find fault with you. Have you ever run into that? If you have a teacher with low self-esteem, there's not much you can do that's right. They'll always try to find something wrong with you. Same with you. If you're around sarcasm or devaluation, with belittling, hurtful, mean people, their self-esteem level is so low that they're trying to bring you down to their level. "Love thy neighbor like thyself," it was written. I find everybody does, and that's the problem.

So, why do you want to raise your self-image, what would be a good reason? You feel better about yourself, you perform better, your moods are better. You market yourself better when it comes to getting that job you want. You stand up for yourself. You stand up for your rights, and you don't let people abuse you in any way. You won't put up with or tolerate any of that nonsense. It is totally out of your self-image. You also treat people better.

How are you going to do it? You control your self-talk. You're going to tell yourself when you're good.

## UNIT 12
# Make the Unfamiliar Familiar

## Unit Overview

In our past, when we really didn't want to go somewhere or do something, we found excellent reasons for not going or doing. What we may not have realized is that we were coming face-to-face with our comfort zones. While some comfort zones are good for us, others hold us back; and it is time that we learn how to expand those limiting comfort zones and allow ourselves to grow.

## Unit Objectives

*By the end of this unit, I will:*

*   understand that I am a self-regulating mechanism.

*   be aware of my reactions to situations, and know that these reactions are signals of comfort zone issues that may be holding me back.

*   know an easy process to help me make the unfamiliar familiar, releasing me from the restrictions of my limiting comfort zones.

# OUR COMFORT ZONES
# REGULATE OUR EFFECTIVENESS.

# UNIT 12
# Make the Unfamiliar Familiar

## Key Concepts

- Self-Concept

- Self-Image

- Comfort Zone

- Behavior

- Subconscious

- Visualization

- Potential

- Goals / Goal-Setting

## Notes

# UNIT 12
# Make the Unfamiliar Familiar

**Notes**

## UNIT 12
# Make the Unfamiliar Familiar

## Reflective Questions

- What situation caused me to feel out of my comfort zone? Why did this situation make me feel uncomfortable?

- What activities am I currently avoiding because they are out of my comfort zone?

# UNIT 12
# Make the Unfamiliar Familiar

## Reflective Questions

- Do I resist change? Why?

- How can expanding my comfort zones help me be more successful at school? At work?

## UNIT 12
# Make the Unfamiliar Familiar

## Interview

Imagine you are going for a job interview; the type of job is your choice. You will be meeting with the department head or manager, someone you have never met before. Your interview time is 9:00 am, one week from today.

On your own, think about this scenario. Using your "Going For An Interview" Worksheet answers below, visualize the interview. See yourself giving the interview of a lifetime, and getting the job.

### Going for an Interview work sheet

Where am I going to be interviewed?

How am I going to get there?

What time will I need to get out of bed?

How should I be dressed?

Who do I need to take me there?

What questions am I likely to be asked?

What questions do I want to ask?

What qualities is the interviewer probably looking for?

What sort of attitude should I have at the interview?

What is the best possible outcome for me?

If I am successful, what do I see as my next step?

# UNIT 12
# Make the Unfamiliar Familiar

## Summary

Do you remember when I talked about going into the wrong rest room? Let me explain to you how your mind works and why that is upsetting to you – or at least it should be. Your self-concept, or your self-image, is related to what we call your "comfort zone." As long as you stay relatively close to behaving like you know you are, as long as you behave pretty much like your conscience tells you to behave, you're OK. When you violate your conscience, how do you feel? Not good, do you? And what do you want to do? You want to correct it. You want to make amends.

When we're talking about your self-concept, your self-image, and your comfort zone, it could be environmentally when you're out of place or it could be when you're socially out of place. It could be when you're academically out of place, or you're racially out of place. It could be when you're around others you think are too wealthy for you or not wealthy enough. What you're doing is you are bouncing your perceptions off of your stored reality of the way you think things should be, for you – the way the world "is." Now, when your perceptions don't match, when you feel that the world outside isn't matching the way you think it should, that's called being out of your comfort zone.

When you're in your comfort zone, you think all right. You are at your best, relaxed, and you flow. When you're out of your comfort zone, you can't think. You feel uptight. One of the things that happens when you're out of your comfort zone, subconsciously, is you stimulate creativity that tells you to go back where you belong. Go back to your old neighborhood; go back to your school; go back to your family; go back to your old friends. "Go back" to the old way – go back to the familiar.

You need to understand that everybody seeks what's familiar subconsciously, not consciously. We're seeking what's familiar. When we find ourselves in unfamiliar situations, here's what happens: When you're out of place you become forgetful. Your memory is interfered with and your mind goes blank. Have you ever had that happen? Your mind doesn't need to go blank, if you visualize ahead. But because you find yourself out of place, you can't think of what you know.

Also, when you are out of your comfort zone socially, academically, environmentally, whatever it might be, people will talk to you, but you don't hear or understand what they're saying. Have you ever gone someplace socially and been introduced to someone, get their name and then forget it? When you're out of your comfort zone, you block the input of information. Then your subconscious says, "Don't do it again. Stay home. Stay with your friends. Stay where you belong." You don't tell yourself in exactly those words. You get creative and say, "That's dumb, I don't need to go there. I have other things to do." You rationalize yourself to stay with the familiar. You need to watch that. Perhaps you are thinking about starting a new business, and here you are in Seattle. Maybe you want to open up in Los Angeles, or maybe San Francisco. If leaving Seattle is out of your comfort zone, you'll tell yourself why you shouldn't go.

# UNIT 12
# Make the Unfamiliar Familiar

Another thing that happens when you're out of your comfort zone is your voice changes. People will know if you're out of your comfort zone, because your vocal cords get stretched and your voice gets higher and starts to crack. When you're lying, your voice changes. Now, you can't remember, you can't get information out, and your voice is changing. So you say to yourself, "I sure look stupid, don't I? I'd better stay where I'm already good."

The other thing that happens when you're out of your comfort zone is your upper body starts to constrict. The muscles tighten up. Have you heard anybody say, "I've been under pressure lately," or "I feel uptight about this"? Being uptight and under pressure comes when you detect yourself being out of place – and it's instantaneous. Your muscles start to squeeze down on your rib cage. Underneath your rib cage happens to be your lungs, so your lungs are being squeezed (under pressure). "I feel uptight," describes the muscles tightening up in your back and your neck. This is where those phrases came from, but what causes it, psychologically, is when you're out of place.

Now, you can be out of place worse than you normally are, but you get the same feeling if you're better than you normally are. It's when things are different that you feel that way. Different than what? Than what's "normal" for you. You need to learn to change normal for you. You want to raise "normal." You must change "normal," or you'll be constantly under stress.

If you need fine motor skills, like athletes or fighter pilots, and you're out of your comfort zone, you blow the game, or you kill yourself, because you need fine motor skills to keep yourself alive or win the game. Remember, when you're out of place, you don't think clearly. You get uptight. You don't kick the ball, you don't catch the ball. If you're playing tennis, you serve the net. Las Vegas knows that, and that's why they give the home team six points or seven points advantage. Teams always seem to play better when they're at home than when they're away, because the crowd is different, the hotels are different. When you're out of your comfort zone, it doesn't mean that you're not brave. It just means your not thinking clearly and you don't use your fine motor skills.

Why is change hard? Why do people want to stay the same? Because your stomach secretes more digestive juice than it needs. Have you ever said, "This makes me sick at my stomach"? When you're out of place, your stomach secretes more digestive juice and so you get nauseated. If you persist, you get ulcers. An ulcer isn't so much from what you've eaten, as it is what's eating you. It's your stomach digesting itself. You are trying to force yourself to be better or do better or to be different without using your imagination to expand your self-image. This happens to everybody.

Now, that's not all. Moisture occurs immediately on the surface of your skin. When you're out of place, whether it be social or business, you start to perspire. This is how the lie detector, the polygraph, works. They attach electrodes to the surface of your skin. They'll ask your mother's

# UNIT 12
# Make the Unfamiliar Familiar

name, which they already know, or your address, which they already know, and then they ask if you robbed the bank. As you answer about your mother's name, the needle goes on an even keel. When they ask, "Did you rob the bank?" and you answer, "Nope," the machine shorts out immediately, just from lying.

Now, that's not all. You're knees get shaky, so you lose balance. You can't remember; you can't get anything in; your voice is changing; your rib cage is caving down on your lungs; you're throwing up; you're sweating like mad, and now, you're losing your balance.

This is why people stay the same. They stay in the same neighborhood with the same job, maybe in the same city. They won't let themselves think about going to school outside of where they live. They won't let themselves think too much about getting a job different than what their parents had. They don't let themselves think about changing their social life and walking into places like a fancy restaurant. "This is too good for me. That's not good enough for me." It's all comfort zone. You're going to learn how to expand your comfort zone. You're going to learn how to visualize in your mind. Goal-setting is familiarizing yourself with your future, safely.

Remember that little five year old we talked about going to school? Their comfort zone was home. If you didn't talk about school and help them visualize something about school, they are scared. If you just dropped them off, rush back to your car, you think you escaped. But when you get home, that five year old is still attached to the bumper of your car. "What's the matter with this kid? School is going to be good for them." Oh, no, it's not!

Have you been out of your comfort zone? Of course, you have. If somebody says, "Well, I don't need this. I've never been out of my comfort zone," then you are staying with the same friends, doing the same thing in the same school doing the same job, the same kind of vehicle, in the same church, going to the same store. Of course, you don't need it. As long as you stay in your comfort zone, you don't need this information at all. But, if you choose to use your potential, then you'd better learn how to visualize correctly.

It's a matter of taking your imagination into the future. You practice in your mind with people that normally make you upset. You take yourself into the way your life is going to be in the future. You practice taking yourself and familiarizing yourself with where you want the job and who you want to be with. You allow yourself to travel there, safely, over and over and over. You're going to see later on that if I can't visualize the future with safety, I won't do it. I won't do it, or I'll just do it once. Then, back I go. But I won't admit to myself the truth. I'll just say to myself, "It was stupid. I didn't like it. It rained too much." You will find reasons to go back.

Watch yourself in your comfort zone. School could have been out of your comfort zone. Universities could be out of your comfort zone. "Used to be" out of your comfort zone, right? Going into business for yourself could be out of your comfort zone. Now, you could be very comfortable in school, but when you go to get a job, you're out of your comfort zone in the interview. If you get

# UNIT 12
# Make the Unfamiliar Familiar

into an environment that doesn't look like school, because you didn't visualize it, from the outside, it looks like you didn't learn a thing. Do you act stupid because you didn't learn anything? No, you act stupid because you didn't visualize yourself safely, so you can't remember.

I'm going to teach you how to visualize. Goal-setting is all for your future. You can familiarize yourself with a better way of life, and you decide what that is. Once you move forward, then where you live now is out of your comfort zone. Think about that. As you visualize yourself into your future job, you won't like being in school. "I gotta get out of here!" What you are going to learn is that as you visualize yourself into the new, you make yourself dissatisfied with the old – and you won't grow on your own until you're dissatisfied.

# UNIT 13
# The Next Time . . .

## Unit Overview

We now know how powerful our self-talk is, and how it has affected our thinking and behavior in the past. In fact, for many of us, our self-talk has been pretty negative. So far in this course, we have been working toward changing our self-talk from negative to positive, and now we go one step further by learning to give ourselves "next time" goals to create that new picture of ourselves in our subconscious.

## Unit Objectives

*By the end of this unit, I will:*

* understand how my self-talk controls my performance reality.

* stop my negative self-talk about my performance and give myself new performance goals with the phrase, "The next time, I intend to . . ."

## I'M BETTER THAN THAT.
## THE NEXT TIME,
## I INTEND TO . . .

## UNIT 13
# The Next Time . . .

## Key Concepts

- Affirmation

- Goal

- Self-Talk

- Self-Image

- Neuron

- Performance Reality

- Belief

- Replacement Picture(s)

- Assimilate / Assimilation

- Attitudinal Balance Scale

- Mentor

## Notes

# UNIT 13
# The Next Time . . .

**Notes**

# The Next Time . . .

## Reflective Questions

- If I let go and let the real me flow, how is it?

- What are some positive words I could use in my conversations that trigger a positive image in my mind?

# UNIT 13
# The Next Time . . .

## Reflective Questions

- What are some negative words I should avoid when speaking because they trigger a negative picture in my mind?

- As I look forward to learning more about goals and my future, what are some important goals I have in each of these areas? Spiritual, Marriage/Relationships, Family, Physical Health, Mental Health, Personal, Social, Vocational/Job, Retirement, Recreation/Leisure time, Community Service?

## UNIT 13
# The Next Time . . .

## Exercise: The Next Time.../Self-Talk

Get out a test, or a project, or an assignment from earlier in the term. Review how the self-talk cycle applies to each phase.

- What were my initial thoughts about the test or project?

- Did I reflect back on how I have always done in a subject like this?

**Self-Talk**

**Self-Image**

**Real Performance**

- Did the performance on the test or the project reflect how I spoke to myself about the old me or the new me?

- Did I reinforce an existing image of myself or did I give myself a new one?

## UNIT 13
# The Next Time . . .

## Summary

How do you speak to yourself when you make a mistake? How do you speak to yourself when you do something right? It's very interesting, because your mind is pretty tricky. If we're going to make the changes, it isn't just going to be the written affirmations and goals I'm going to teach you. It needs to become an everyday discipline in how you control your self-talk, particularly when you make a mistake. If you make a mistake and then if you speak to yourself incorrectly, you're going to solidify in your self-image who you really don't want to be. I thought what I would do is review a little bit, then take you forward, because we've gone through a great deal of material up to this point.

You and I have what we call a self-image. That self-image is really nothing that I've made up. It is your reality that's stored in the neuron of your brain. That self-image controls how you act or how you behave. I'm going to call how you act or behave your "performance reality." It's how you are, if you're not faking it. Your self-image automatically controls the real you. Now, you can override it. You can try hard to be better, sweeter, nicer, friendlier, or happier. Inside, you know, "Wow! If I let go of control, they'd see the real me." I'm talking about the real you.

What we're saying is, "As I think, I am." This controls your automatic, free flowing behavior of the way you automatically act. What caused that to occur in the first place was how you spoke to yourself with your self-talk. Remember, self-talk is that three dimensional form of thought – words, pictures, and emotion. Another word for self-talk might be "affirmation."

What's an affirmation? It's just a statement of fact, or a statement of belief. You make thousands of them every day. "I like this, I don't like that." "That's like me; that's not like me." You're constantly talking to yourself. That self-talk forms your self-image and still does. What makes it difficult for us to change is this: Let's say you make a mistake. You see yourself making a fool of yourself or messing up in some way. As you observe how you messed up, you tell yourself, "Well, that's always been like me." Remember, your self-talk goes, "That's like me. I've always been a screw up. I've always made a fool of myself. I've always been forgetful. That's normal for me. That's like me." This self-talk reinforces your already existing self-image that isn't good enough for you. So, when you make a mistake, I want you to say to yourself, "That's not like me. I'm better than that."

Up to this point, it may not be true, because you can start arguing with yourself. "Who am I kidding? I've been like this since I was four, okay? I was like this yesterday, and now I tell myself it's not like me?" You want to say to yourself, "That is no longer who I am. I'm much better than that." Then you need to tell yourself, "The next time…" – that's the key phrase – "the next time I intend to," and you go on to tell yourself what you intend to do. The next time I intend to think before I talk. The next time I intend to control my temper. The next time I intend to… Otherwise, if you don't do that, your self-talk goes, "What's the matter with me anyway? How could I have

# UNIT 13
# The Next Time . . .

been so stupid?" Then you get caught in that stream of negative self-talk describing to yourself what's wrong with you. Do you ever do that? It's like, "There I go again. What's the matter with me? I've always been that way." All of this then hardens the self-image, which makes sure you behave like that the rest of your life, until you change it.

Good athletes don't dwell on their mistakes. Great athletes quickly make the correction in their mind. Remember, it's all about replacement pictures. You need to give yourself a replacement picture for the way you're behaving now. If you remember, I said to you how necessary goals were, that if you don't give yourself a new one, all you do is do the old one. This is all about giving yourself replacement pictures for your social life, for your personal life, for how you feel about yourself, how you think about yourself. It's how you want to live. It is about how much money you want to accumulate, It's whether you see yourself as poor or wealthy, or see yourself as smart or dumb.

It's all about a replacement picture, and the key phrase for the replacement picture is "The next time…" It shuts off all the negative self-talk, if you tell yourself what you're going to do the next time. If you tell yourself, "No more. That's not like me," and you give yourself "the next time," it gives you the image to seek.

Years ago, when I was a high school football coach, I had this kid who was a punter. It was a very important game. I had this kid take the ball and kick it, and it went only 10 yards down the field, and right out of bounds. Geez, that made me mad! That wasn't at all what we needed. So he came out of the game, and I said, "Hey, stupid. You're kicking the ball off the side of your foot. Sit down and think about it." I don't make these up. So, the kid is sitting there thinking, "I'm kicking the ball with the side of my foot. I'm kicking the ball with the side of my foot." He goes out the second time to kick one, it was just like the first one. He comes out, and I said, "Didn't I just tell you you're kicking it off the side of your foot? "He said, "Yeah." I said, "Well, don't you care? Sit down and concentrate." The kid is sitting on the bench doing what with his self-talk? He's thinking about his mistake. Three times in the same game.

He came out of the game the third time, and tried to hide from me; but I found him. I put him on the bench and said, "You may not play again the rest of the game, let alone the rest of your life. Besides that, you don't even get good grades." You always threw those in when you got a chance. We coaches got accused of not stressing academics. Now, the young person was doing exactly what I was telling him to do. I was telling him what to do wrong. Remember the kid with the bicycle heading to the rock; as you dwell on the rock, you run into the rock. Remember the race car driver. If the car is going out of control and you look where you don't want your car to go, bam, you run right into the wall.

It's all about replacement pictures. Stop telling yourself what you don't want, and tell yourself what you do want. You'll become good parents. You're going to become good spouses. You're

# UNIT 13
# The Next Time . . .

going to become great leaders, great managers, because you're going to be different than most people. People will say, "Wow, I don't know why it is, but your people seem to do better than everybody else's." You are telling them what to do right instead of what to do wrong.

That doesn't mean you tolerate poor performance. Being positive doesn't mean you're soft or weak. Being positive just means tell them how to drop the ball right. Drop it with the nose up. I should have said to that punter, "You're better than that. Stop it. You're too good to be doing that." And if I had been a good coach, I would have said, "The next time you go out there, just drop it with the nose up." You stop the behavior and the picture. Otherwise he'll be thinking, "Oh, I'm sorry. I didn't mean to." But, you do that all the time, don't you? Up until now. No more, no more. You're going to start correcting your own behavior.

One more piece to this. When you do something right for the first time, you know, you always knew you were a screw up, and this time it went well for you in something; you may say to yourself, "Wow, that's not like me either. I always blow it." Do you ever do that? People say, "Wow, you were really good at that." "Are you kidding? I don't know what happened. I got lucky." You deny that you can be good. Don't do that. You want to assimilate into your mind the new you. You don't want to deny what you are capable of being.

When you do something you like about yourself, I want you to tell yourself this, "That's like me." You say, "Yes!" to yourself. Yes, I am good at that. But do it quietly. If somebody says, "My, but you do that well," you say, "Yeah, I really did didn't I? I'm really special," they say, "That's the last time I'm ever going to talk to you." You can't push compliments away. You need to accept them. Learn to say, "Thank you," when somebody pays you a compliment. Then give credit where credit is due. Inside, with your self-talk, it is, "Yes!" Each time you do, you put a positive weight on your attitudinal balance scale. You're putting a positive weight on your attitudinal balance scale. You're changing your image of yourself.

You're learning to mentor yourself. Remember, a good mentor always sees more in you than you see in yourself. That's what you're doing here. You want to stop affirming the behaviors and the traits you don't want. Then, when you do something right, you tell yourself, "You know, I'm much better than I thought. This is me. I am this good." Now, when you make a mistake, it is, "That's not like me," and then you're going to say to yourself, "The next time I intend to," and then you give yourself the replacement picture. Just give yourself the replacement picture. If you don't, you say, "Well, I could have; I should have; if only I would have," and you just go on to a cycle that just runs you into a rut, a depression, and keeps you into a slump. Practice this, and you'll get better at it all the time.

Here's what I want you to do: For the next 24 hours, I want you to play a game with yourself. No negative affirmations, no negative self-talk for 24 hours. I know what you're thinking, "I might as well go home and go to bed, right now." "That's not like me." It is going to be like you. You are

# UNIT 13
# The Next Time . . .

going to do it.

When you catch yourself making a negative affirmation, you just tell yourself, "That used to be the way I talked. I don't do that anymore. I'm better than that." Then what you're going to say to yourself is, "The next time, I will make sure I control how I think." What I'm asking you to do is to control your thoughts. It will become a habit for you. Just like the times tables and tying your shoes. It took focused concentration, but you learned. It's going to take the same kind of behavioral pattern.

You want to develop the habit pattern of controlling your self-talk. When you get around people that are negative and destructive, don't get trapped by them. When you're correcting your friends, when they make a mistake, you're going to help them out. You will tell them, "You know, I see you as a lot better than that." You don't have to tell them, "That's stupid of you," and, "There you go again." You don't have to teach them a course. Just say, "You know, I don't see you that way at all." It will shock them. They think, "You don't? But, I've always been this way." Well, up until now. You're much better than that. How you're going to treat them is very constructive and very positive. You are not going to take anything wrong, but you're not going to be devaluing or demeaning to them. You're going to be very strong. Being positive is very strong.

I was very firm with that kicker after I learned how to do it right. I said, "Stop it. Don't do that anymore. You're better than that." I raised his self-image, but that wasn't good enough. He needed a replacement picture. I had to give him a replacement picture. You will do the same thing for yourself.

# UNIT 14
# Putting Life on a Want-to

## Unit Overview

We have all felt, at one time or another, like we were being forced into doing something against our will. We may have done it, but we rebelled every step of the way. We felt pushed and we pushed back, and it used up a lot of energy while it made us feel unhappy. What if we put life on a "want to" basis, and used all of that energy and creativity to make a happy life for ourselves and those around us?

## Unit Objectives

*By the end of this unit, I will:*

- understand fear-based "have to" restrictive motivation.

- understand value-based "want to" constructive motivation.

- know how to put my life on a want-to basis.

- take accountability for my decisions and accept the consequences.

## PUT YOUR LIFE ON A "WANT TO" BASIS.

# UNIT 14
# Putting Life on a Want-to

## Key Concepts

- Motivation

- Energy

- Fear

- Coercion

- Push / Push Back

- Have to

- Or else…

- Intimidation

- Creative Avoidance

- Procrastination

- Consequences

- Subconscious

- Constructive

- Want to

- Value

- Self-Esteem

- Self-Image

## Notes

# UNIT 14
# Putting Life on a Want-to

**Notes**

## UNIT 14
# Putting Life on a Want-to

## Reflective Questions

- What are some have-to's that I have in my life?

- Now that I realize there are no have-to's in my life, what are some of the reasons I choose to do what I do?

## UNIT 14
# Putting Life on a Want-to

## Reflective Questions

- Where have I let other people affect my self-esteem?

- Where do I give up accountability to someone else? Why?

## UNIT 14
# Putting Life on a Want-to

## Exercise: Math Test

In the following simple arithmetic problems, a plus (+) sign means to multiply, a divide (÷) means to add, a minus (-) sign means to divide and a multiplication (x) sign means to subtract. Complete the problems below. You must complete the test in 1-1/2 minutes.

| | |
|---|---|
| 8 + 2 = | 7 x 2 = |
| 9 + 11 = | 9 + 2 = |
| 4 x 3 = | 8 – 4 = |
| 9 – 3 = | 9 + 6 = |
| 7 x 4 = | 8 ÷ 4 = |
| 4 + 4 = | 8 x 7 = |
| 12 x 2 = | 13 – 1 = |
| 2 - 10 = | 16 – 4 = |
| 9 – 1 = | 8 x 2 = |
| 5 + 6 = | 6 x 2 = |
| 2 x 1 = | 8 + 4 = |
| 10 – 5 = | 10 – 2 = |
| 12 + 2 = | 4 – 1 = |
| 6 ÷ 2 = | 28 + 2 = |
| 8 + 5 = | 8 + 2 = |
| 6 + 6 = | 14 ÷ 2 = |

## UNIT 14
# Putting Life on a Want-to

## Exercise: Have to's

Check either "Have to" or "Want to" for each of the examples below. In the empty spaces, list a few of your own activities, and whether they are "Have to" or "Want to".

| Have To's | | Want To's |
|---|---|---|
| | Go to class | |
| | Study | |
| | Do homework | |
| | Read | |
| | See a tutor | |
| | Ask questions in class | |
| | | |
| | | |
| | | |
| | | |

## Are they really have to's?

...............................................................................................................................................

...............................................................................................................................................

## UNIT 14
# Putting Life on a Want-to

## Summary

I think, if I would title this unit for you, it would be, "Who's In Charge, Them or Me?" Just who is the "them"? Well, it could be almost anybody. In order to be the super effective person that you're capable of being, it is essential that you embody and practice what I am about to teach you. It has to do with getting yourself motivated. When I talk about motivation, I'm not talking about inspiration, hallelujah and all of that. No pep assembly. I'm talking about putting a passion inside of yourself, a drive inside of yourself.

In order to accomplish the big things you're going to accomplish, you're going to need to drive yourself. "I am completely self-determined. Nobody outside of me is making me do this." Nobody is making me become wealthy. Nobody is making me become who I want to be in this business. Nobody is making me, and quite frankly, nobody can make you do anything.

You need to recognize that you're operating from free will, as a human being. You're not necessarily operating as if you are being told what to do. "I'm being bossed around by some power outside of me." God, if there is a God (and I believe there is), created human beings with choice. You get a choice. You get a choice to behave or not behave. You get a choice to act or not act. You get a choice, and this is a way of thinking.

There are two forms of energy or motivation. One is based on fear. You'll see that is where you feel like you're being made to do something against your will, or you're being pushed or coerced. In the example where I held my hand out, and pushed against one of the audience members, what happened? He pushed back. When pushed, human beings push back.

What does it feel like to be pushed? How do you know when you're being pushed? It's when you're being told you "have to" do something, or else be punished or made to look silly. "Or else," I'll withhold something that you want. If you don't do what the teacher wants, in the old days, they would withhold your grade. They may even withhold your diploma. They may keep you from graduating. So, you did what they asked, not because you really chose to do, but because, in your mind, you thought, "If I don't, something awful will happen to me." Some of you live your life that way. You live your life recognizing, "I have to do this work," or, "I have to do whatever I'm doing, because if I don't, something awful will happen to me." And you let yourself dwell on the awful.

If you've been around coaches, and people like me in the old days, it was, "Shape up or ship out." Have you ever heard that one? "If you don't like it, quit." "If you don't like it, get out of the house. My rules or out of the house." Do it, or else something awful is going to happen to you, and let me tell you about the awful. When I didn't know how to teach any better, I'd just tell kids, "Do your studies. You've got to get up, and if you don't get up and do that in front of the class, it's all right. I'm going to flunk you. And if I flunk you" – now get this, I'm directing the movie in their mind to motivate them – "if you don't do it, then not only will I flunk you, but you won't graduate from the school. I'll see to it. Now, do you want to do it?" The kid says, "No." "Well, if you don't graduate from school, you'll never go to college. If you don't go to college, you won't get a good job. If you don't get a good job, you'll be rolling in your puke in the gutter for the rest of your life.

# UNIT 14
# Putting Life on a Want-to

Now, do you want to study?" "Yeah." "You like the class?" "Hate it." Then why are you studying? "Because I don't want to roll in my puke in the gutter for the rest of my life."

The old way was you needed to be able to intimidate people. Also, many religions would intimidate us. I was raised a Catholic, and you couldn't eat meat on Friday or you'd go to hell. Good gosh! I was in the first grade, and I got it. Those nuns painted a picture of hell that would scare an adult! Now, some of the kids in my neighborhood, they weren't Catholic, and so they'd say come over for dinner on Friday. I'd say, "What are you having?" Hot dogs. "Not me. I ain't going to hell. You go ahead." You couldn't have pried my mouth open on Friday and put meat in it, because I knew I was going to go to hell. My behavior wasn't because I chose to be good. I was trying to outrun the flames of hell licking at my butt! I just didn't want to go to hell.

Some of you live your whole life that way. Wherever you're being told you "have to," that person is coercing you, or at least trying to. What they're doing is pushing you, and so you push back, but not physically. Do you know how you push back when somebody tells you, "You have to" do something? You slow down. You take longer to do the job than necessary. The other thing you do is you find other things to do that don't even need to be done, because you don't want to do what they're telling you to do. Another thing is you only do the work good enough to get the people that are pushing you to shut up. It's creative avoidance, procrastination and work in kind of a minimal way, never really using your potential.

From now on, do what you want to do, don't do it if you don't want to, just accept the consequences for your decision. That's the key, accept the consequence. You might get fired. The teacher may fail you, but you are your own person, and it's your choice. Live your life, the goals that you're seeking, on a want to, choose to, like it, love it basis, and you'll see an abundance of energy coming inside of you. Have you ever been around people who are in a world of "have to"? They are exhausted. Try it on yourself. Tell yourself, "I have to do my homework." Do you know what you'll do? You will wait until the last moment to study. See, it doesn't matter if I tell you, "You have to," or if you tell yourself you have to.

You must eliminate the "have to" as much as you can. You can't say, "Oh, I really didn't mean I have to." Well, your subconscious is a literal mechanism. It doesn't know you didn't mean it. You just said you had to, so it tries to get you out of it. Where you're having difficulty using your potential, see if perhaps you're telling yourself you have to do something. Your subconscious says, "Oh, no, you don't. Let me show you how to get out of it." Really! You procrastinate, or you find things to do, or you slow down. See, your subconscious is there to protect you from coercion. It's trying to keep you from being shoved against your will.

The second form of motivation, rather than the fear and coercion, is called Constructive. You need to tell yourself why you want to change. You sell yourself on your future, tell yourself why you want to study, why you want to develop, why you want to read the book. You don't have to read a book. You don't have to take a test. You don't have to pass the test. You don't have to apply for the job. You don't have to get up in the morning, quite frankly. You can stay in bed. "But, if I stay in bed, I'll fail the class. If I fail the class, then my career might be damaged." That's true, so shut up and get up. It's your idea.

# UNIT 14
# Putting Life on a Want-to

What you need to do is to switch it from a "have to," to a "want to, choose to, like it, love it." Tell yourself why you want the change, the goal, why you want what you're seeking. You need to sell yourself on your future. Then when you write your goals out, you're going to tell yourself, emotionally, what the pay value is in it for you. What's it going to be for me when I achieve what I want to achieve, when I have the relationships that I want, when I have the family I want, when I have the goals that I want? What's in it for me? I'm going to eliminate the "have to."

By the way, when you tell yourself you "have to," you lower your self-esteem. It's subtle, isn't it? How would that happen? Because you're saying you're not your own person. "Somebody is making me do this. If I had my way, I would rather be doing something else. Since I don't have my way, I'm a victim. It's not my fault. I'm being coerced. I'm weak. I'm small." Your subconscious just shrinks, and then you behave like it.

All of your goals need to be your idea. Go back to that theological example. Many people spend their whole life trying to be good because they don't want to go to hell. What if you wanted to be good because it was the right thing to do? What if you saw the value in being good and the possession of a supreme being? You will attack the future. I want you to create a passion in your life for everything you want to change, because you won't change any other way. You're too stubborn, aren't you? You're too stubborn. Nobody can push you.

If I told my kids, "Get in there and wash the dishes, or else you can't use the car, or you can't go out tonight." You need to have an "or else" in there. Do you know what they'd say? "I've got to do my homework." Homework? They didn't even think homework until I said wash the dishes. That's kind of a replacement for not wanting to be bullied into washing the dishes. Then they'd wash the dishes but not the pots and pans, not the silverware, not the cups. I come in and say, "I thought I told you to wash the dishes?" They'd say, "I did. You didn't say pots and pans. You didn't say silverware." Minimal compliance. You're that way, too, aren't you? And then it would take them an hour to do a 10 minute job. They slowed down.

Stop doing that! Take the consequence, or shut up and do it. Tell yourself why you want to. Can you do it? I think so. And you're going to get better at it, and better at it, and better at it. Listen to people around you. You'll hear, "I have to do this and I have to do that, and I have to go here and I have to…" No, you don't, quite frankly. I have heard people say, "I have to change diapers." No, you don't. Leave them on the kid. "Are you kidding?" No, I'm serious; just accept the consequences. "I don't want to leave them on." Then shut up and change the kid's diapers. You want to. It's your idea. It's all a matter of free will. You don't have to obey the law. You can break the speed limits, you can cheat, and you can steal. You can do anything you want. When you get caught, shut up. It was your choice.

Do what you want to do, just accept the consequences. "Free at last, free at last. Thank God Almighty, I'm free at last." You will absolutely love it and enjoy your life. Just remember to switch from "have to" to "want to," and you will be different. You will be different.

# UNIT 15
# Making the Pictures Match

## Unit Overview

When the world outside doesn't match the picture of the world we hold in our minds, we have a problem. The creative subconscious goes to work to make the pictures match. We get lots of energy, and we get very creative. This is human nature. However, we can take hold of this process and use it to help us make the positive changes we want in our lives, using our power of visualization to reach our goals.

## Unit Objectives

*By the end of this unit, I will:*

- understand that I am always working for order in my mind.

- learn that I can create my own energy by changing my internal picture.

- know that my subconscious doesn't care if I go back to my old picture or the new picture; it goes in the direction of the strongest picture.

- use visualization as I set my goals, to make the outside world match my new internal picture.

# AS WE CORRECTLY VISUALIZE THE NEW, WE BECOME DISSATISFIED WITH THE OLD.

## UNIT 15
# Making the Pictures Match

## Key Concepts

- Self-Image

- Reality

- Gestalt

- Energy

- Goals / Goal-Setting

- Out of Order / Into Order

- Visualization

- Drive

- Creativity

- Subconscious

- Potential

- Self-Motivation

- Replacement Pictures

## Notes

# UNIT 15
# Making the Pictures Match

**Notes**

# UNIT 15
# Making the Pictures Match

## Reflective Questions

- What are my goals after graduation?

- What goals have I set to make my vision of the future a reality?

# UNIT 15
# Making the Pictures Match

## Reflective Questions

- What is good enough for me?

- Where am I not living up to my own expectations?

## UNIT 15
# Making the Pictures Match

## Exercise: "Now is the winter of our discontent..."

On the left, list some of your favorite commercials, radio or television. On the right, list the discontent they are trying to create in you.

_____     _____

_____     _____

_____     _____

_____     _____

_____     _____

# UNIT 15
# Making the Pictures Match

## Exercise: List 10 Things

In the left-hand column, list 10 things you want to do before you die. The right-hand column will be used in Unit 16.

### Current Appraisal

Move to a happier place

Get a job @ a resort spa

go to school in San Fran for Graphic Design

Work for Apple, Inc. or a Mag. doing G.D. or MT

Have a house + a family

Make enough $$ to live comfortably

take a long vacation

tone up + stay fit

Keep my car for as long as I can

continue w/ drawing, photography, + graphic design
and massage therapy

# UNIT 15
# Making the Pictures Match

## Summary

When I give you this information, you'll understand how to create the power inside yourself and, again, why it's important to change your mind. This is so essential. Knowing this, you'll have an advantage over everybody that doesn't know it. I swear to you, you'll have a great advantage. You're going to be competing for jobs and careers and stuff like that, and people will be amazed. "How do you do this? How do you get there? How come?" Because you know how your mind works.

Remember, when we talked about the self-image, you have a stored reality of how you know your house looks, your room looks, or what's normal for you. It's inside you. Then, when through your senses you perceive information that is different or contrary to the way you know things are supposed to be, you throw your whole inner system out of order.

As an example, if I was born with my fingers stuck together, then every time I wake up and look and they're still stuck together, I'll feel okay. I'll be free of anxiety, free of tension, because that's the way it is. That's the way it's supposed to be. If I wake up one morning and my fingers are apart, that doesn't look right to me. That's called a problem. A problem is when the world outside of you doesn't match your idea of what is normal for you or how things are supposed to be. When you're out of order, that's called Gestalt. Human beings are always working for order in their minds. Order just means that the outside picture must match the inside picture. I will try to straighten up the outside to match the inside. I must put things back together.

Have you ever walked into a room or down the hall and seen a painting on the wall and it's crooked. Does it bother you? That's what I'm talking about. You get the simple idea. It doesn't look the way it's supposed to be. "It doesn't look right to me." Most of you didn't deliberately put into your mind the level of excellence, or the level of life that you want. You just let it happen. Now, when it doesn't look right, you get upset, just like you do with the painting on the wall. When you see the picture crooked on the wall, what do you do? "Fix it." How? By putting it back the way it's supposed to be. Who said it was supposed to be that way? You do, don't you? We tell ourselves, "That's not right. I gotta fix it."

You are doing this all the time. When you move away from the picture you hold in your mind of your social life, or your grades, anything, you have an urgent feeling inside yourself to fix it. Even if it's better, you want to fix it back. If it's below your standard, you fix it up. But if it's above your standard, it still bothers you, because it's different.

So, when you're out of order, energy is created. Do you need any energy if the picture is the way it's supposed to be? No, I don't need energy, because it looks okay to me. Energy comes when it doesn't look all right. Goal-setting will be to deliberately see yourself differently than you actually are. You will see yourself having a new car, while you're still driving this old junk heap. You will see yourself with a beautiful apartment, but you're still living at home. You will see yourself graduated but you're still in school. You will see yourself making money but you're still poor.

# UNIT 15
# Making the Pictures Match

You have a problem. That's where the energy comes in. You don't need energy if things look the same, if they look all right to you. You need energy when you throw your whole inner mind out of order. That's what goal-setting is: to visualize yourself having something you don't have, being something you are not. Then, you look at how you actually are, and the difference between the two motivates you, and gives you drive.

Watch what happens once you arrive at a goal that you've set. Once you put the picture back together, your energy shuts off. So, you want to be careful. Some of you goal-set to go to school, but not to study. Isn't that amazing? You did what you set out to do. Your mind shuts off. Some people will goal-set to go to school, but not to graduate. Then they hang out and socialize. Some people goal-set to graduate, and then live at home for another year because they are so tired. They forgot to goal-set to get a job.

In your mind, you want to goal-set ahead. That's what creates the drive and the energy. Some people goal-set too short. Some people goal-set to get home and have dinner. Then they don't have enough energy to go to bed. You goal-set to a weekend, but you didn't tell yourself what you wanted to do on the weekend so you just sit in front of the TV with the remote. The whole idea is to goal-set through. Keep your mind goal-setting instead of up to a point, goal-set through the point. That's what I teach athletes. Don't goal-set to go to the Olympics, goal-set to win it. If they goal-set to go there, they wonder why they aren't motivated when they get there.

Remember, when you're out of order, energy comes to complete the order. The other thing you get is ideas, or creativity. If the picture is crooked, I've got to figure out how I'm going to fix it. Your subconscious comes up with, "Well, let's just do this and this and this, and straighten it up." When you're out of order, you are at your creative best. When you set a goal, you invent how to achieve it. When you set a goal, you come up with ideas on how to get it done. You don't need to know any ideas of how you're going to do something before you set the goal. You set the goal and your subconscious gives you the ideas on how to do it.

Some people will set their goal only as big as they know how to accomplish it. "Do you know how to do it?" "No, I don't know." "Well then, back it up to what you do know." No, set the goal based upon what you want, and your subconscious will create a way. If you don't have enough knowledge inside you, your subconscious will have you read a book. It will have you meet people, have you study. What you're doing is creating, inside yourself, the thirst for knowledge. "I've gotta have it, gotta have it." I've given myself this problem.

When you're out of order, it's natural inside of a human being to create order. Your job will be to throw your system out of order by visualizing yourself already achieving the goal, being the person you want, having the income you want, having the business that you want, having the family, having the home, having the apartment, whatever it is you want. You will see it as though you actually have it.

# UNIT 15
# Making the Pictures Match

One thing: when you're out of order, your subconscious doesn't care if you go back to your old way, go home, go back to what your old way of living, or go to the new way. It doesn't care which way you go, which way you use your energy or your creativity. What determines the direction you're going is the strongest picture. This is very important.

Goal-setting will be creating the future that you're seeking, in all parts of your life where you want to use your potential. All you need to do is get the picture, but you must make it so strong in your mind that where you are now is beneath you. You're not satisfied with where you are. You don't hate it. It's just that, "I can hardly wait. I can hardly wait. I want to hurry up, hurry up, hurry up, hurry up."

That's how commercials work on television. They get you to drive a new car, then you can't stand your old car. Fashions change, and you see yourself in the new fashions. "I couldn't go outside looking like this. I mean I just can't. I've gotta get that new dress. I gotta get the new shoes. I've gotta get my hair done." Funny, but it was alright yesterday. As you visualize the new, you become dissatisfied with the old.

Your job is to create dissatisfaction in yourself, which is self-motivation. Create dissatisfaction in yourself by visualizing yourself already having graduated, already having the career, already having the job, already having the business. It isn't like, "I'm going to." It is, "I am. I have it." When you write your goals, you want to write them out as I'm going to teach you. They need to be in the first person, present tense. It's as though I already have... I've won the game. I have the business. I have graduated. I have the income. Your subconscious looks around and says, "You don't have it. You have a problem." You are supposed to have problems.

If I say, "I will be nice. I will be a good person. Someday, I will own a car," that doesn't do it. You want to create the drive in you. See what you want as though you have it. Your senses will tell you, "No, you don't." If I throw my system out of order, I can't sit still. I want to study. I need to develop myself. This isn't magic. If I'm going to be in business, then I want to learn about the business. I am driven to study. You don't have to study, you love it.

This is what the Gestalt is all about. It's why you're going to goal-set. If you don't, then you're going to live your life the way it is, right now. I can be a fortune teller for you. I can tell you the kind of guys you're going to hang out with. I can tell you the kind of ladies you're going to seek. I can tell you the kind of businesses you're going to be in. I can tell you what your income is going to be – not much different than it is now. Do you know why? You didn't change the picture. Once you change the picture, whoosh, off you go. That's what we're teaching you, how to change the picture. Part of it is self-talk, part of it is writing out your goals. It's all about replacement pictures. If you don't give yourself the replacement picture, life is just like it is now.

## UNIT 16
# I Can See It!

## Unit Overview

It is a fact of life – literally – human beings need goals. If we have no goals, we die. Our survival instinct is so strong that if we have no new goals, we simply recreate our old ones and life doesn't change very much. We must dream big and give ourselves goals, causing tremendous energy and creativity inside ourselves to achieve these goals.

## Unit Objectives

*By the end of this unit, I will:*

- understand why I need to set goals.

- know that I need new goals, so that I grow into the person I want to be.

- dream bigger, because the bigger the dream, the more energy and creativity I release from inside me to accomplish my goals.

# IT'S ALRIGHT TO BE AFRAID;
# IT IS NOT ALRIGHT TO STAY AFRAID.

## UNIT 16
# I Can See It!

## Key Concepts

- Gestalt

- Out of Order / Into Order

- Goals / Goal-Setting

- Subconscious

- Visualize / Visualization

- Affirmations

- Imagination

- First Person

- Present Tense

- Experiential

- Have-to

- Potential

- Replacement Picture

- Efficacy

- Conscious

- Comfort Zone

- Tension / Anxiety

- Dynamic Balance Principles

- Resiliency

- Persistency

- Forethought

- Performance

**UNIT 16**
# I Can See It!

**Notes**

## UNIT 16
# I Can See It!

## Reflective Questions

- What is my vision for my income level and lifestyle?

- Where have I already achieved a goal and need to set a new one?

- Why am I going to school?

# UNIT 16
# I Can See It!

## Reflective Questions

- What is my current reality in relation to why I am going to school?

- Who do I feel has power over me at home and away from home?

## UNIT 16
# I Can See It!

## Exercise: Mini Balance Wheel

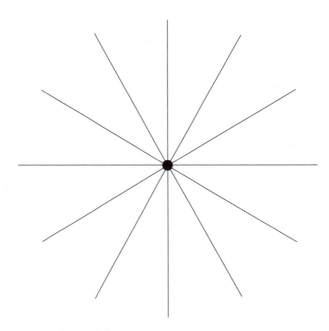

In the segments of this Mini Balance Wheel, list your course schedule. With zero in the middle, and 10 at the end of each spoke, use a pen to mark where you see yourself, right now, in each course. Then, take a pencil, and mark each course where you expect yourself to be.

What is your current appraisal of your ability to get the grade you want for each course?

## UNIT 16
# I Can See It!

## Looking Ahead

What courses will you have next term? What is your current appraisal of your ability to cause the grades you want?

_____    _____

_____    _____

_____    _____

_____    _____

_____    _____

## Looking Back to Move Ahead

Refer back to your "List 10 Things" from Unit 15 on page 159. On a scale of 1 to 5, with 5 being the strongest, rate each item on your list with your current Efficacy Rating – can you actually see each happening?

If you've given yourself a 5, then you can really SEE it and you can feel the emotions of hope, passion, drive and excitement. If you've given yourself a 1, and get feelings of intimidation or anxiety, then it doesn't mean this is a bad goal. You just can't see yourself in it yet. Don't give up on the goal; begin visualizing yourself, bit by bit, and create a new comfort zone for yourself.

# UNIT 16
# I Can See It!

## Summary

In our last session, we talked about the Gestalt and throwing your system out of order. How far can you take yourself at one time? How far can you visualize? The reason this is important is because I'm going to teach you how to write your goals out. You must write them out, otherwise your subconscious causes you to forget. I'm talking about really taking charge of your life here, not just leaving it to chance, accident, maybe, and so on.

It's very important that you learn to write out 10 to 15 goals at a time. As you accomplish some of these and move towards them, you can change them again and again and again and again. The kinds of goals you're going to write are ones that will change your inner strength, the kind of person you are. You're going to be able to design yourself. You're going to design a new you. You can do that. Otherwise, what you've done is just leave it up to chance and you just are who you are based upon what people told you and who you were.

Then, you're going to learn to visualize your goals two or three times a day. Visualizing isn't hard; it's very simple. You're going to write the affirmations, or the statements of fact, which are goals, and every time you read them correctly, your imagination will take you as though you already have what you're seeking. You already are that person. Remember, it needs to be first person, present tense – and experiential imagery. It's not like you're sitting up in the stands watching yourself play on the field. You need to be in your mind playing on the field. You only see that what you would see if, in fact, you are doing it. In basketball, you wouldn't see yourself out there as in a video. You'd see yourself, in your mind, shooting, checking, doing what you're supposed to be doing. You run your patterns and stuff in your own mind.

How far can we take ourselves? Let me give you an example. One time I had one of my sons-in-law having lunch with me, in West Seattle at a restaurant. I was trying to explain to him this concept about how far. As I looked out the window of the restaurant, across the street was this derelict getting into a garbage can, sorting stuff out. So, I said, "Look." He looked and I didn't say anything. Then, I said, "Do you suppose if you keep looking at that guy, you'll become a bum? Because if you image and visualize what it is you're thinking about, it does change your mind, and then you become it." His reply was, "I could never see myself living like that." I said, "That's my point." You can observe other people and you can see things. However, you don't change like them until you imagine yourself being or having, owning, that which you're visualizing. It always belongs to somebody else.

Do you know the difference between what somebody else has and what you have? Of course you do. So I said to him, "You know, if it worked the other way, I'd take you and put you out in front of Bill Gates' house. You could watch Bill Gates for months until you changed your mind about being rich. Then you could come back and support your father-in-law for the rest of his life." But

# UNIT 16
# I Can See It!

you're going to say, "Oh, I can't see myself living like that either." You need to see yourself living like that.

When you write out your goals, you want to write them out first person, present tense. You've already won the game. You already are what you want. You already have what you want. You only are limited by how far you can get your imagination to see yourself. Now that you know the process of goal-setting, you can do it again and again and again and again.

You'll put your goals out there just far enough that it creates a passion to seek. You're going to tell yourself why you want it. No have to's. You won't do it; you're too stubborn. You need to sell yourself on what you want. Once you do, you can't take it all the way to your potential. You're going to take it to where you can see yourself doing it. At first you'll almost laugh. "Me? I don't think so." Then you'll start looking around and say, "Well, I see other people doing it." And then you go, "Hmm, I think maybe I can do it." Then pretty soon you say, "Hmm, I am doing it." That's the sequence. It is all about the picture in your mind. It's all about a replacement picture.

I'm going to give you a little bit more on the depth of goal-setting, because we could go on two to three days with that. The way you are made as a human being, I think I mentioned to you, if you don't have a goal, you either recreate the one you have in your mind or you die; death occurs. There's a book that would be good for you to read. It's by Viktor Frankl, "Man's Search for Meaning." It's a little tiny book. Frankl was a psychiatrist, interned in a Nazi prison camp. As he observed people, even if survival or revenge was a goal, they would stay alive. Otherwise they just died, under extreme, extreme circumstances.

During the Korean conflict, the same thing occurred. The North Korean communists, or the Chinese communists, who had captured prisoners, would take away hope. They would take away the future of 18 to 23 year olds, and they had a system of doing so. They would send them bad news, or they would give them history of people the prisoners thought were heroes that really weren't. Then they'd have the prisoners inform on one another. They were creating, in their minds of the prisoners, that it's useless to go on. We lost more prisoners of war in Korea than any war in the history of America. This is how they died: they just gave up living. They'd crawl into their bunk, pull a blanket over their head, and die within 48 hours. Just quit living. You'll see the same thing with your grandparents, if they've been married for a long time. One dies, and the other one may go right afterwards.

Goals are so essential, and here's another reason why I'm giving this to you: If you don't give yourself your own goals, you become so susceptible to the strongest voice at school, when you're out at a party, or from whoever you're hanging around. You become very susceptible. Everybody does. You become susceptible to being influenced, because you're seeking. You're seeking something to do, subconsciously. You want to goal-set by intent, not by default. Look at your areas of your life where you've goal-set by default. You became what you have become,

# UNIT 16
# I Can See It!

because you didn't even think about something bigger or better. I want you to remember, from here forward, you're going to take charge of your life. You're going to take charge. You're going to set your own goals and your outcomes.

I'm leading you into the next step, which is called "efficacy." I had to look that up myself, so don't worry. "Efficacy" just means your appraisal of your own ability to make your life what you want to make it. "Oh, I can't do that." "That's too hard for me." "I can't afford that." "We can't buy that." "I don't have enough money." Those are all inefficacious statements. You're telling yourself you can't do it, that you're not good enough.

Many of you have enormous potential. Your appraisal of your own ability to cause, to make happen and to bring about, that's what efficacy is. Your appraisal of your own ability to cause something, to make something happen, to bring something about, is what needs to be increased. The dreams you have are in direct proportion to how good you think you are. Out of Stanford University, by Dr. Al Bandura, who is the best in the world in the research of this, said to me one time, "We don't let ourselves want what we don't believe we can cause," even though the potential is inside of ourselves. What does he mean by that? Well, I was a high school teacher and had taken the vow of poverty by mistake. I mean, we were poor. The cars we were driving were junk heaps. Just wrecks. Every summer we'd say, "We've got to get a new car." Now listen to that statement, a "new" car. I wasn't even thinking of a new car. Do you know what I was thinking? A new junk heap. I didn't think a new car and back it up to a junk heap. A new car never came to my mind. How big you dream isn't because of your potential; it's because of your appraisal of how good you are.

When you set a goal, the question of efficacy in your mind is this: is this goal bigger than me right now or am I bigger than it? Can I pull it off? Do I know how to do it? Do I have the knowledge? Do I have the skill? Do I have the money to buy it? Do I have the money to create the business I want? Do I have the ability to take the courses I want to get the job I want to get the degree I want?

If you start to feel scared, subconsciously, you start backing away from the goal. You start backing up the goal. You start creating negative avoidance inside your mind. You start telling yourself, "Oh, my gosh, I will lose everything. I'll be embarrassed." You wake up at 2:00 in the morning with, "It won't work. It won't work!" When people set a goal bigger than their present capability, if they don't know any better, they become sensible. They become realistic, and back up the goal. "Let's be sensible about this." What does that mean to most people? It means don't set a goal bigger than what you presently know how to do. You're not qualified.

Here's what I want you to do: Set the goals beyond your present capability, always. Set your goals outside of your comfort zone. Set your goals based upon what you really love to do. Yes, when you do that you're going to get the tension inside of yourself, but what that does, if you

# UNIT 16
# I Can See It!

do it right, it causes you to study. We're talking about dynamic balance principles here, the way your mind works. Like Gestalt, you throw your mind out of order with the right goal for yourself, and you must close it down. "But, I don't have enough money. I don't have enough knowledge. I don't have enough people." So you study, you go to school, you learn. You find new friends. "I have this dream, but I don't have the resources right now." That creates the appetite to grow. No goal, no appetite. Little tiny goal, little tiny appetite.

Your goals may trigger in you negative creativity. Don't be afraid. Like I tell my grandkids now, it's all right to start off afraid. It's not all right to stay afraid. We're going to grow. We're going to grow. We're going to grow, and that's what I want to encourage you to do. That's why I'm giving you all this information. Look at the potential you have inside yourself. Look at how good you really are.

Efficacy also means you need to be resilient and persistent. You want to make goals and strengthen your inner resiliency. What is resiliency? Well, you've had some tough times in your life, haven't you? I'd like to have you write a list of maybe five the things in your life that were just devastating. Could have been the death of a loved one. It could have been you tried for a job and didn't get it. You turned out for something and you got rejected, whatever. Now, why in the dickens would I want you to think about that? Remember, that's like the rock in the road, isn't it? Now, I don't want you to remember and dwell on the rock. I want you to remember how well you recovered. You go back and say, "I lived through that. I thought I was going to die. I thought it would be terrible when I lost my boyfriend." "I thought it would be terrible when I failed that class." "Hey, look at me now. Look at me now."

This is the way you grow. It's how you deal with the hard things. Now, why do you want that? Because every time you're going after a goal, you're going to get knocked down. You're going to get flattened. There's lots of stuff that will blow the wind right out of you. But, you're going to get up quick. You're not going to stay down, see? You're not going to stay down. You build yourself to be tough. As you write down those five things, go back and remember, "I got through that." Then, you take your forethought, which is visualization – what great, efficacious people do – and you see the goal you're seeking. You say to yourself, "Well, what if I don't get it? I'll live through it. I'm tough."

Persistence is the same. Persistence means you're going to stick to it. You're not going to quit easy. If you're low in efficacy, it's only because you don't have the inner strength, or you are listening to the people you've been hanging around. Forethought is what human beings use to move into the future. It's using your imagination to look into the future.

People with great potential, but who don't persist and quit on themselves, they look at what they want in school, or a career, or whatever, and they "what if" that happens. They see awful things in front of them, like problems and obstacles and things that will get in the way of their goals.

# UNIT 16
# I Can See It!

Now, they'll still go after the goal, but if you're inefficacious, you hope that the bad stuff doesn't come. If it does come, the first slap in the face causes them to quit – quit school, quit their career, quit their dream, quit. So, what do efficacious people think like? They look forward, and if they see an obstacle, which you will from now on, you're going to see how you're going to handle it. "If that happens, I'll do this. If that happens, I'll go here." It's all about using your imagination and building yourself strongly.

Go back and remember the good things you've done, I don't care if it was the fifth grade or sixth grade or seventh grade. What did you do that you're so proud of? Write a list of five to 10 of them. Now, this is what high performance people do naturally. Go back and remember how you felt. Then, as you remember how you felt, I want you to take yourself into that job, into that career, into that interview. I want you to take the same emotion you had and drop it out into your future. You color your future with your old emotion of success.

You're going to learn to control your anxiety and pressure inside yourself. It's all right to be afraid; it's not all right to stay afraid. You know you're going to come up with negative ideas. But, if you can visualize the value in it and make sure you have your mind set on what you really want in your life, then you can fight hell with a bucket of water. You are so tough, nothing's going to stop you.

## UNIT 17
# If It's to Be, It's Up to Me

## Unit Overview

The best way for us to see our goals achieved is to write them down and visualize them happening. We need to "see" ourselves into a successful future before we ever get there. It's all about growing into our goals and dreams and we can speed up that process with effective visualization.

## Unit Objectives

*By the end of this unit, I will:*

- learn lasting change must come from the inside, and cannot be imposed from the outside.

- understand that I need to write down my goals and use visualization to see myself into the future I desire as though it is already accomplished.

- know that I must throw myself out of order, so that I cause energy and creativity to put myself back in to order at the new level.

# ALL MEANINGFUL AND LASTING CHANGE STARTS FIRST ON THE INSIDE, THEN WORKS ITS WAY OUT.

## UNIT 17
# If It's to Be, It's Up to Me

## Key Concepts

- Self-Image

- Conscious

- Motivation

- Dominant Idea

- Visualize / Visualization

- Goal / Goal-Setting

- Imagination

- Subconscious

- Current Reality

- Creative Subconscious

- Mentor

- Vision

- Dissonance

- Tension

## Notes

## UNIT 17
# If It's to Be, It's Up to Me

**Notes**

## UNIT 17
# If It's to Be, It's Up to Me

## Reflective Questions

- Where have I forced myself to change for a particular situation, and when it was over, went right back to the "old" me?

- What is my ideal or perfect career? What am I presently doing to make my vision a reality?

## UNIT 17
# If It's to Be, It's Up to Me

## Reflective Questions

- My present thoughts determine my future. What am I thinking about today that will have a positive impact on my future?

- Where do I find myself looking to others for approval?

## UNIT 17
# If It's to Be, It's Up to Me

## Exercise: Imagination[2]

Answer the questions below, using the most vivid words possible. Really "draw the picture" with the words you use.

| | |
|---|---|
| What do I want to do for a living? | |
| What responsibilities do I want to have? | |
| Where do I want to live? | |
| What will my home look like? | |
| What model will my next car be? | |
| What will my family look like? | |
| What kind of people surround me? | |
| What conversations would I have with the people who surround me? | |

## UNIT 17
# If It's to Be, It's Up to Me

## Summary

Here are some principles. Now, "principle" is just something very practical that has broad application. You can use it in every part of your life. One of the important principles is that, "All meaningful and lasting change starts first on the inside in my imagination and works its way out into my life." Now, two words, "meaningful" and "lasting," are important. You can override your self-image and try hard to be different for a little while, but when you let go of your conscious control, what do you do? You go back to being yourself.

You can see, in history, where people tried to impose change on other countries or other people. When they let go, like in Iraq, they'll go back to being themselves. You can't force change on people. Your parents can't force change on you. They'll try to force it. A teacher can't, a coach can't force you to change. You'll pretend for awhile. You'll do what they want in a compliant way. But the moment they release the push or the external motivation, you always go back to your dominant idea of who you are. Your job is to change the dominant idea of who you are or what you have. It's a matter of visualizing it correctly with your mind. I've talked to you about this before, but it's a matter of, in your mind, seeing yourself at the level that you choose to be.

There's a little problem here, because if you had a five year old little brother or sister and you were talking to them about going to college, they're not going to connect. Someday, they will be in college. But you're talking too far beyond them, so they can't catch the dream. If you talk about first grade or second grade, maybe. If you talk to a five year old and say, "Do you go to school yet?" "No, no, no. The big kids go to school. I'm still a little kid." You need to see that this is the way your mind has always worked. Someday, they'll be in the university. They'll be a doctoral candidate or doing something in their own. Right now, they just can't see it.

You take yourself and your goals where it causes you to be able to experience yourself at that level. Now, as you approach your goal, you're not going to wait until you get there. You're going to change it again. Change it, re-set it again. As you approach the new goal, then change it again. You don't want to arrive and flatten out. You don't wait until you achieve the goal before you set another goal. You set the goal, and because you can't imagine yourself being at your full potential, as you get closer to it, you say, "Wow, I can do more." Remember, there's always a horizon past the horizon. It looks like that's the end, but once you get there, you realize that there's another one. That's the way I want you to think of your life.

If I was going to be your mentor, which in a way I am right now, the one thing that will make you unique from everybody is not setting the goal based upon how good you presently are. Set the goal based upon what you want. That's called a vision. How do you get a vision? You get a vision by just asking yourself the question, "What do I want for a social life? What do I want in the way of a bank account? What do I want in the way of a job? What do I want in the way of a home?" What do I want? That gives you the vision.

# UNIT 17
# If It's to Be, It's Up to Me

Right now, you are into what's called "current reality." That's the now, that's how things are now. Don't get stuck in the now. People will say, "Well, I'm talking real stuff. You're talking vision; you're talking imagination. I'm talking real stuff. This is the way things are." The problem is the way we are right now is only temporary. If you could hold that vision of what you want in your mind, hold it clearly and make the vision stronger than the way you're living now, the dissonance or the tension inside yourself becomes great. If you hold the vision in your mind and you then look at the way things are, you're completely out of order inside yourself.

Now, if you're doing it right and the vision is strong enough, the question is, will you take current reality and move it to the vision through finding the way, and inventing the how? Your subconscious is a genius. You don't need to know how to set the goal. If, in fact, you set the goal based upon your present how, your goal would be too low. Does that make sense? If you set the goal based upon what you want, and because of the tension inside you, you create and you invent the way to your goal. You don't need to know how. Remember, all you need to do is to know how to invent the how – by setting the goal in your mind and looking at the truth as it is. That gap causes you to feel, "I need to do something."

Do you not take a good picture, are you not photogenic? Do you know anybody else that doesn't? "I don't take good pictures." See, I look at a picture, and I say, "Well, that doesn't look like me." And they say, "Yes, it does." "No, no, no it doesn't. I look too fat in this picture." "Well, you are." See, it's like I don't want to see it. Or, I don't want to step on the scale, because if I step on the weighing scale, it doesn't match what in my mind I want to be. It ruins my day. So, you know how I keep from ruining my day? I don't step on the scale. Don't look at the truth. What you need to be able to do is set the goal in your mind, make it strong, and you need to constantly look at the truth of how things are. That's what causes you to invent the how. That's what creates your energy.

You have the vision in one direction, and here you are in current reality. There are two ways of going. If the goal isn't stronger than where you're living now, your subconscious has to make the pictures match. You'll make excuses, you'll find reasons, you'll find fault – all to go back to the way you were. So, no excuses. No way out for yourself and those goals. You must be committed. "This is what I'm going do."

Remember that all meaningful and lasting change starts on the inside, in my imagination, and works its way out into my relationships, into my income, into the environment. There is a direct relationship between the way I want my life to look, my world to look, and the way it actually looks. Here's an interesting bit on this. You might say, "Well, where is the money coming from? How can I live like that? How could I buy that? How could I get the car? How could I have a flat like that or a house like that or apartment like that? I mean don't I have to have the money? Yes. Your subconscious will create and sustain your present reality. So as you envision the life style you want, you'll find yourself earning the money. You don't wait to earn the money, you set the aspirational life style, and then what courses you take, what businesses you start, how your

# UNIT 17
# If It's to Be, It's Up to Me

imagination works, all help you create enough money to live the way you want to live.

Your subconscious, remember, does what's in your job description and no more. Your job description is the way you want to live, the style in which you want to live. You create that in your mind, and your creative subconscious will get you to study or change businesses or grow a business or find the money to support your life style.

Here's another principle: Yesterday's dreams become today's necessities. Today's necessities are tomorrow's opportunities. "Tomorrow" is the way you're going to live. Your present thoughts determine your future. The way you think presently is the way your future is going to be. Remember, I told you the three time frames. Can you think of where yesterday's dreams became today's necessities? Cell phones, computers. You can't live without them, now, right? There was a time when there wasn't any cell phone. There was a time when there weren't these computer programs. Somebody started visualizing…

As you visualize today, that's the way your future is going to be. That's the way change takes place. It's all in your imagination. So, yesterday's dreams become today's necessities. You don't want to go backwards. You don't want to go back. You don't want to go back to living with your folks. You don't want to go back to grade school anymore, thank you. The desk doesn't fit. So, as you visualize new friends, you will no longer hang around some of the old ones. You'll be at a different level. Yesterday's dreams became today's necessities for you. Now remember, we need to use that again. Today's dreams are the way your future is going to be. Now, it isn't a guarantee, but that's the way you're leading yourself into it. It's what you presently think about.

These are very important concepts, extremely important. That's why you write your goals out. You're going to do it every day, because you're not going to leave it to chance. You're not going to fool around about this. You're going to visualize the way you want to live next month, six months from now, a year from now, and three years from now. The further out you can do it, the greater the likelihood that it will occur. As you visualize being an architect, or running a business, or having a home on the ocean or in the mountains, it's going to take you time to gather the information to do what you need to do in order to get the goal or develop yourself.

# UNIT 17
# If It's to Be, It's Up to Me

## UNIT 18
# My Better Future

## Unit Overview

It is normal for us to want to know "how" we are going to get where we want to go. But, we really don't need to know the "how" in order to set our goals. In fact, if we demand to know "how" first, we will usually back up our goals to match our current abilities, and we don't grow very much. The idea here is to see the end result.

## Unit Objectives

*By the end of this unit, I will:*

- understand that my mind is so powerful that I don't need to know "how" to grow in order to set and achieve my goals. I will invent the way.

- know why it is important to see the end result.

- know that I am good enough to invent my way to my goals.

# THE GOAL COMES FIRST
# AND THEN YOU SEE.
# YOU DON'T SEE FIRST.

# UNIT 18
# My Better Future

## Key Concepts

- Visualize / Visualization

- Goals

- Affirmations

- Vision

- Reticular Activating System (RAS)

## Notes

# UNIT 18
# My Better Future

**Notes**

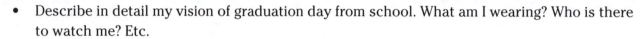

**UNIT 18**
# My Better Future

## Reflective Questions

- Describe in detail my vision of graduation day from school. What am I wearing? Who is there to watch me? Etc.

- What new goals do I need to set now, for my future after graduation?

# UNIT 18
# My Better Future

## Reflective Questions

- Where has my current opinion of myself held me back?

- What are my three most important goals at this time?

## UNIT 18
# My Better Future

## Exercise: Family Timeline

Create a timeline of your immediate family and other special people in your life. Construct a graph on the next page with one axis listing all family members and the other axis charting the next 10 years. After each family member's name, list that person's age and project that age through the next ten years.

Now, look at the chart as you address these questions to yourself:

- If you are still planning to build that big house for the kids, how much time do you have left to do it and have them live in it?

- When will the college expenses hit? What's your plan?

- How much work time do you have left? When will retirement come?

- Can you tell when your grandchildren will be born?

- Are there certain years you might like to plan to stay close to home?

- When would be the best time to travel? To write a book?

- What can you learn about the timing of your business investments? Starting a new venture?

- How old will your parents be 10 years from now?

- How about special vacations when the kids are at just that right age?

- When should you plan to give your children your religious values, your business values, your family values?

- What will the holidays be like 10 years from now?

- What are you getting ready for?

# UNIT 18
# My Better Future

|  | Today | 1 Year | 5 Years | 10 Years |
|---|---|---|---|---|
| Self |  |  |  |  |
| Spouse |  |  |  |  |
| Son |  |  |  |  |
| Daughter |  |  |  |  |
| Father |  |  |  |  |
| Mother |  |  |  |  |
| Grandfather |  |  |  |  |
| Grandmother |  |  |  |  |
| Grandson |  |  |  |  |
| Granddaughter |  |  |  |  |
| Brother |  |  |  |  |
| Sister |  |  |  |  |
| Niece |  |  |  |  |
| Nephew |  |  |  |  |
| Friend |  |  |  |  |
| Friend |  |  |  |  |

# UNIT 18
# My Better Future

## Exercise: Be / Have / Change / Do

Let's focus a little further, and discover what we can see for the next 12 months. In the chart below, in the left hand column, list your Balance Wheel areas from the Overview chapter of this book. Then, take each Balance Wheel area and project out over the 12 months. Where will you Be? What will you Have? What do you want to Change? What do you want to Do?

| Balance Wheel Areas | 1st Quarter Key Words | 2nd Quarter Key Words | 3rd Quarter Key Words | 4th Quarter Key Words |
|---|---|---|---|---|
| | | | | |
| | | | | |
| | | | | |
| | | | | |
| | | | | |
| | | | | |
| | | | | |

# UNIT 18
# My Better Future

## Summary

Remember I talked about Gene Juarez, earlier? When I first started, I had guys like Gene and people like that trying to help me. I dressed like a schoolteacher, you know. One time, I had one guy watching me, and he said, "Where did you get that suit you're wearing?" It was my only suit. "You look like a crumpled professor." So, that was all right, because I was a rumpled teacher, but it was my only suit. So, Diane decided she would buy me a new suit. Now, she went out and bought me a brown polyester suit (this was all we could "see"). You may not know what polyester is, but it won't wrinkle. However, if you smoked or somebody else smoked and they dropped ashes on you, your pant leg melted.

So here I am, with Gene and others coaching me. I didn't know anything about business, as I'd just come out of teaching. Here I am, with my new brown polyester suit, at the Washington Athletic Club. They belonged, I didn't. It was out of my comfort zone. So Gene kept admiring my new suit, and I didn't want him to think it was a new suit. I wanted him to think I always dressed this way. Keep in mind that polyester wasn't really at their level either. My comfort zone was a little bit below the rest of those guys. Anyway, he kept admiring my new suit. Later, I went into the lavatory, and as I was washing my hands and combing my hair, there in the mirror I looked, and I still had the tags on the sleeve of my suit. I had been wearing that suit for weeks, wherever I went! Luckily, things have changed.

We have a ranch. When I visualized the ranch, I could see exactly what I wanted. I had described almost 170 things I wanted in it, very clearly. Yet, as I visualized as though I already had it, it would drive me crazy. It took me 10 years to get it. 10 years! Every year, I thought I was going to get it. Honest to God. And every year, it was, "Where is it? Where is it?" Do you see what you're doing to yourself? Now, some people say, "Oh, who needs to live like that? This is too much." Not for me. It's necessary. This is the way I live. If you come to my house in Seattle, it's as nice, or nicer, than the one at the ranch. "Two of them? That's too much." No, no, not for me. It's necessary.

When I left teaching and started doing this, my house payment was $105 a month. That was it. But, you see, that was all a schoolteacher could afford, about like a schoolteacher would live. The cars we were driving were junk heaps. I couldn't tell you how many cars I have now, because they are between the ranch and Seattle. You need to make your future necessary, not a "wish for." Some people only wish for something, want it, love to have it. You know, "Oh, wouldn't that be wonderful?" No. It needs to become necessary. Your goals must become necessary. It isn't an "extra." It's not extra money. It's not an extra life style. It is what I need. This is what I need.

You need to be able to visualize what you want and create within yourself the need, or you won't do it. That's why yesterday's dreams become today's necessities. It's a necessity that I live this way. It's a necessity. There was a time I couldn't go more than 150 miles because I didn't have a

# UNIT 18
# My Better Future

spare tire in my car. We couldn't go any further than the tires could take us. We used to count how much gas money we had. I didn't jump from there to the way I'm living now. I visualized what I wanted, and then it became, "I gotta live this way." That's the key I'm teaching you.

As you do your visualizations, write your goals out. Your affirmations need to be written out, and then you imprint them into your mind, so strongly, so strongly that you cannot live without them. It's not extra money. We give to charity, Diane and I, a lot. It's because it is necessary. We just do that. The income I generate worldwide is because I've created a life style that expects it. I need to do that. Where I wouldn't let myself go 150 miles from home, we can fly to Mexico and back in the same day. We can do business, then come home. Or we head on down to Peru, do something, come back, and then head off to China. Remember, when I first started, I wouldn't go where there wasn't a football coach.

When you set the vision, set the goal, you open your Reticular Activating System. Once you set the goal, you are declaring a new significance for yourself. Now you hear information like the baby's cry, or like you see parking spots. Instead, you're going to see information in the world that will help you achieve your goal. So, you set the goal, and now you find what you need. Now, when you think this way, your goals can be much higher than the people you live with or are around. Usually, they're setting goals based upon, "Where are we going to get the help? Where are we going to get the money?" They back up their goals to where they do know how.

One time, when I was teaching at Kennedy High School years ago, I wanted to make some money for the school. I got these 10 kids to fight these other 10 kids. They were going to fight in the street anyway, so I figured we might as well sell tickets to it. So, we did. I sold about 2,000 tickets, and they agreed they wanted to fight each other in front of the school. What I needed was a boxing ring. I needed some boxing gloves and stuff, because I wanted to protect them. I needed a referee and so on. I looked and looked and couldn't find them anyplace. So, people were saying, "You'd better give the money back," because here it was Wednesday and the fight was to be next Tuesday. I looked for a month.

Now, I'm teaching this night school class of adults, and I'm still selling tickets. "Why don't you come to the fight? Why don't you come to the fight?" This one guy said he'd like that as he used to be a boxer when in the Army, in the Pacific. Nobody cares, it's not of value, that information. But then he said, "And I've got a friend that runs a boxing club in Auburn," a little town next to Seattle. I said, "Wow, you do? I wonder if he knows where I can get a boxing ring." See, my reticular activating system is open now to clues and information. Nobody else in the class could care. Big deal. The information is there, not important.

So I called the guy, and he said, no, he didn't have one, but he had a friend in Kent, a little town next to Auburn. This guy rents his out. I called the guy, and I said, "Man, I understand you've got a boxing ring. I need to rent it. How much?" He said $50. I said, "I'll take it." Then I said, "By the

# UNIT 18
# My Better Future

way, I can't use your boxing ring if you don't know where I can get a referee." He said he'd referee. "For the same price?" He said, yeah. I said, "Well, don't come and ref if you don't have those helmets you wear and the boxing gloves." So the guy said, "What do you have?" I said, "Nothing, just the tickets sold and the kids to fight. So if you've got the bell and the stool they sit on, you better bring them, too."

Now, my point is this: How many people would have waited until they had the boxing ring, the boxing gloves and the referee before they sold the tickets? Most of us. Boxing rings are trivia. It's not important to you. The only thing that gets through is that which is significant or important. When you set a goal, what you're doing is making that which you're seeking significant to you. Now you hear information. It's all over the place. Does that make sense how you're going to set your goals in the future?

I could tell you story after story after story. But don't look at where I am now and say, "Oh, I could never get there." You ought to see where I was when I was your age or when I started. Stop comparing yourself to people that are far out where you want to be and then making yourself feel "less than." Find out where they were when they began and visualize yourself at the level that they were. Study them. "How did you get there? How did you get there?" If you don't, you just quit, because things seem too big for you. Now, you're catching on.

# UNIT 18
# My Better Future

## UNIT 19
# My Goals – My Vision – My Future

## Unit Overview

We have learned about the importance of setting goals, and we have learned how to visualize what we want for our lives. Now it is time to learn how to write out our goals effectively, for the maximum positive impact on our futures.

## Unit Objectives

*By the end of this unit, I will:*

- have learned the steps to writing effective affirmations.

- know that I must see my future as already having happened, which creates the energy to move into that future.

- visualize my goals as affirmations at least two times a day; more times, if I want to make the change quicker.

**READ THE WORDS;
SEE THE PICTURES;
AND FEEL THE EMOTIONS
WELLING UP INSIDE YOU.**

## UNIT 19
# My Goals – My Vision – My Future

## Key Concepts

- Goals

- Visualize / Visualization

- Attitudes

- Emotional History

- Flick-back / Flick-up

- Affirmation

- Fear

- Assimilate / Assimilation

- Replacement Pictures

- Self-Talk

- Words – Pictures – Emotions

- Read – Picture – Feel

- Subconscious

- Reality

- Mentor

## Notes

# UNIT 19
# My Goals – My Vision – My Future

**Notes**

## UNIT 19
# My Goals – My Vision – My Future

## Reflective Questions

- "People can become successful as soon as they decide to be." —Harvey Mackay 1999. Where in my life have I decided to be successful?

- What pictures and emotions do I need to change in order to make my affirmations come true?

## UNIT 19
# My Goals – My Vision – My Future

## Reflective Questions

- What are my general expectations for my life, now and in the next ten years?

- Review my affirmations. Am I able to read, picture and feel each one strong enough to make them come true?

## UNIT 19
# My Goals – My Vision – My Future

## Summary

When you're setting goals, you need to change yourself, too. You want to build a better you. We've taught you a little bit about how to write goals, but let me emphasize now. Here's what you do. Look into the future. If this was July, can you look into October and see yourself as though the changes that you want to make in yourself have already occurred? Can you see the car you wanted or the apartment as already yours? How would you describe yourself? Well, you'd say, "I am..." I'd say, "Tell me about yourself. Not what you were in July, but that what you become in October now."

Now, write down the description. You step ahead into October, if this were July, and you ask yourself, well, if the change has already been made, how would I act? How would I behave? How would I describe myself? Let's suppose you had a bad temper and you always blew up when something happened. You say I want to change that. So, you step into October, and say, "When this happens, I remain calm and poised and blow it off. No big deal. I'm completely in control of my emotion." Write it down, and come back to July. Read the affirmation, "I'm calm and relaxed. I just blow it off. No big deal."

You visualize that occurring in October, whatever it would be that would make you mad and get you upset. You visualize that, but with a new emotion. What you're doing is preparing your emotion for your future. You're not going to live with the one you presently have. When you're afraid of things, you wouldn't let yourself do something, your attitudes were kind of avoidant – like me and the guy and the purse. I wouldn't say, "Go out and try hard" to do it. I visualized myself with somebody doing things that are different from me, but I do so with a calm or even emotion that I want. I'm changing my emotional history in my mind for a better future.

There's a technique called Flick back/Flick up. Let's suppose you can't talk in front of a large group. You get nervous or something like that. It's hard for you to talk to people you don't know socially or something like that. What you do is you find somebody in your own life – your best friend or somebody you can talk to that's easy. You write your affirmation like this: "It's as easy for me to talk to new people or large groups as it is to my best friend." You visualize yourself with your best friend emotionally, how you feel. Easy. Now, you transfer that emotion into the picture of October, and you see yourself speaking to new people at a party, or new people socially, or to someone you don't even know, and you're interviewing for a job. Or you see yourself in front of a large group making a presentation. You borrow the emotion of talking to your best friend, and you color that future for yourself. That's what the affirmations are for, to not let you run into your future with your old history of how you responded emotionally in the past.

When you were afraid of something, you don't need to be afraid of it in the future. If you avoided stuff, you don't need to avoid it in the future. See, avoiding is looking at the negative outcome so you won't let yourself do it. If you set a new goal, then you write the affirmation about, "I have

# UNIT 19
# My Goals – My Vision – My Future

this and this is the way I am." Then you borrow back and you project into the future. Borrow what went well for you, let yourself feel it, and then come forward into that which is scaring you. Write the affirmation, "I remain calm and poised whenever I'm in an interview." Most of you are living in your past. You're coloring your future in your present with old emotion, so you won't let yourself do the things that you're capable of doing, because your emotion won't let you do it.

Affirmations are to give yourself the right emotion and the right picture. You put into your mind the pictures of who you are now and how you want to feel. That's why you write out your affirmations correctly. However, writing them out is not enough. That isn't the end. The end is not even the end I'm giving you. The end is getting what you want, being who you want to be. You don't make affirmations because you wake up one morning and say, "You know, I think I need to make some affirmations." You're making affirmations to get what you want, the life you want, the business you want, become the person you want to be. So the question is, "What do I want?"

I'd recommend you make about 10 to 15 affirmations. Do you want to grow socially? Do you want to grow with more poise and confidence inside yourself? People treat you as they perceive you, so if you come off shy or not confident, they'll act towards you like you're shy. They read your body language. They read the way you tip your head. They read the way you stand. You can strengthen yourself on the inside with the way you want to be by finding, "I like her. I like him. I like what they're doing," and then you see yourself, not somebody else, doing it.

It isn't like you admire somebody, like, "I admire that movie star," or, "I admire that person." It stops right there. What I don't want you to do is just to admire them. I want you to assimilate, to embody what you like about them in your mind. I want you to take that characteristic or that quality and make it you, inside you. What is it you admire about them? Write that out as though you own it. It's me, I am. And then, take it in.

Then you visualize yourself where you are tomorrow or the next day or next week. You see situations where you would have responded like you used to, but instead of that now, you see your new self in your mind, just in your imagination is all. When you're doing that, don't go out and try hard to be it, because you'd be faking it. You're changing your mind. You're changing your picture. Just visualize it, just visualize it, just visualize it. If, in fact, you get into a situation and you still screw up like you used to, you say to yourself, "No more, I'm better that." Then, tell yourself again what you're going to do the next time.

You're creating replacement pictures for your income, for your life, for your relationships, for your future family. You're creating new pictures for your environment. You're deliberately giving your mind the ideas that you want to create. Remember, all meaningful and lasting change starts first on the inside and works its way out. It isn't going to be luck outside. It's because you change the picture on the inside. Then, as you look at the truth, "It ain't that way; I've gotta fix this."

# UNIT 19
# My Goals – My Vision – My Future

Once you've made the affirmation or written it, now it comes time to put it inside you. It's not hard to do. It's very easy. It's a three step process. Remember way back, we talked about the self-talk and the three dimensions? Words, pictures, and feeling or emotion. You've written it out now, and the words will describe the emotion you want to have.

Now, just before you fall asleep at night, you're closest to what is called the alpha state of consciousness. That's daydreaming. You sit back, read your words of your affirmation. It's one sentence long. You read it, and then you say, "Where would I be if this was occurring?" You take yourself into tomorrow or next week or take yourself into October if it's July. Give yourself the picture that these words describe. Give yourself the feeling that the words and the pictures bring you. That's all there is to it. That's all there is to it. That's all there is to it.

Then you go to your second affirmation. And because you've written it correctly, you read the words, close your eyes, see yourself having or being, feel what you feel like, and then go on your next affirmation. That's all it takes. That's all it takes. That's all it takes. Does this work? Absolutely.

I want you to think about, How good can I be? How good can I be? Do you see how you do it? It's as easy as that. The more time you spend doing this, I promise you the greater your life will go. Before you fall asleep, tell yourself how you want to wake up. Tell yourself exactly what time you want to wake up. You'd be surprised, even in a different time frame, you do that. You wake up at the exact time, if you're in Turkey or if you're in Europe or if you're in the United States. Your subconscious is that strong. Tell yourself how you want to feel when you wake up. Tell yourself how you want your morning to go. Tell yourself how you want your afternoon to go. Tell yourself how you want your evening to go. If you have a special date, a special party, talk to yourself about how you want it to come out. Visualize it. Don't leave it to chance. Don't walk in with your old history, unless your old history is good enough. Prepare yourself for the day. Prepare yourself for a meeting. Prepare yourself for the class. Visualize yourself into it.

It's best if you write them out. The reason is your subconscious is trying to keep you as you used to be, or as you are now. It isn't trying to make you be the new. Your creative subconscious' job is to keep the status quo, keep you as you are. You're messing around with your mind here, folks. You're just saying, "No, I'm changing." Your subconscious says, "Forget the affirmations. Blow 'em off, forget it," because what you're doing is messing around with your own reality.

Remember I said that a mentor throws you out and you catch up? That's what you're doing with this. You're mentoring yourself. This way, you're not dependent on having somebody around you who loves you and cares about you and will mentor you. They may be there. If they're not there, it isn't matter. It's not going to stop you, because you're going to do it yourself. It's the same thing. A mentor takes you into the future and describes you as they see you as though you actually are, and you catch up. Your affirmation takes you into the future as though you actually are, and you make yourself catch up. Can you do it, do you think? I know you can. Now, will you do it? That's a good question.

# Affirmation Workshop

## Affirmation Workshop

In this session, you learn how to write affirmations and practice writing them. You will use the goal ideas you have worked on. An affirmation is a statement of fact or belief. When written correctly, an affirmation will trigger a picture in your mind of your goal already accomplished. Your affirmations are your tools to deliberately control your own forethought. As you have learned, this is how successful, high-performance people win so frequently. You can paint your own positive scenarios, change your picture on the inside first, and automatically gravitate toward your goals by using these tools. There are eleven basic guidelines for writing affirmations. Review them closely.

1.  **Personal:** Affirmations are written with the word "I" in them. You can only affirm for yourself. The desired change will come about because of something you do, and it is your own inner picture that will change because of your affirmation.

2.  **Positive:** Always describe what you want in your affirmation. Describe what you want to move toward, not what you want to move away from. What would it look like if it were fixed?

3.  **Present Tense:** Affirmations are written as though they are happening right now. This requires using your imagination and becomes easier with practice.

4.  **Indicate Achievement:** Eliminate words such as, "can, will, should, and want to" etc., from your affirmations. Include phrases such as, "I am, I do," or "I have." It is important to give your subconscious a clear picture of the end result as though it is already accomplished.

5.  **No Comparisons:** Comparing yourself to others is ineffective. The technique of affirming is a personal process. Your measurement of growth is based on yourself.

6.  **Action Words:** Use terms that describe and trigger action pictures, such as "easily, quickly, thrive on, energetically, confidently," in your affirmations.

7.  **Emotion Words:** These are of critical importance. The more positive emotion you feel when picturing your accomplished goal, the faster your affirmation will work for you.

8.  **Accuracy:** If your goal is to exercise regularly, what kind of exercise? Is it jogging, walking, swimming, aerobics, or something else? How regularly? Three times a week? If so, on what days? What time of day and for how long? This is how accurate your affirmations must be. If written in general terms, the picture is too vague, and it gives you too many escape routes.

9.  **Balance:** Set goals, and write affirmations in all areas of your life.

10. **Realistic:** After you have written your affirmation, close your eyes and picture it. Can you see yourself there? You need to be able to see it, visualize it, and imagine it.

11. **Confidential:** Share your affirmations with only those you are certain will support and help you achieve them. Most of your personal affirmations need not be shared.

# Affirmation Workshop

## Affirmation Preparation

What are some of my important goals for these areas?

- Personal


- Family


- Health/Physical


- Health/Mental


- Spiritual


- Social


- Career/Vocation


- Education


- Recreation/Leisure Time


- Community Service

# Affirmation Workshop

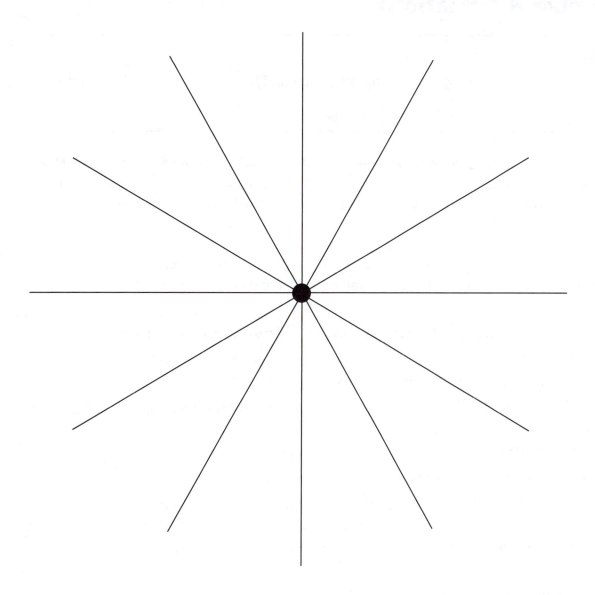

- Education

- Finances

- Relationship with Parents/Siblings

- Relationship with Significant Other

- Relationship with Kids

- Relationship with Friends

- Spiritual Life, Physical Health

- Community Life

- Current PT or FT Job

- School Involvement

- Relationship with Faculty/Staff

# Affirmation Workshop

## Sample Affirmations

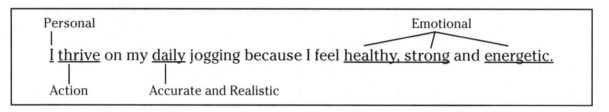

The following list has a variety of sample affirmations that may be helpful. Some may fit your career situation, others focus on your personal life, and some may overlap. If some of these affirmations work for you, please use them, but be sure to rewrite them so that they are you talking to you.

1. I like and respect myself because I know that I am a worthy, capable, and valuable person.

2. I enjoy my life and my relationships with other people.

3. I have an excellent, free-flowing memory with clear and easy recall.

4. It is easy and fun to write and imprint affirmations daily.

5. I enjoy making my affirmations daily because of the positive and quick results I get.

6. I have a positive expectancy of earning good grades, and I see all setbacks as temporary.

7. I have pride in my ability to find quality, affordable and dependable day care for my child/children.

8. I enthusiastically arrive at school on time and attend my classes daily with an open mind and a positive attitude.

9. I am very effective and efficient especially in stressful situations.

10. I have pride in my educational performance and positive expectations of my future.

11. I express myself well, and I know others respect my point of view.

12. I quietly do helpful and worthwhile things for others.

13. I look for ways of uplifting myself and others, and I do it with ease every day.

14. I am accountable for the results of my decisions and actions.

15. I reinforce my successes and positively correct for errors.

16. I am my own expert, and I accept only positive attitudes and opinions from others.

17. Because of the warmth and love I show my children, I teach them to show warmth and love to each other.

18. I develop feelings of self-respect and self-esteem in others and myself.

19. Because I sincerely care about myself and the quality of my life, I am financially responsible.

# Affirmation Workshop

## Sample Affirmations

20. My family and friends are benefiting from the successes that have come from my hard work and commitment to my education.

21. Taking tests is easy for me because I study and prepare for them well in advance.

22. Because of my careful, advance planning, I am well-rested for my exams.

23. I am healthy and energetic because I treat my body with the love and respect I deserve.

24. Because I am well organized and plan ahead, I have reliable transportation to school and back.

25. I am calm, relaxed, and clear-headed when I ask questions in class.

26. Giving presentations in front of my classmates is fun and uplifting.

27. I speak clearly and calmly and make positive contributions that benefit me and my classmates.

28. My classmates who are young and intelligent enrich my life. I value their contributions and learn many things from them.

29. I sincerely care about my instructors and am open-minded about what they teach me.

30. I am a successful professional and earn $____ per month. I live a comfortable and happy life.

# Affirmation Workshop

## Group Exercise

In groups of three or four, write an affirmation for each of the following situations as if you were the person with the challenge. Recognize that the person in current reality wants to change. The vision is what it looks like without the challenge. Refer to the checklist on page 213 and the samples on pages 208 and 209.

| Current Reality | Vision |
|---|---|
| Denise feels she is too old to learn anything new, but she wants to use computers. | |
| **Affirmation:** | |
| Melanie is often late for work. She feels guilty and knows her boss is beginning to notice. | |
| **Affirmation:** | |
| Juanita has ongoing transportation problems she would like to be able to solve. | |
| **Affirmation:** | |
| Maurice gets so nervous before making presentations that he "blows it" at meetings. He wants to do well. | |
| **Affirmation:** | |
| Kurt has been concerned about his home loan. He feels very frustrated and worried. | |
| **Affirmation:** | |

# Affirmation Workshop

## Writing Affirmations

Now, individually, write three sample affirmations for yourself, following the same process with each. Refer to the list of helpful Action/Emotion Words on pages 215 through 217 and the Affirmation Checklist on page 213.

| Current Reality (to move away from) | Vision (to include in your affirmation) |
| --- | --- |
| bad temper | calm, clear minded |
| lazy | energetic |
| procrastinate | accomplish immediately |

**Current Reality**                    **Vision**

**Affirmation:**

**Current Reality**                    **Vision**

**Affirmation:**

**Current Reality**                    **Vision**

**Affirmation:**

# Affirmation Workshop

## Writing Affirmations

**Current Reality**                    **Vision**

**Affirmation:**

**Current Reality**                    **Vision**

**Affirmation:**

**Current Reality**                    **Vision**

**Affirmation:**

**Current Reality**                    **Vision**

**Affirmation:**

# Affirmation Workshop

## Affirmation Checklist

❑ **Personal** – Include *I* or *me.*

❑ **Positive** – Describe what you want instead of what you don't want.

❑ **Present Tense** – Write like it's happening right now.

❑ **Indicate Achievement** – Use phrases such as *I have, I am* and *I do.* Do not include terms like *can, will, want to* and *should.*

❑ **No Comparisons** – Picture your own change and growth instead of comparing yourself to someone else.

❑ **Action Words** – Create pictures of yourself performing in an easy, anxiety-free manner.

❑ **Emotion Words** – Cause you to feel exactly how you want to feel when it is achieved. Refer to pages 215-217 for Affirmation Action/Emotion Words.

❑ **Accuracy** – Specific and detailed. Are there any escape routes?

❑ **Balance** – Coordinate well with goals you have in other areas of your life.

| | | |
|---|---|---|
| • Family | • Recreation | • Social |
| • Spiritual | • Education | • Business |
| • Health | • Relationship | • Career |
| • Financial | • Other | |

❑ **Realistic** - Can you see yourself achieving it?

❑ **Confidential** - With whom do you choose to share this affirmation? Who will really support and help you to achieve it? Most of your personal affirmations need not be shared.

# Affirmation Workshop

## Create Your Own Balance Wheel

On the Balance Wheel, list the areas of your life you would like to improve or change. For example: career, spiritual, family, physical and mental health, education, financial, etc. Refer to the ideas you have written in previous units.

On page 212, write an affirmation for each area listed on your Balance Wheel using the process of Vision, Current Reality, Affirmation. Refer to the Affirmation Checklist on page 213, and the Action/Emotion Words on pages 215-217. When you have completed this transfer them to 3x5 cards, and insert them into your affirmation folder.

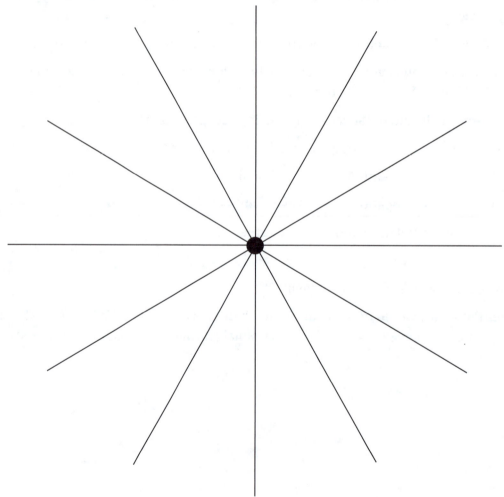

- Education
- Finances
- Relationship with Parents/Siblings
- Relationship with Significant Other

- Relationship with Kids
- Relationship with Friends
- Spiritual Life, Physical Health
- Community Life

- Current PT or FT Job
- School Involvement
- Relationship with Faculty/Staff

# Affirmation Workshop

## Action/Emotion Words

Accepted
Accomplish
Achieve
Acknowledge
Active
Adaptable
Admire
Adorable
Adventurous
Affectionate
Agreeable
Aggressive
Alert
Amazing
Ambitious
Articulate
Aspiring
Assertive
Assured
Attentive
Beautiful
Beloved
Blessed
Blissful
Brave
Bright
Brilliant
Calm
Capable
Caring
Charming
Cheerful
Clean
Clear
Clever
Colorful
Comfortable

Comic
Compassionate
Competent
Complete
Complimentary
Composed
Concise
Confident
Conscientious
Considerate
Constructive
Content
Cooperative
Courteous
Creative
Cultured
Curious
Dazzling
Decisive
Delightful
Dependable
Deserving
Determined
Devote
Dignified
Diligent
Diplomatic
Disciplined
Dramatic
Dutiful
Dynamic
Eager
Easy
Effective
Efficient
Effortless
Electric

Elegant
Eloquent
Embrace
Encouraging
Endearing
Enduring
Energetic
Enjoyable
Enlightened
Enterprising
Entertaining
Enthused
Enthusiastic
Excellent
Exceptional
Exciting
Expectant
Expressive
Faithful
Famous
Fantastic
Fascinating
Fearless
Feminine
Fervent
Festive
Flexible
Fluent
Forceful
Forgiving
Fortunate
Fresh
Friendly
Frugal
Fulfilling
Fun
Gallant

Generous
Genial
Gentle
Genuine
Gifted
Giving
Glad
Glorious
Good
Graceful
Gracious
Grammatical
Grand
Great
Growing
Handy
Happy
Harmonious
Healthy
Hearty
Helpful
Honest
Honorable
Hospitable
Humble
Humorous
Idealistic
Illustrious
Immense
Impartial
Impeccable
Important
Impressive
Independent
Individualistic
Industrious
Influential

# Affirmation Workshop

## Action/Emotion Words

| | | | |
|---|---|---|---|
| Ingenious | Mighty | Proficient | Seeking |
| Innovative | Modest | Progressive | Selective |
| Inspiring | Moral | Promising | Self-confident |
| Inspirational | Motivated | Prosperous | Self-contained |
| Instrumental | Musical | Proud | Self-reliant |
| Intellectual | Myself | Prudent | Sensational |
| Intelligent | Natural | Punctual | Sensible |
| Intense | Neighborly | Pure | Sensitive |
| Intentional | Noble | Purposeful | Sentimental |
| Intuitive | Nourishing | Qualified | Serene |
| Inventive | Obedient | Quick | Sharing |
| Jolly | Obliging | Quiet | Significant |
| Jovial | Outstanding | Quotable | Simply |
| Joyous | Passionate | Radiant | Sincere |
| Jubilant | Patient | Rapid | Skillful |
| Just | Patriotic | Rational | Smiling |
| Kind | Peaceful | Realistic | Smart |
| Knowing | Perceptive | Reasonable | Smooth |
| Knowledgeable | Persevering | Receptive | Sociable |
| Learned | Personable | Refined | Sophisticated |
| Likeable | Placid | Refreshing | Sparkling |
| Lively | Pleasant | Regal | Special |
| Lovable | Pleasing | Relaxed | Spectacular |
| Lovely | Pleasurable | Reliable | Speedy |
| Loving | Polite | Reputable | Spirited |
| Loyal | Positive | Resourceful | Spiritual |
| Lucky | Powerful | Respectable | Splendid |
| Luminous | Practical | Respected | Spontaneous |
| Lyrical | Praiseworthy | Respectful | Sporting |
| Magnetic | Precise | Responsible | Stable |
| Magnificent | Prepared | Retentive | Stalwart |
| Marvelous | Presentable | Reverent | Steadfast |
| Meaningful | Prestigious | Rich | Steady |
| Mellow | Principled | Safe | Strong |
| Melodious | Privileged | Scholarly | Strengthen |
| Memorable | Productive | Secure | Stylish |
| Merry | Professional | Seeing | Stunning |

# Affirmation Workshop

## Action/Emotion Words

Sturdy
Successful
Super
Superb
Supportive
Sure
Survivor
Swift
Sympathetic
Systematic
Tactful
Teachable
Tender
Terrific
Thankful
Thorough

Thrifty
Thriving
Timely
Tireless
Tolerant
Tranquil
Treasured
Thoughtful
Triumphant
True
Trusted
Trustworthy
Truthful
Understanding
Unforgettable
Universal

Uplifting
Useful
Valiant
Valuable
Venturesome
Vibrant
Victorious
Vigorous
Virtuous
Visible
Visionary
Visual
Vital
Vivacious
Vivid
Warm
Wealthy

Welcome
Well
Wholesome
Willing
Winner
Winning
Wonderful
Working
Worthwhile
Worthy
Young
Youthful
Zealously
Zestful

## Words to Avoid Using

Better
But
Can
Could
Even if
Going to
Have to
Hope to
Less
Maybe
Might
More
Need to
Never

Not
Should
Some
Something
Try
Want to
Will
Wish
Would
Would like to

# Affirmation Workshop

**UNIT 20**
# If I Want It, I Can Create It

## Unit Overview

By growing stronger on the inside, we allow ourselves to dream bigger and set bigger goals. In order to grow stronger on the inside, we need to escalate our self-efficacy – our belief in our own ability to make things happen in our lives. We look forward to success, and not fear of failure; and if we don't reach our goals, we are resilient. We pick ourselves up, and start again.

## Unit Objectives

*By the end of this unit, I will:*

* have learned how to develop my sense of personal efficacy.

* look forward and see success.

* not be afraid of failure, as I know that I am resilient and persistent.

* dream big.

# WHENEVER POSSIBLE, DRIVE FEAR OUT OF YOUR LIFE.

**UNIT 20**
# If I Want It, I Can Create It

## Key Concepts

- Fear

- Consequences

- Attitude

- Comfort Zone

- Value

- Visualize / Visualization

- Emotion

- Self-Esteem

## Notes

# UNIT 20
# If I Want It, I Can Create It

**Notes**

# UNIT 20
# If I Want It, I Can Create It

## Reflective Questions

- What kind of adversity have I overcome? And how did it make me a stronger person?

- Where can I look forward and see success?

- I have high self-efficacy in these areas because . . .

# UNIT 20
# If I Want It, I Can Create It

## Reflective Questions

- What gives real meaning to my life?

- Select a challenge. What attitudes, beliefs, comfort zones, self-talk, habits and goals do I want to adjust to overcome this challenge?

## UNIT 20
# If I Want It, I Can Create It

## Exercise: Play Without Fear

In the chart below, list some things that scare you. They could be things that scare you a little or a lot – your choice. In the next column, describe how life would look if you weren't scared. In the final column, write an affirmation that helps you move to that new vision of life without fear.

| Things that Scare Me | What would it look like without the fear? | An Affirmation to Move Me Past My Fear |
|---|---|---|
|  |  |  |
|  |  |  |
|  |  |  |
|  |  |  |
|  |  |  |
|  |  |  |
|  |  |  |

# UNIT 20
# If I Want It, I Can Create It

## Summary

I would encourage you, if you can, to drive fear out of your life. You're afraid you won't be accepted. You're afraid you won't get the job. You're afraid that you won't look good. I don't know what it might be. Fear is so debilitating. Fear causes you not to be your best. Fear is a terrible way to live.

Now, I didn't say to live without consequences. But you don't need to fear the consequence. What you need to do is to drive fear out of your life. Remember when I said, as you were growing up, you might have been raised theologically to outrun the flames of hell licking at your butt. The only reason you are good is because you don't want to go to hell. So, you live your whole life fearful that you're going to go to hell, instead of visualizing you're going to possess the good.

There was a lady that came to work for me years ago called Marilyn Thornton. Marilyn used to work for the Governor of Colorado. He'd been governor for 12 years, and now he couldn't run anymore, so he called and asked if I would take her for a job. I said of course, and so on. Anyway, when I talked about efficacy one time, Marilyn was telling this story. She was raised in New England, the only child of a very conservative Catholic family. She was about 19, and her mother would say, "Where you going tonight?" To a dance. "How are you going to get there?" Drive the car. "Well, what time are you going to be home?" About 1 AM. 'Well, what happens if you are coming home and you get a flat tire, in the dark?" Now listen, "what if's" everywhere. Mother's getting her to think in a negative scenario. So Marilyn says, I'll get out, get the spare and change the tire. "Well, what happens if, while you're changing the tire, somebody drives up and tries to attack you?" (Sound like anyone you know?) Then, I'll hit him with the jack handle. "Well, what if he's bigger than you?" then, I'll run. "What if he's faster?" You're right, Mom. I shouldn't go.

Now listen to that. That was a beautiful scenario, which many of us have run into. Isn't that right? Your friends will what-if you, family will what-if you, almost to the point where you say, "Gosh, you're right, you know. You've told me enough. I quit." But you can do the same to yourself. You can what-if yourself to death.

One more example. Let's say there is a beam or a plank, and it would go the length of the classroom to where you're seated now. I'd ask you to go down to one end. The plank is going to be as high off the floor as a table. I'd say if you walk from down there where you are to where I am and not step off of this plank, I'll give you a thousand dollars. Would you try it? Probably. Come one down for a thousand dollars. You have the skill, the balance, and the reward is good. See that attitude?

Now watch this, I'm going to do one thing. I'm going to raise the plank 50 stories up in the air – 50 stories high, between two buildings, maybe in New York. You're going to be on that side on the roof, and I'm going to be on this side. I'm going to say I have a thousand dollars for you. Walk across and it's yours. Step off and you won't get it. (And I would say that.)

# UNIT 20
# If I Want It, I Can Create It

You have the skill to walk it at table height. You have the balance to walk it and you can see the reward. You focus on the reward, and you just walk across gracefully. But, if I raise it 50 stories up in the air, what's the difference? You might fall. Yes. And what does that do to your balance? It throws you off. Remember being out of your comfort zone, how it throws you off, how you get uptight, and you can't use your skills? What is the difference? The width is the same, the length is the same, the skill is still inside you. It's the fear of death, the fear of dying. Do you see that fear would make you less effective?

You can see why I encourage you to stop using fear on yourself. If I apply for the job, I won't get it. If I ask her for a date, I won't get it. If you play with fear, it impedes how you play. What you want to do is to see, "How good can I be?" Ask yourself, "What's the value in this?" Then, you visualize and put that kind of an emotion in. Some of the emotion you have of fear isn't because you put it in. It's almost like you don't know how you got it. What you need to do is beat the fear or you won't let yourself take the job. You won't let yourself move away from your old friends. You won't let yourself go to school, or let yourself graduate. You just stop yourself. If you do go out socially, you just blow it because you act stupid, because you're out of your comfort zone. You can't override your fear. You need to beat it.

If the plank was 50 stories high, all you want to do is see yourself getting the reward. Focus on the reward, and you can come across without stepping off. But it's hard to do because your mind goes, "What if I…" Just like the mother that I was talking to you about, of the lady that used to work for me. "What if the guy comes to attack you?" "I'll hit him with the jack handle." "What if he's bigger?" "Then I'll run." "Well, what if he's faster." "Ah, you're right, I shouldn't go." Do you see what you're doing to yourself? It may be all right to start with, but you keep what-ifing yourself or you let others do it, and before long, "I give up; I quit." What if you put all that time into developing a business? What if you spend all that time in school and you don't get the career you want? Well, you're right, I shouldn't go.

Who are you hanging around? Who's talking to you like that? What kind of people are encouraging you to quit or triggering fear pictures in your mind? There are a lot of people around you you're going to need to drop. I don't know who they are. I needed to drop them. There are a lot of people who will try to trigger fear pictures. In your own mind, you need to ask, "Who are you to tell me that? Maybe for you, but not for me." Develop your self-esteem inside yourself, and you can conquer the fear.

## UNIT 21
# Rites of Passage

## Unit Overview

While we have learned that in order to make a change in ourselves, we need to read our affirmations at least twice a day, for several weeks, there is something even more powerful at work in us. A vow – a one-time affirmation – made with great emotion can change your life forever. Rites of passage do the same, especially when sanctioned by a "who-said of the greatest magnitude." We are about to embark on our own rite of passage as we conclude this course.

## Unit Objectives

*By the end of this unit, I will:*

• understand the power of one-time affirmations, or vows.

• have learned the influence rites of passage can have on the changes I want.

• be a positive wizard in the lives of my family, friends and co-workers.

# A VOW:
# ONE STATEMENT OF FACT
# MADE WITH TREMENDOUS EMOTION,
# CAN CHANGE YOU FOREVER.

# UNIT 21
# Rites of Passage

## Key Concepts

- Vow

- Accountable

- Beliefs

- Affirmation Process

- Scotomas

- Behavior

- Rite of Passage

- Who-Said

- Negative Wizard

- Positive Wizard

## Notes

# UNIT 21
# Rites of Passage

**Notes**

**UNIT 21**
# Rites of Passage

## Reflective Questions

- Who are two positive wizards in my life? How have those individuals influenced me?

- Have I ever experienced a negative wizard? What impact did that person have on my life?

## UNIT 21
# Rites of Passage

## Reflective Questions

- In what ways do I limit myself because I have listened to others tell me what was wrong with me?

- Examples of rite of passage situations in my life have been:

**UNIT 21**
# Rites of Passage

## Exercise: Future Check

Put an "x" on either the "need more" or "need less" line, in the proper place for you.

| Need less | OK | | OK | Need more |
|---|---|---|---|---|
| ← | → | Dependability | ← | → |
| ← | → | Honesty | ← | → |
| ← | → | Good Attitude | ← | → |
| ← | → | Critical Thinking Skills | ← | → |
| ← | → | Intrinsic Motivation | ← | → |
| ← | → | Creativity / Innovation | ← | → |
| ← | → | Self-Esteem / Self-Efficacy | ← | → |
| ← | → | Accountability | ← | → |
| ← | → | Goal-Setting / End-Result Thinking | ← | → |
| ← | → | Resiliency | ← | → |
| ← | → | Making Effective Decisions | ← | → |
| ← | → | Empowering / Mentoring Others | ← | → |
| ← | → | Team Player | ← | → |
| ← | → | Culturally Diverse | ← | → |
| ← | → | Flexible & Multi-Skilled | ← | → |
| ← | → | Planning & Organization | ← | → |
| ← | → | Take Action / Proactive | ← | → |
| ← | → | Professional | ← | → |
| ← | → | Ability to Handle Change | ← | → |
| ← | → | | ← | → |
| ← | → | | ← | → |

## UNIT 21
# Rites of Passage

## Summary

Do ever remember making a vow when you were a kid? Here, eat your mush. "No!" Eat your spinach. "No!" Liver. "No! I hate it. I'll never eat it." Vows are like that third level of self-talk. "I quit. No more. That's it. No more." Let's suppose 10 years from now somebody serves you liver and onions. You haven't had it for 10 years. It's in your mind, the vow you made. So when it shows up, "Nope." That's how powerful your mind is.

I can remember years ago, when my father died. I was about 12. He died just before I turned 13. We were very poor, because we didn't have any money then. We were on welfare. I thought my grandfather on my mother's side would help out, and he didn't. At 13 years old, I just got so angry about it. I'm raising my brothers now, I'm trying to. My mother was on welfare. I'm trying to earn enough money to take care of my brothers and so on. I just said, "I'll always take care of my family." That was a vow made by a 13 year old. Now, I don't know if the circumstances were that way or not, but that was my impression of it.

I am very loyal to my family. I do take care of my family and so on. My family can be my business family or my friends. We have 11 foster and adopted children. I take good care of many of them, and we have a lot of grandchildren. We help out, take care, watch for them. We help them with college and things like that. And I take care of friends who are in trouble. That vow serves me well, but the problem was with that vow.

In my company I'd have people who told me the were going to do something and not do it. I come back from being out of town, and I thought it was going to be done. It made me mad that it didn't higher get done. Then we just go out and have a beer. They knew I'd never fire them. So, that vow, made as a young person, served me well in some ways, but I was wondering why I'd have all these people who weren't very accountable. It was me. I was enabling them because of the vow that served me well. You want to look inside yourself. Where did you make promises to yourself that may be in your way now?

I was having dinner one time with a friend of mine who really was a great football player and became a great businessman in Seattle. I coached him in high school, and then he went on to play in the pros. I'm a godfather for his son. We were sitting at this restaurant in Burien called Angelo's, my wife and his wife, and he was saying to me, "Lou, you're a teacher, you're a coach, and you're always so darn poor. Give me a thousand dollars of your money, I'll put it with nine or ten of mine and I'll invest it and help you out." I didn't want to tell him I didn't have a thousand, so I said, "Well, making money is all right for you. But for me, when people name a kid after me, like you have, or ask me to be the godfather or whatever, that's really what I want out of life. Making money can be okay for you. That's not for me." This kid was about 22 years old, and I can still see where he was sitting 40 some years later. He looked across the table, he said, "Who in the hell said you had to be poor do that?" I did. I said you had to be poor to do that.

# UNIT 21
# Rites of Passage

See, you get certain beliefs in your mind like you can't be wealthy or you're going to go to hell. Everybody making money must be bad people or something like that. Where do you get that? I don't know, but I had it. Now, I changed my mind and immediately got wealthier. But if I kept that, I would never be in this business. I wouldn't be doing what I'm doing, because it takes money to help my company grow, and so on. My attitude and belief and my vows about money and wealthy people were interfering with my success.

You need to find your own. What are some of the things you told yourself that are interfering with your own growth now? You use the affirmation process to change that. I needed to make affirmations about "I always take care of my family." I hold them accountable. I need to make sure that they take care of themselves when they're capable. I needed to change things that I grew up with. I had lots of them. But I needed insights, because I had scotomas. I couldn't see my own behavior. I can't see it sometimes. I don't know what's causing me to behave the way I am, but when I've got it in me, I keep acting like this isn't working.

Do you know how important and powerful vows are? You have two people who are single, unmarried. They behave single. But they go to a rite of passage like a wedding. A rite of passage usually has a "who-said of the greatest magnitude" present. In the old days for you, it was a teacher, a coach, a scout leader. Typically, they're powerful, and have authority. So you go through a rite of passage, like a wedding ceremony. The who-said, which is the minister, priest, the rabbi, the judge, this person who you think has the power says, "Do you take this man to be?" And with one vow you say, "I do." "Do you take this woman to be?" And with one vow, one affirmation, you say, "I do." This person says, "By the power vested in me, given to me by the State of Washington, the State of California, the Holy Church, I now pronounce you man and wife." Now you believe you're married. You come in single, you go out married. That's all there is to it. That's how powerful belief is. See, you changed your mind, then you act like you're married for the rest of your life. It's all in your mind.

Or you're married and you want to get a divorce. You go before the magistrate or the judge or something like that. He says, "I dissolve this relationship," and now you're single. That's how powerful your mind is.

Now, for the most part you were raised by always having somebody tell you that you can go to the second grade if you're in the first. "Oh, thank you." Will I ever get to the sixth grade? "Oh, thank you." Then you're going to go into junior high school or middle school. "Oh, thank you. I wonder if they're going to let me go." Then will they let me go to high school? "Oh, thank you. They gave me permission." Who is "they"? These teachers; these who-saids. Then it's, "Will I graduate from high school? Will they let me go into college? Will this guy hire me? Will they give me a raise?" Many of us let somebody else give us the permission before we take ourselves there. You doubt your own self enough. It's important to have those rights of passage, but the affirmation process will move you beyond waiting for permission.

# UNIT 21
# Rites of Passage

I want you to give yourself the power to affirm yourself into your future. You don't need to wait for the permission. Of course, you can't go out and do something without being qualified by the State and so on. But you need to stop waiting for people to tell you you're beautiful, or capable, or you could start your own business, or you can live your own life.

Now, here's my final way of giving you a picture that you can carry with you. Have you ever seen the movie "The Wizard of Oz?" You know, I think it's been translated into every language! This is my version I tell my grandkids, so I've kind of changed it a little bit. Dorothy lived in Kansas. A tornado came, blew her house out of town. Darn the bad luck, when it landed, it landed on a witch, the Wicked Witch (of the East). Killed her dead. Dorothy gets out, looks around, and doesn't know where she is. She sees the Wicked Witch's legs sticking out underneath the house with these beautiful shoes on. Dorothy figures the Witch isn't going to use them anymore, and puts them on. Along came the Wicked Witch's sister, sees the shoes on Dorothy, which makes her mad. Now Dorothy has got to get out of town, because the Wicked Witch (of the West) is after her.

The Good Witch Glinda, shows up, and Glinda says, "My dear, the only way back to Kansas is you've got to go see the Wizard in the land of Oz." So here was Dorothy, off to see the Wizard, the wonderful Wizard of Oz. How come? Because the Wizard could help her get where she wanted to go.

Now, on her way to see the Wizard, Dorothy ran into somebody without brains, she ran into somebody without courage and someone without a heart. But being a very up person, she just fought off all the monkeys with the wings, the fire and stuff like that. When she finally got to the land of Oz, the Wizard (Frank Morgan was the actor) hid behind a screen, trying to scare them away. "What do you want?" What did the Cowardly Lion need? The lion didn't have any courage, right? So the Wizard said, just like getting married, "I can understand why you aren't courageous. Every brave person has a medal. I notice you're not wearing any medals. For all the brave things you did for Dorothy and Toto, I give you a medal. Now you have courage; go act like it." The Lion starts to roar, "Wow, I got it now!" That was a onetime affirmation, accepted by that person, in this case the person was the Cowardly Lion. Off he goes, he's brave.

Now, the Scarecrow, his head was full of stuffin', he couldn't think and his mind was nothing. No brains. The Wizard said, "I can understand why. Every smart person has a diploma. I notice you don't have a diploma. So by the power vested in me, the great Wizard of Oz, I give you diploma. Now you have brains; go act like it." A onetime affirmation, through a rite of passage, just like getting married, and off he goes.

Now, it was the Tin Man didn't have a heart. No feeling. No emotion. The Wizard said, "Well, I can understand why. Everybody who has a heart can hear it tick." So he gave him a clock, and put it inside of him. "Now you have a heart; go act like it." A onetime affirmation through a rite of passage.

# UNIT 21
# Rites of Passage

Now, it's important to know, when I thought of this whole example I was in Hawaii talking to the native Hawaiian. It is believed they never get out of the eighth grade. They're looked upon as not very strong. It would be like the Native American oftentimes is thought of. They just won't go to school. They don't care, whatever. That was the impression. I was working with them, and I told them this story I just told you.

I told them that the difference is that so many of them came across negative wizards as they were growing up. They told you that you weren't smart, didn't have brains or didn't have courage. It could have been coaches, teachers, grandparents, parents. It could have been people outside of you, other kids teasing you. And I said, the problem was you accepted it. You let those negative wizards in your world describe you for you. You took it on, because you didn't know any better. You didn't want to be that way. You tried pushing it off, but pretty soon, "OK, I guess I am," and then you acted like it forever.

I'm going to encourage all of you to watch out for the negative wizards. They'll be in your social world. They'll be on television. They can be in your music. They are people taking your future away. They're describing you as they see you, and because you didn't know any better, you gave them sanction. "Ah, I got it. It's me. I don't want to be that way, but I guess I am." Only hang around and find good, positive wizards in your life.

For you, I want you to think about how powerful you're going to be to your friends and your future family and the people around you. See, I want you to be a positive wizard. I want you to affirm greatness in them. I want you to see them and tell them how much you care about them, how much you love them, how smart they are, how capable they are. You don't have to lie about it. You can see the good. You can look for the good. It's not enough to just see it. You want to tell them. If they respect you and like you and love you, you are just like that person that says, "Now you're married." "Oh, I am? Wow!" You can be a tremendously powerful, positive influence for the rest of your life.

Do you ever get a song stuck in your head that you can't get out? Put this one in and try it. You know that song in The Wizard of Oz – "I'm off to see the Wizard, the wonderful Wizard of Oz." She's skipping down the yellow brick road? What I want you to be thinking is this: Just change a couple words. "I'm off to *be* the Wizard, the wonderful Wizard of Oz. I'm off to *be* the Wizard because of the wonderful things *I* does." I got the touch. I got the touch. And you have the touch. You want to keep it, develop it and use it. Use it for your brothers and sisters, your mothers, your fathers. Use it with the people around you. Affirm them, tell them how good they are, but for yourself also. Watch out for the negative wizards, don't let them touch you, don't let them get you. Be open to constructive criticism, but not to the negative stuff that they're using to try and tear your heart out. So my final act: By the power vested in me, given to me by me, I now pronounce you Associate Wizards. That's your graduation ceremony. Go and live like it.

## UNIT 21
# Rites of Passage

## Personal Beliefs Inventory

Please read each statement and place a check in the box that most accurately describes your beliefs and/or feelings.

| | | Strongly Agree | Agree | Mildly Agree | No Opinion | Mildly Disagree | Disagree | Strongly Disagree |
|---|---|---|---|---|---|---|---|---|
| 1 | When I enter a new situation, I typically see others as smarter than me. | | | | | | | |
| 2 | My past successes are due to luck. | | | | | | | |
| 3 | I expect to be successful in life. | | | | | | | |
| 4 | When life events are difficult, I can adapt. | | | | | | | |
| 5 | I have complete control of my attitude. | | | | | | | |
| 6 | I have virtually no alternatives in my life. | | | | | | | |
| 7 | Outside events have a great impact on my life. | | | | | | | |
| 8 | When my mind is made up, there is no changing it. | | | | | | | |
| 9 | My past successes are because of me. | | | | | | | |
| 10 | I can change if I want to change. | | | | | | | |
| 11 | I know how my self-talk impacts my attitude. | | | | | | | |
| 12 | I am responsible for my own happiness. | | | | | | | |
| 13 | My happiness is increased when my goals are met. | | | | | | | |
| 14 | Goal-setting is worthwhile. | | | | | | | |
| 15 | I like me. | | | | | | | |
| 16 | I know how to set goals. | | | | | | | |
| 17 | I am satisfied with my current situation. | | | | | | | |
| 18 | I rarely miss a day of work or school due to illness. | | | | | | | |
| 19 | I rely on others to motivate me. | | | | | | | |
| 20 | Good things happen because I cause them to happen. | | | | | | | |
| 21 | I am capable of making changes in my personal life. | | | | | | | |

## DAY 1
# Getting Started

## Journal

# DAY 1
# Getting Started

## Audio Summary

Well, I know what you're thinking. "I think I'll wait until tomorrow to do my affirmations. Today I'm so busy." Well, let's talk about that for a moment.

One of the things that happens is you were so engrossed in those days of intense learning that it consumed your whole time, didn't it? Remember, once you arrive at a goal that you set, what do we do? We flatten out. And if the goal was to go to the seminar and not through the seminar, here we are, flattening out. Oh, maybe not flattened completely, because the F card and the old lady or the young lady was fun. But I know what you want to do now. You want to go out and just teach the whole seminar, don't you? You're just going to teach them off the F card or you're going to show them the old lady, show them the young lady, but that's not what it's all about. It is where your enthusiasm is right now, but we need to take it past that one point of either flattening out or "What can I do to go out and shape up my spouse, or my children, or somebody at work. I know all these people that really need it, but I don't know that I do."

So don't wait; we're going to start right now. I'm your coach. My job now is to take you past the video burst. We're really going to get serious now about assimilating what it was that we learned. I'm not going to start at the beginning like we did with the first unit in the video. That's not the way to do it. The way to do it is to start like on the fourth day. If you went through three days of video burst, you don't need to start at the beginning. Where you need to start is with the new knowledge that you have, and how you are going to apply it and how you are going to use it.

So if you were sitting with me right now, the first thing I think I'd talk to you about is using your forethought correctly, because that's so simple and it's so easy. So, let's just talk about using our forethought. Now, forethought really is what? Using your imagination, which is unique to a human being, to look forward. To look forward to what? Well, let's not make this too mysterious. Let's just look forward to breakfast. Let's look forward to dinner. What are you going to have for breakfast? What are you going to have for lunch? What are you going to have for dinner? What are you going to do in the morning? What are you going to do in the afternoon? What are you going to do this evening? That's forethought. What are you going to do at work, if it's a work day. What are we going to do? Who's going to be around us? What are our plans? That's forethought.

You know, another thing about forethought – it's so simple if you stop and think about it – forethought is like writing a grocery list. You write a grocery list, and what it does is it triggers your thought forward, forethought, triggers it forward. It lets you imagine yourself going to the store, but you even go past the store, don't you? What you do if you're cooking or preparing a meal, is you go past the cooking and you go right to the preparation. No, you might even go past the preparation and go all the way to enjoying the meal and seeing the people around you enjoy the meal. Well, that's forethought. Nothing mysterious. So forethought isn't something that we need to relearn or something that we need to start with. This is something we've been doing all the time.

# DAY 1
# Getting Started

Do you know another example of forethought? As you drive to work or you drive home or you're driving someplace today, look for the road signs. You might see a sign that says "Danger" with a swervy little line or something like that. Well, what that is doing is triggering your thought forward so that you can imagine what's coming up. That's forethought.

Now, can we make road signs for ourselves? Yes, they are the affirmation process. But even more so, if you never write an affirmation (which is a mistake), and let's just suppose you don't write an affirmation, the only thing you're going to get out of this whole course is to every day plan the next day. When should you do it? Well, the best time to do it would be when you're in the alpha state of consciousness. That's just before you fall asleep. Just before you fall asleep, if you could plan the next day for yourself, not only do you look through the day, but you mentally rehearse it. You practice in your mind, with your forethought, the way you want your morning to go, the way you want your afternoon to go, the way you want your evening to go. That's forethought. That's a practice of forethought.

Now, you not only take yourself through it with logic, but you take yourself through it with emotion. How do you want to feel? What's the emotion you're going to flavor it with? Let's flavor the day with emotion. Now, remember we spoke a little bit in the past about the Pygmalion principle. What you're going to do is you're going to Pygmalion your day. You're going to sculpt your day. You're going to create your day with your thought. Now, you've done that many times when you've had a special occasion or a special day. It could have been a special religious holiday, or it could have been a birthday or something like that. What you've done is you've taken your time, as we mentioned, and you carefully thought your way through the whole day, the gifts you're going to give. You've thought yourself through who's going to be there. You've decorated the whole environment in your mind. You've put in fun, joyous emotion, the happiness, the joy, whatever it was that you wanted to flavor it with, and you saw the dinner and how you're going to plan the dinner around and so on. All that is just the use of your forethought.

But you didn't start that very day. You didn't even start the evening before. What you did, if I think right, was you started several days before, several weeks before. And in doing so, as you rehearsed it over and over in your mind, you said, "Well, no, I think I'd rather have it this way or I think I'd rather have it that way." And as you did, as you built that, and did it over and over in your mind, with enough time involved, it almost matched perfectly, didn't it? Almost matched perfectly.

Well, that's the power of forethought. That's also why we're going to write our affirmations, because our affirmations will control the forethought about the party or about the day. But what we're going to do instead of doing it on that special religious day or that special day, we're going to do it every day. We don't want to just do it the night before. What I'd like for you to do, if you're going to use your forethought, is to start thinking about not only the first day, but what are you going to do, say, towards the end of the week? What are we going to do one week away?

# DAY 1
# Getting Started

Can we use our forethought to plan one week away, and then back it up and plan the day before, the day before that, and the day before that, and the day before that?

So what can we do? Eventually what you're going to see yourself doing is plan out maybe two weeks in advance. Not only are you going to plan out two weeks, you're going to plan out three and four; and then what you're going to learn to do is to plan a month ahead, and you might even think a year ahead. The more we can use our forethought to look forward and see the way we would like our business to be – the way we'd like our family to be, the relationships to be, our life to be, our health to be – the further out we can do this, the greater the likelihood that we can cause it. It's going to take some time for us, if we think big enough, and we start thinking magis enough, outrageous enough, we're going to need to grow into that dream. We're going to need to grow into what it is that we want to be. The most important thing is looking forward, thinking forward, seeing what it is that we want, and mentally taking ourselves through it. This needs to become a habit – this is a new habit.

So this is the first lesson. I want you now to just take your time. If you can only think forward for the next three hours, do so. But if you can take yourself six, do so. If you can take yourself 24, do so. It's using very practical things that you're doing today or you're looking forward to today, and then let's see what we can do about tomorrow. So I'll see you soon.

# DAY 1
# Getting Started

# DAY 2
# Forethought

## Key Concepts

Adventure; Affirmation; Efficacious Mood; Goal; Imagination; Negative, Forethought; Positive Forethought; Scotoma; Visualization.

*Efficacious people look forward and see success.*

## Main Concepts

**The most important ideas and insights I have gained from this session are:**

## Choice Of Activities

**One situation I am looking forward to is:**

I look forward and visualize clearly all the details, and feel the positive emotion of achievement of the end result.

# DAY 2
# Forethought

One way to achieve:

Second way to achieve:

Third way to achieve:

I use my forethought in a very positive way, to look forward to the following event within the next week and see two alternative plans to achieve this result:

•

•

## DAY 2
# Forethought

## Affirmations

Write your own Forethought Affirmations using your ideas gained from this session, your review of related information and notes, as well as affirmation ideas from your Participant Manual.

- Refer to the Action/Emotion Word List on pages 215 through 217 for appropriate words.

- Review the Affirmation Checklist on page 213 to be sure you are writing them effectively.

It may be helpful to write down the current reality first, and then describe what it will be like when it is fixed. Use this as the basis to write your affirmations. Transfer your completed affirmations to 3 x 5 cards and place them in your Affirmation Folder.

### My Affirmations

### Assimilation

Refer to the Affirmation Imprinting Reminders on page 240 as you go through your affirmations.

*I get a clear and vivid picture in my mind and I feel the wonderful emotion and mood of already achieving my goal. I dwell on this feeling of achievement, which gives life to my affirmations. I do this for each affirmation. I set aside time at least twice daily to imprint them.*

# DAY 2
# Forethought

## Journal

# DAY 2
# Forethought

## Audio Summary

Some of the questions that you might have in regards to the use of forethought: Will I lose my flexibility? I mean if I just keep planning my day, do I then not have any spontaneity? No, not at all would this interfere with spontaneity or flexibility. In fact, what you might do, in using your forethought, is create several scenarios. You cannot necessarily control all the things that are going to happen around you at work or what might happen to you as you drive down the road in traffic. So, what you need to do is use your forethought to look for alternatives, to look for ways of overcoming a blocked traffic pattern. Well, not just a blocked traffic pattern, but it might be some problem that jumps out at you at work. How will you deal with that? It might be a problem with a child. It might be a problem with a family member. It might be that you get some serious news about an illness or something that you have no control over. Well, how are you going to deal with that? Not only how are you going to deal with it, but how are you going to help others with their forethought?

Remember, now, we can look forward two ways, can't we? Highly efficacious people look forward, and they see success. It doesn't mean that they see it smooth and perfect. They may see, what would I do should my child, who's two, have a serious accident? What would we do if we had a fire in our home in the middle of the night? What would we do should I hear the news that my father was ill and my mother was seriously ill? How would I handle that? That's forethought.

So forethought doesn't mean that you build scotomas to the bad or the negative or the awful that will go on. Forethought means, how are you going to control your mood? How are you going to control your actions and your behavior? Are you going to throw yourself into a panic? Are you going to lose your ability to think effectively? Is your anxiety going to go so high that you're out of control and you lose your memory or your recall or you don't hear people around you? Or, if you use your forethought without dwelling on the awful things that might occur, you can see them as obstacles; you see them as setbacks; you see them as difficulties. They're in everyone's life. But if we're going to really use our forethought correctly and develop our efficacy, what we do is we see the situation and then we create a plan to deal with it, to handle it.

What we also want to do is not just work for the alternative going around to the left or going to the right, or going over or going under it. We need also to program in the flavor of the mood that we need. The second lesson is, as you look forward, you might see what would block you from achieving the goal at work or the goal on the way to work, the goal home, or when you call and invite somebody over and they say no. You can see those things as you look forward that might turn out to be challenges or problems. Well, don't stop there.

Now, remember, once you arrive at a goal that you set, you flatten out. So you not only use it to goal-set through, but here you're going to use it to look at one, two, three, four ways to reach your objective or your goal. Now, we're using simple and small things to think about right now,

# DAY 2
# Forethought

because we're going to extend this into very outrageous goal-setting. The important thing now is to develop the habit, develop the skill of using your forethought correctly.

So now as we look forward and we see all these obstacles in our way, you ask, "How am I going to get past this? If this occurs, I'll do this. If this occurs, I'll do that. If this occurs, I'll do this. Nothing is going to stop me." Now, if we don't think that way, what is the other way? Well, the other way is to look forward, and while we still see the desired outcome in our mind with our forethought, we also, if we're not careful, is scare ourselves. We could look forward and say, "Well, if I apply for the job and not get it, look at how disappointed I'll be." Or, "If we invest our money and lose it, oh, my gosh." "Why, if we merge the company and it doesn't work out . . ."

So, you see, using your forethought and coming up with scary end results, scary situations, what do you suppose that's going to do to you? Is it going to cause you to seek it out or cause you to go forward almost cautiously? You will go forward not boldly, not energetically, not enthusiastically, but go forward as if it comes out all right the next step, I'll take another step. And if that one is good, I'll take another step.

Well, that's not the way to go forward, is it? You must go forward boldly and confidently, because you need to inspire others around you to go confidently and boldly. If they see you hesitantly or tip-toeingly or fearfully moving forward, you can't then collect the people around you, the team you need, in order to bring them forward. The first time an obstacle occurs, I know what you do; you'll quit, you'll abort your effort.

What we want to do now is to learn to look through the day. We're going to see challenges that might jump up, but what we're going to do is have another way to go. We won't have just one way to reach the goal. We're going to have many ways to reach the goal. Today, it's very important, particularly in your businesses; because in your businesses, there are so many things that happen that cause you to abort your plan. You start off with a goal, and somebody says this is how we're going to reach it; and then sure enough, something happens and somebody – might be somebody in authority over you, changes the plan. There it goes.

Well, in order to reach an objective or a goal today, what we need to learn is the goal we're going to lock onto – the goal, the end result – is what we're going to really focus on, as well as the way we're going to get there. We may start out this way, and we're blocked. We're going to need to back up and go to the right. We're going to need to back up and go to the left, need to go over or jump it. We cannot really put all of our faith and trust in the plan. We're going to invent the plan, remember? We're going to create the way, remember? So it isn't a matter of us getting disappointed and stopping because we're blocked.

What we're going to do is hold our trust on the end result or the goal. We're going to invent the way and create the way, but we need to do our forethought work the night before, the day before. We must look through the weeks. We need to see and fiercely lock on. Now we're go-

# DAY 2
# Forethought

ing to be around a lot of people who are inefficacious, who are going to be intimidated. How is that self-talk going to influence you? How are you going to influence them? That's a part of your forethought. See, as you're going forward, some of these monumental and big goals that you're setting for yourself are no easy task. There's going to be a lot of difficulty, a lot of land mines, a lot of things that are going to get in the way. You're going to have a lot of people who are going to try to talk you out of it because they aren't as tough as you, aren't becoming as resilient as you.

So using your forethought now is extremely important – at work, at home, with your family. It doesn't mean that we're not going to look forward and see the obstacle. We're going to look forward and see the obstacle, but we're not going to stop there, remember? What we're going to do is we're going to develop our plan. Now, do that with just your morning. Do it with the evening. Practice on the way to work. Practice in traffic. Practice and see. Nothing is going to stop you. Don't make it too big today. Just make it easy, make it easy. This is just rehearsal, rehearsal for the big time.

Everything we're doing now is similar to using the affirmation process, and we haven't even got you focused on your written affirmations, although I expect you to be doing this. What we're doing now is just talking about forethought control, the use of your imagination, a wonderful gift at looking forward and planning the way you want things to be. It doesn't mean that we're not going to be knocked down and hurt and damaged and emotionally, but it means that we're not going to stay there. We're going to get up and go past it. What I want you to do now is to look through the day, look through the week; if you can, look through the month. Just plan something special. See you soon.

## DAY 2
# Forethought

# DAY 3
# Half-Step Method

## Key Concepts

Affirmation; Current Reality; Forethought; Goal; Half-Step Method; LO/LO; Reflective Thinking; Vision.

*The life that is not reflected upon is not worth living.*

## Main Concepts

**The most important ideas and insights I have gained from this session are:**

## Choice Of Activities

**A small project I am thinking about doing or something I would like to change is:**

# DAY 3
# Half-Step Method

And my half-step method to completing the project is:

Step 1: Aware of situation and how I feel about it:

Step 2: Examine in depth:

Step 3: Explore "what if?":

Step 4: Experiment:

Step 5: Decision: Move Forward? Abandon? Need more information?

Step 6: Commitment:

Step 7: Let go:

## DAY 3
# Half-Step Method

## Affirmations

Write your own Half-Step Method Affirmations using your ideas gained from this session, your review of related information and notes, as well as affirmation ideas from your Participant Manual.

• Refer to the Action/Emotion Word List on pages 215 through 217 for appropriate words.

• Review the Affirmation Checklist on page 213 to be sure you are writing them effectively.

It may be helpful to write down the current reality first, and then describe what it will be like when it is fixed. Use this as the basis to write your affirmations. Transfer your completed affirmations to 3 x 5 cards and place them in your Affirmation Folder.

### My Affirmations

**Read**
▼
**Picture**
▼
**Feel**

### Assimilation

Refer to the Affirmation Imprinting Reminders on page 240 as you go through your affirmations.

*I get a clear and vivid picture in my mind and I feel the wonderful emotion and mood of already achieving my goal. I dwell on this feeling of achievement, which gives life to my affirmations. I do this for each affirmation. I set aside time at least twice daily to imprint them.*

# DAY 3
# Half-Step Method

## Journal

# DAY 3
# Half-Step Method

## Audio Summary

If you are, why are you hesitant in getting started on your affirmation process? Why are you hesitant in setting goals for yourself? Well, maybe one of the reasons might be that if you do get there and you do achieve it, what happens if it's not what I want? Perhaps I wanted to be a teacher, and I get there, and I say, "Ah, this isn't what I wanted." Or maybe you say to yourself, what if I choose to open my own business and I get there, and it's not what I want? What if I go to medical school and find out it's not what I wanted? What if?

Okay, there's a half-step method that I'd like to have you explore, and you want to keep doing this, not once, but do it a lot of ways. Every time you're starting to make a change in your life, use this half-step method. One of the problems is if you don't commit – like the old lady, young lady – you know that if you lock-on, you lock-out, don't you? You know now all about that lock-on/lock-out stuff. "I might not want to get started on this affirmation process just in case I'm locking onto the wrong thing, right?" Okay. Now, keeping your options open causes paralysis, doesn't it? There's no movement. So, let's go back to the half-step method.

One of the things you need to do with your reflective thinking process – and remember that reflective thinking is keeping a diary, keeping your thoughts, doing this every morning – is write out one page, two page, three pages a day. Just let your thoughts come. Let your ideas come. That's an essential. That's something that we can't skip. In fact, you'll enjoy this, I think, as you do it. Keep it private.

But now what you're doing, as you're doing your reflective thinking, I want you to reflect on the first step in this seven step process, and that is to really become aware of the parts of your life that are incomplete. Become aware of the parts of your life that are kind of dull, the parts of your life where things aren't going well for you, the parts of the life where you've had this nagging toothache or headache, or this knot in your stomach about it. It's like, "I just feel dull. I feel despair when I'm in this environment. I feel unhappy when I'm around these people. I feel like I'm under living my life. I feel like there must be more."

Most people do not take the time to find out what is it that they don't like about the last weekend? What is it I don't like about my job? What is it I don't like about the friends I have? What is it I don't like about the house I live in? What is it that I don't like about the way I've spent my last year? Well, you need to do some serious work if you're going to get some serious growth. This is very powerful information. It will move you in that direction, and so you ought to be a little concerned about what it's going to be like when you get there. If you don't really do a good job of choosing, you're going to end up wherever "there" is, saying, "Holy cow, this isn't what I wanted at all." So you need to do that awareness work.

Then the next step is where you need to do some real good examining and become aware – really get into the depth of examining. What is it about the friends, what is it about the job, what

# DAY 3
# Half-Step Method

is it about the way my life is going, what is it about the way I spent last year? Really get into the examining of it. Take it past that superficial level and go into some depth. It might take you a day or three days or five days to go back over what you wrote and look at it. Take it another step, go back to the next layer, and the next layer and the next layer.

So if you were afraid to look in-depth at your marriage or your relationship, or what it is about you don't like, how are we going to fix it? How are we going correct it? You must be courageous enough to do this. So, the second step is to examine.

Now, the third step is to explore. Explore, very simply, is using your forethought, your imagination. "I wonder what it would be like to not work at all. I wonder what it would be like to be wealthy. I wonder what it would be like to be poor. I wonder what it would be like to..." and you go on and you let your imagination take you in the exploration. See how you feel; see in your imagination what it might look like. It doesn't mean you need to do it, but some people won't even let themselves think about that, and it's because of the fear feedback. Maybe I shouldn't even let myself think about that." No, right now it's healthy. Let yourself wonder, way past the present reality. I'm not asking you to actually do it; just let yourself wonder.

Now let's go to the next step. We're going to experiment a little. Experimenting very simply is, "How are we going to try it just a little bit." Maybe what you'll do is make a visit. You might take a trip. You might take a vacation someplace that's unique or different. Maybe you just go out and bum around a little bit. Let's say, you decide, in your wondering, that you wanted to live on a farm. "Ah, that's what I wanted. I'd love to live in the country, live on a farm and have animals. What a wonderful life that would be." But now you find that it's cold and you need to get up and milk the cows. "Oh, I don't want to get up." But the cows aren't going to wait, and they smell bad. They have manure on their tail and they slap you in the face when you're trying to milk them. Then they kick the bucket, step on your foot and knock you into the manure. And you say to yourself, "Oh, I wish I hadn't bought the farm." Well, don't buy it. Go live on one for a week. That's experimenting. You might say, "I love it," and you might say, "I don't love it, and I'm sure glad I didn't pay all that money and didn't commit myself to it."

What you're doing is gathering information that you didn't have before. This is a process of leading you to the next step of making a decision. Now we have enough information to make a decision – a decision to buy or to change what it was that I thought I wanted. Decisions can be to move forward, to abandon the thought, or the decision can be, "I need more information." See, you can't jump from awareness to decision-making, so don't get down on yourself. You haven't taken the time. You can't go from experimentation to decision-making either. I mean it takes some time to be able to make the decision, so don't be in a hurry. That's all right.

But now the next step, after decision-making, is to make a commitment. Now you can't go from awareness to commitment. A lot of people do. They're aware they don't like their marriage. They

# DAY 3
# Half-Step Method

examine it and dump the marriage, and commit to somebody they just met. That one didn't work out either. Or, they don't like the boss so they quit the job. Out they go, and they don't even have another one.

It takes some time and some work. Now we can make a commitment. But don't worry about committing yet. You haven't done enough exploring. In those areas where you're hesitant and holding back and unable to make decisions to move forward boldly, you have some more work to do. Now that you made the commitment, you can let go. We can let go of where we're living. We can let go of what we're doing. We can let go of the old friends.

And, by the way, this letting go process may not be a conscious decision. You'll just find yourself spending less time with the friends than you used to spend, or doing the things that you used to do. And, it isn't a matter of, "Oh, I've got to decide to let go." It's a natural process. You just start filling your life with those things that you now want to do, and you squeeze out those things that you don't want to do. You'll find that true of friends, the way you're spending your money and everything else you're spending.

It's a good idea to do some serious thinking, because this affirmation process, and this whole course on how to be effective and cause your future, really works. If you're going to apply it, let's apply it to those things that we spend a lot of time thinking about and really know that this is what we want. In doing so, by the way, it will make that fierce, fierce lock-on to that future, that family, that job, that commitment. It comes from doing all this examining. Keep using your forethought correctly, just for today, for the week, for the month.

# DAY 3
# Half-Step Method

## DAY 4
# The Next Time

## Key Concepts

Attitude; Negative Self-Talk; Positive Self-Talk; Pygmalion; RAS; Sanction; Second Nature; Self-Esteem.

## *People are selective information gatherers.*

## Main Concepts

**The most important ideas and insights I have gained from this session are:**

## Choice Of Activities

**The last occasion at home when I corrected someone incorrectly was:**

How would I use the three stages or steps to constructively handle the situation?

• Step 1

• Step 2

• Step 3

# DAY 4
# The Next Time

**One thing I do well is:**

When I do it well my self-talk is:

and I feel:

**One thing I do not do well is:**

When I do it well my self-talk says:

and I feel:

When I don't do it well, my self-talk is:

and I feel:

**I am focusing on the following ways to handle the talk of others towards me:**

## DAY 4
# The Next Time

## Affirmations

Write your own Next Time Affirmations using your ideas gained from this session, your review of related information and notes, as well as affirmation ideas from your Participant Manual.

*   Refer to the Action/Emotion Word List on pages 215 through 217 for appropriate words.

*   Review the Affirmation Checklist on page 213 to be sure you are writing them effectively.

It may be helpful to write down the current reality first, and then describe what it will be like when it is fixed. Use this as the basis to write your affirmations. Transfer your completed affirmations to 3 x 5 cards and place them in your Affirmation Folder.

### My Affirmations

### Assimilation

Refer to the Affirmation Imprinting Reminders on page 240 as you go through your affirmations.

*I get a clear and vivid picture in my mind and I feel the wonderful emotion and mood of already achieving my goal. I dwell on this feeling of achievement, which gives life to my affirmations. I do this for each affirmation. I set aside time at least twice daily to imprint them.*

## DAY 4
# The Next Time

## Journal

# DAY 4
# The Next Time

## Audio Summary

Well, how's your day going? Some of the things you might have noticed is how negative the world is. You've noticed it in the newspaper. You've noticed it on television. You've noticed it in your family. You've noticed it at work. Isn't it amazing how negative people are? "Negative" in that they become very critical of others, very demeaning. You have probably noticed a great deal of sarcasm, too. You've noticed people talking about what's wrong with the world instead of what's right with the world.

It's always been there; it's just that your reticular activating system is picking it up. You're hearing things because you have a whole new awareness and you didn't even know it. You need to be careful you don't have the tendency to want to shape them up. They don't really know what they're doing, but don't you get caught up in it. You can see where you were getting caught up in the past. You'd go into wherever you have coffee at work, and it is complain, ain't it awful, and what about this. Do you know what that does to your perception if you give sanction to it? Well, you know that your self-talk affects your perception, because once you get an opinion about the way someone is or this situation is, you become a selective perceiver. So these people are really seeing what it is that they're preparing themselves to see.

Let's take a look, if you have children, at how you can help your children through this. When you hear your children with negative self-talk, make a positive suggestion. Take them right past it. Don't argue with them. Just make a positive affirmation, a positive suggestion to them. When your spouse is making a negative, ain't it awful, things aren't going right comment, what you need to do is not argue or teach the course. What you do is you just be a very positive wizard, a positive Pygmalion, and you make a statement about seeing something in a different way, and you affirm them right past it. "I see it as," or "There's a lot of opportunity here," or "Have you ever thought about," and just change the subject. Switch them past it. Bring up something positive. Bring up something good. Lead them past that.

You do the same at work. You do the same socially. What you're going to do, probably, is find yourself not socializing or hanging around those kinds of people. However, there are some situations that you can't ignore, where those people who you love and are committed to, are in that negative state. It could be a parent. Oftentimes, you get a parent who comes over and, if you have children, that parent may be the one who is negatively affirming your children. Are you going to shape up that parent? I might have a private talk with that person, if I were you. Now that you know the power of negative affirmations on the people that you care about, what you're going to need to do is not embarrass them in front of someone. You know, "I found some new information, and I know you really don't mean to, but what if," and you go on to name the child, "What if they really believe or think that they are the way you're describing them? What if they never change and what if they just stay that way? My goodness. What would their life be like?"

# DAY 4
# The Next Time

What do you suppose it would be like? Let's just try an experiment. When we see the behavior we don't like in that person, what if we tell them, "I see you as being," and you go on to describe the way you'd like to see them. Instead of telling them, "There you go again. You've been doing it for all your life, you'll never change," what you might say, in some way, maybe even firmly, is, "Stop it. You're too good for that," and you go on to describe the way you positively see them or want them to be.

Remember, the more we affirm the behavior in a person that we don't want, the more they become like it. Now, what I want you to do is become very aware of people who are affirming you when you don't even know it. "That's like you" kind of affirmations are coming your way that really don't fit the way you would like to be. You want to listen for them at work; you want to listen for them at home; you want to listen for them when you're out socially. You're going to hear people telling you and describing you as they see you; and you've given sanction to it unknowingly, and it's negative or it's limiting. Have you ever noticed how hard it is to overcome somebody who has an opinion of how you really are? And you try. Growing now with the affirmation process you're using and applying to your life, you're also living around people who want to keep you as you are, even though the way you are isn't a happy way and isn't fully utilizing your full potential as a person. Yet they know how you are, and they keep telling you, "Why don't you," or "Here's how I see you." Sometimes you need to change your friends. You can't change your family, and I wouldn't recommend that. But what you need to do is not give sanction to those people who are affirming you.

This piece is so essential. Remember what you need to say when they affirm you as "You've always been this way." You could say to yourself, "Well, up until now I might have been, but no longer." And you go on to describe yourself as you are in the future, but in the present tense. Remember you are going to think future in the present tense. You're going to talk to yourself about the way you intend to be as though you already are. You can't get into arguments with people all the time because they see you as you are. But in your own mind, you're just going to say, "That's not like me. That is not like me."

When you do make mistakes – and sometimes your self-talk is more brutal on you than the people you're working with or the people you're living with – remember the whole key is to say to yourself in some way, "No more, that's not like me," and use the phrase, "The next time I intend to." The next time I intend to go this way in the traffic pattern. The next time I intend to say this. The next time I intend to. The next time I intend to be better prepared. The next time I intend to control my temper. The next time I intend to. "The next time, the next time, the next time, the next time, the next time," is what I want you to use.

This whole week, if there were three words that are going to stick in your mind like a song, it is going to be "the next time." And then I want you to add, "I intend to." That's going to control your forethought to be positive instead of repeating the mistake or the pattern, the habit, the

## DAY 4
# The Next Time

behavior or the action. It is going to control your forethought, remember. It's going to push your forethought forward with a positive change, with the way you would really do it the next time. Now, remember, we're trying to make this second nature to ourselves, automatic. So it doesn't need to be great big things in life; it can be little things in life. This just becomes the way we think every day. This is natural. This is the way you speak to the people around you. How would you do it right, or how would you do it better, or what would you do the next time.

# DAY 4
# The Next Time

## DAY 5
# Second Nature

## Key Concepts

Affirmation; Assimilation; Attitude; Belief; Forethought; Goal; First Nature; Second Nature; Habit; I x V = R; Potential; Pygmalion; Self-Image.

*I enjoy making my affirmations daily.*

## Main Concepts

**The most important ideas and insights I have gained from this session are:**

## Choice Of Activities

**Stepping ahead five months, I see one concrete fun goal for myself which is:**

The benefit(s) its achievement would bring me is (are):

# DAY 5
# Second Nature

My feeling(s) of achievement would be:

One aspect of my life, and my second nature, where I definitely know that I have potential that I'm not using is:

The benefit(s) I would get from increasing the use of that potential is (are):

The attitudes I have about myself that might be hindering me are:

My feelings of satisfaction in the achievement of this increase would be:

**DAY 5**
# Second Nature

## Affirmations

Write your own Second Nature Affirmations using your ideas gained from this session, your review of related information and notes, as well as affirmation ideas from your Participant Manual.

*   Refer to the Action/Emotion Word List on pages 215 through 217 for appropriate words.

*   Review the Affirmation Checklist on page 213 to be sure you are writing them effectively.

It may be helpful to write down the current reality first, and then describe what it will be like when it is fixed. Use this as the basis to write your affirmations. Transfer your completed affirmations to 3 x 5 cards and place them in your Affirmation Folder.

### My Affirmations

**Read**
▼
**Picture**
▼
**Feel**

### Assimilation

Refer to the Affirmation Imprinting Reminders on page 240 as you go through your affirmations.

*I get a clear and vivid picture in my mind and I feel the wonderful emotion and mood of already achieving my goal. I dwell on this feeling of achievement, which gives life to my affirmations. I do this for each affirmation. I set aside time at least twice daily to imprint them.*

# DAY 5
# Second Nature

## Journal

# DAY 5
# Second Nature

## Audio Summary

We've gone a couple of days now, and we haven't insisted that you do your affirmations. Negligence on my part; negligence on yours; but only if you're not making them. So I'll make the assumption that you are. Those days of the video burst inspired you to do your work and you're writing your affirmations and making your affirmations.

Well, let's talk about affirmations and which ones we should make to start with. Well, let's talk about first nature and second nature. First nature has a lot to do with what you inherited through your parents, right? Your coloring, height, etc., and everything else that goes along with what your genes provide you. We don't know about temperament and musical ability and a lot of those things that perhaps are part of what you inherit.

Let's talk about second nature, the way you run your day. That's the way you run your week. That's the way you run your job. That's the way you run your life. Pretty much all of it is second nature. Second nature is what you have assimilated habitually, attitudinally; it's knowledge and skill, and has been assimilated to where it free flows pretty much automatically. Well, how's your day going? How's your work going? How's your life going? How are your finances going? You'll hear people say, "Well, this is just the way I was born. It's because I'm ..." Well, some of it is, some of it isn't. I don't know which is, and I don't know that you do. But let's act as though most of it is second nature. It was acquired or learned or assimilated, and if that was so, then why don't we use the affirmation process that we learned in the video burst to see if we can improve our second nature?

Where do we want to improve our second nature? Where do we want to free flow? What if we didn't need to try hard to make more money, we just made more money? But what good would it do us to make more money if we don't invest our money or save our money? I know people who would increase their income, maybe double it, but spend a little bit more. Then they'd make more and spend more, make more and spend more. Maybe we need to look at not just making more money, but look at what we want to do with the money. Let's look at our habits and what our second nature is when it comes to dealing with money. What are your beliefs about money?

Now, let's not just talk money. The money is the fuel, isn't it, that causes you to send your kids to school or allows you to live in the style or with the freedom or creature comforts that you wish for or you want. It allows you to build the industry, the business. Maybe, you even have an attitude about making money that needs to be examined, and perhaps changed, in order to release the potential inside yourself.

Oftentimes, I think a lot of people really do want to attack that one issue or that one problem. So I would recommend that as a fun place to start. That's an interesting place to start. It's a nice emotional place to start, because a lot of other things really do connect to whether I have enough money to take the trip or buy the car, or to pay the bills, or give to the church or give to charity. So money is important, and your attitude toward it, your beliefs toward it, have a great to deal to do with the way your world goes. I wonder if the beliefs you hold on the inside are what you create on the outside. That's what we've been talking about.

The affirmations that you want to make about changing the quality of your environment, or the way your work goes or your life goes, might have a lot to do with your attitude towards wealth, money and finance. I would encourage you to start right there. Don't try to start with something way out so far out that you can't imagine it. Let's just practice for a couple of months and see what happens. Make some affirmations that aren't so far out right now, because we're really trying to learn this information. We're trying to make this information second nature to us.

Now, what are some other areas that you want to examine? One of the ways of doing it is to look and say to yourself, "Where do I have some potential that I'm not using?" – potential in relationships, potential in being a more loving human being, a more responsive human being, a more appreciative human being. What value would that be to you at work, at home, in your community? What changes would transpire if you changed instead of waiting for the other person to change? "I wonder if I changed the way I appreciate people, whether they would be different around me. I wonder if I looked at them with love instead of disdain and disrespect, I wonder how they would be around me. I wonder if I was more thoughtful, I wonder how they would be around me." In a sense, what you're going to do is Pygmalion the people outside of you by changing you on the inside. Not conscious level, "I think I'll do it today because it's a good idea." Remember the affirmations that we're going to use. What they're there for is to cause this to be second nature, automatic, free flow. It's learned, it's assimilated, it's part of me, but I wasn't born this way.

Really, what I'm saying is you look at every area that you feel is important for you, and step ahead three or four months – maybe five months – and say, "I think that what I would like to do is to be," and then you go on to describe that person. Then you back it up and you make the affirmations that would cause you to become, in a second nature way, that which you have the potential to be, that you can see the profitability in being.

It isn't my job to tell you what affirmations to make. I am here to inspire you to build a new second nature; and not just once, but we want to do this in three years, in five years, in ten years. This is an ongoing process, because it's pretty hard for you to see yourself perfect. What you're doing is striving toward not necessarily perfection, but just improvement. You're going to see, in your reflection or in your daily encounters with other human beings, all kinds of opportunities to improve your second nature through the affirmation process – to unleash this beautiful potential inside of each one of you. Remember now, this isn't a conscious level thing. It's conscious level as we write it out. It's conscious level while we're affirming it. But the reason to affirm it over and over with the formula I x V = R – imagination times vividness becomes reality – is really just another way of using your forethought, isn't it? You mentally rehearse as though you are. You mentally rehearse as though you are, over and over.

## DAY 5
# *Second Nature*

Now how often you want to make the affirmations each day has a lot to do with how fast you want this assimilated and habituated, so that you free flow in your second nature. You can do it once a week, if you want. I don't care if you do once a month, but once a month might take you about two years to change your second nature. If you do it a couple of times a day and do it with emotion and clarity and really using your forethought in a focused way, you might be able to recognize this new second nature within just a month or two. You're worth it, and it's worth it. So pick out something that would be easy and fun in order for you to make the change. Work on maybe 10 or 12 changes, just to see if it works.

# DAY 5
# Second Nature

# DAY 6
# Wondering About Affirmations

## Key Concepts

Act in Accordance with the Truth; Affirmation; Assimilation; Belief; Comfort Zone; Forethought; Potential; Reality; Second Nature; Standard.

*We act not in accordance with the truth, but the truth as we believe it to be.*

## Main Concepts

**The most important ideas and insights I have gained from this session are:**

## Choice Of Activities

I use my forethought to visualize the following examples of a better standard closer to my potential in the areas of:

Income:

Alternative, additional or future ways of earning a living:

Relationships with spouse, child, colleague:

# DAY 6
# Wondering About Affirmations

**One aspect of my life to which I have become accustomed is:**

It is good enough for me?

I can improve it by:

**A missed opportunity, which could have made a marked difference in my life, is:**

I missed it because:

If a similar opportunity occurred now, I would take advantage of it by:

**One belief (about myself, a relationship, work or money), which is seriously holding me back, is:**

The basis, in reality, for that belief is:

That belief might be based on erroneous opinion and imagination because:

**One event of my life in which I was extremely successful and the best for me was:**

My affirmation to change, so that the very best I could imagine becomes a new standard, would look like:

And the good feelings of achievement would be:

## DAY 6
# Wondering About Affirmations

## Affirmations

Write your own Wondering About Affirmations using your ideas gained from this session, your review of related information and notes, as well as affirmation ideas from your Participant Manual.

- Refer to the Action/Emotion Word List on pages 215 through 217 for appropriate words.

- Review the Affirmation Checklist on page 213 to be sure you are writing them effectively.

It may be helpful to write down the current reality first, and then describe what it will be like when it is fixed. Use this as the basis to write your affirmations. Transfer your completed affirmations to 3 x 5 cards and place them in your Affirmation Folder.

### My Affirmations

### Assimilation

Refer to the Affirmation Imprinting Reminders on page 240 as you go through your affirmations.

*I get a clear and vivid picture in my mind and I feel the wonderful emotion and mood of already achieving my goal. I dwell on this feeling of achievement, which gives life to my affirmations. I do this for each affirmation. I set aside time at least twice daily to imprint them.*

## DAY 6
# Wondering About Affirmations

## Journal

# DAY 6
# Wondering About Affirmations

## Audio Summary

Let's take a look at the affirmation process in more depth. I want you to wonder if you could raise your expectations, which we call a standard, through the affirmation process, like raising the bar that you're going to jump over. I want you to wonder if the affirmation process could cause you to expect a higher income. "I wonder if it could cause me to expect people to treat me better, or me to treat people better. I wonder if it could cause me to expect to live or work in a better environment." I wonder, in every area in which you're now working or performing, whether it be the arts or music, whether it be athletics, or no matter what it is, if you can use the affirmation process to change your internal standards, raise your comfort zone, broaden your comfort zone. Because what you're receiving in an automatic second nature way is controlled by your level of expectation on the inside.

Very simply, use the affirmation process to expect a little more of yourself. Now, you might really take off too big a bite. Remember, what we're doing is making this information not Lou Tice's information, but my information. "This isn't the way Lou Tice thinks, this is the way I think. This isn't the way Lou Tice does it. This is the way I do it." I just want you to wonder – which is a part of using your forethought, part of that exploring, part of that experimenting in your mind, taking yourself into the future – if you raised your expectation about communications, what would happen? "I wonder what this quality movement is all about – improving the quality of my work life, my home life, my spiritual life, my social life." I just want you to wonder, "Where I could improve the quality," which is an internal standard, by using the affirmation process.

So up the standard on yourself just a little bit. Don't take off the big bite yet; just see if you can bump it up a little bit. Then if it works, in two or three months do it again. If that works, do it again, do it again, do it again, do it again, do it again, do it again. We are acting in accordance with the truth as we believe it; that's the whole premise of the curriculum. We behave not in accordance with the truth as it really is, but what we do believe it to be. If it's not the truth, it doesn't make any difference; we're limited by it. We're limited by our beliefs.

Ask yourself, "What was the most outrageous, best day I had last year? What was the best workday I had? What was the best I ever performed athletically? What was the best? What was so special? What was, when I look back, once in a lifetime?" And you look at all those areas of your life where throughout last year – or your lifetime, if you want – where you were absolutely, outrageously different than you ever have been, better than you ever have been. Then you say to yourself, "I wonder what it would be like if this would happen all the time. I wonder what it would be like if that was the standard." Well, that's the whole idea of it.

You look at where it was at any part of your life where you want improvement. Those of you who golf, go back. If you had a favorite course that you play, and over the last few years go back and add up the best you ever did on each one of the 18 holes. That would be perhaps an outrageous

## DAY 6
# Wondering About Affirmations

score at the end, wouldn't it? Well, that's your potential. You've actually done it on different days. What you need to do is to put it all together, and you need to expect it, and change that internal standard.

Well, do the same with every part of your work world. Do the same with every part of your social world. Do the same with everything that you have ever done around your family. What is the best you've done? Now, that's where your affirmations come in. We don't really need to go out and try to invent something we want to do new in the future. Maybe what we've been doing has really been fun and exciting and worthwhile, but not often enough, only once or twice. What we want to do is use the affirmation process to visualize ourselves doing it regularly, automatically.

In a sense, this is just the way I am. I know what you're thinking, "If I use up all my specials, my life will be dull." What happens then is you have new peaks, new specials, and then you make that an affirmation process. You keep raising your internal standards, and you keep acting like the person and being like the person you know yourself to be. We're just using this affirmation process to improve "how I'm supposed to be." Does that make sense? See how simple that is? Don't make it hard. Don't make it complicated. Make it easy.

## DAY 7
# Habits

## Key Concepts

Current Reality; Flexibility; Forethought; Goal; Habit; Serendipitous; Superstition.

## *Is this habit necessary?*

## Main Concepts

The most important ideas and insights I have gained from this session are:

## Choice Of Activities

Daily/weekly routines or habits I could spend less time on, or cut out completely, because they hinder my new goals, are:

## DAY 7
# Habits

My superstitious habits, that I would like to change, are:

I would like to change these habits because:

## DAY 7
# Habits

## Affirmations

Write your own Habits Affirmations using your ideas gained from this session, your review of related information and notes, as well as affirmation ideas from your Participant Manual.

- Refer to the Action/Emotion Word List on pages 215 through 217 for appropriate words.

- Review the Affirmation Checklist on page 213 to be sure you are writing them effectively.

It may be helpful to write down the current reality first, and then describe what it will be like when it is fixed. Use this as the basis to write your affirmations. Transfer your completed affirmations to 3 x 5 cards and place them in your Affirmation Folder.

### My Affirmations

**Read**
▼
**Picture**
▼
**Feel**

### Assimilation

Refer to the Affirmation Imprinting Reminders on page 240 as you go through your affirmations.

*I get a clear and vivid picture in my mind and I feel the wonderful emotion and mood of already achieving my goal. I dwell on this feeling of achievement, which gives life to my affirmations. I do this for each affirmation. I set aside time at least twice daily to imprint them.*

# DAY 7
# Habits

## Journal

## DAY 7
# Habits

## Audio Summary

In your own mind you ought to be thinking bigger, having a greater sense of wonderment, aspiring to new things. This will occur on an ongoing basis. One of the things we need to discuss is that once you get an idea about what you want to do – say, at work or do with your family or even something new with you – there doesn't seem to be enough time in the day in order to accomplish what it is you want to accomplish. You're trying to figure out, "Should I stay up more? Do I get up earlier? How am I going to get more time?" Well, you're not going to get more time.

What we need to be able to do is change some habits or routines. Some of the things that we're doing we won't be able to accomplish because you're too busy doing the things you're presently doing. "Well, we always see the Nisses on Thursday night." Well, see them every other Thursday. "Well, Monday is my bowling night." Well, go bowling once a month instead of once a week. You don't need to necessarily let go of these things. It's all right if you do. You don't need to sit down and consciously plan. But as you start visualizing the new end results, a part of your creativity should be to reorganize your day. Some of you are so locked into your day, you're so firm in your routine, that you don't allow yourself to let go of what you do in the morning or what you do in the evening or what you do on the weekend.

You need to become a little more serendipitous now. You need to allow yourself to reorganize your time for you, and let yourself drop some of the things that you have been doing in order to allow yourself to enlarge your life. Some flexibility is needed. Sometimes you can deliberately pattern in a new habit. Sometimes you just let it happen, just let it flow in.

When I was coaching in high school, there was a wonderful person by the name of Joe. (I won't use his last name.) He was the baseball coach, and he was so predictable. I would know that at lunchtime, when I would be sitting in the locker room in the office, he would come in with two cups of soup – one for him, one for me. He would come with crackers in his right pocket. He would kick the door two times because he had soup in both hands, expecting me to get up and open the door. He would come in, and he would set his down and then walk over and set mine down, take the crackers out. This would happen every day for months and months and months. He was so routined. One time when I was coaching and he was one of my assistants, I made the mistake of stopping at Zesto's for a milkshake before I went to the game. He was in the car with me. Now, before every game for two years we needed to stop at Zesto's for a milkshake and it had to be the same flavor. It's called superstition. It's called so locked into a routine that you almost feel guilty or uneasy if you don't follow the same pattern or same routine.

Many of you are that way. You don't have the flexibility to change what you think you might. But that wasn't so bad. Remember about forethought? If we missed the milkshake, guess what he would think? "We're going to lose." How come? "We didn't get a milkshake." What's practice all

# DAY 7
# Habits

week got to do with it then? Why don't we just stop at Zesto's for a milkshake and skip practice all week? Can you imagine what you do to yourself, some of you?

Another thing that I did, which was just to drive him crazy, I would walk to one end zone before a game and I'd pick up chalk and put it in my right pocket off the field. Then I'd go to the other end zone and pick up chalk and put it in my right pocket. And he would always ask me before, "Have you got your chalk?" Have you got your chalk. Like if I didn't get the chalk, we were going to lose? Yeah. That wasn't so bad, but if I didn't get the chalk or if I told him I didn't have it, he would get this feeling, "I don't feel right about the game." And he'd communicate, "I don't feel right about the game" to the kids, the players. Something's wrong. The coach doesn't feel right.

Can you imagine how you get so grooved and so into your routines, almost superstitious about them, that you don't allow yourself a new pattern? You don't allow yourself the inventiveness and the creativity to flow, and you need to have a new pattern in order to accomplish new goals. You are already busy, already doing, filling your day. And if these new goals are coming about – the new, bigger aspirations, or just different ones – it means you can't just jam more into your day. You're going to need to let go. So check yourself for flexibility, look at where you're almost superstitious, look at where you get that inner feeling that, "I'm not doing something right, something's not there."

I can remember when we first started in this business, Diane and I didn't travel much. She was going to go to Colorado, when I was working with the University of Colorado football team for the first time. I came home, and the airplane was going to leave in a couple of hours. (This was before we needed to go through all those security checks.) So I walked into the kitchen, and here was Diane – we still had all of our children – scrubbing the kitchen floor. Now, we're going to catch an airplane to Colorado in two hours, and the airport is about 20 minutes away. And I said, "Diane, what are you doing?" She said, "What's it look like? I'm scrubbing the floor." But what I really meant was, "Aren't you going?" She said, "Yes." "Well, what are you scrubbing the floor for?" "Oh," she said, "I don't feel like a mother unless I scrub the floor." Well, how do you argue with that? You don't. But you don't go to Colorado either. I mean you need to get somebody else to scrub the floor.

You must look inside yourself and ask, "Where are those emotional tugs?" Where are those things that don't let you be what you're capable of being or do what you're capable of doing? What is it to be a mother? What is it to be a father? What is it to be who you are? See, don't be so invested in who you are presently in order to restrict you from becoming who you are going to be in your new you, your new life that you're creating for yourself. Some of those habits, some of those processes, some of those ways, we need to examine. "Maybe there is a better way, and I need to be able to be an option thinker and a creative thinker." We're going to talk about option thinking and creative thinking in some of our next segments, so see you in a little while.

## DAY 8
# Comfort Zones

## Key Concepts

Affirmation; Attitude; Comfort Zone; Creative Subconscious; Flick-Back/Flick-Up; Forethought; Goal; Habit; Self-Talk; Subconscious; Reflective Thinking; Resilience; Second Nature; Self-Esteem; Servo-Mechanism.

*Most of our limitations are self-imposed.*

## Main Concepts

**The most important ideas and insights I have gained from this session are:**

## Choice Of Activities

**A few of my current limitations are:**

I would like to eliminate these limitations by:

# DAY 8
# Comfort Zones

**At home, one thing I have become used to is:**

My reason for changing this is:

**At work, one thing I have become use to is:**

My reason for changing this is:

**DAY 8**
# Comfort Zones

## Affirmations

Write your own Comfort Zone Affirmations using your ideas gained from this session, your review of related information and notes, as well as affirmation ideas from your Participant Manual.

- Refer to the Action/Emotion Word List on pages 215 through 217 for appropriate words.

- Review the Affirmation Checklist on page 213 to be sure you are writing them effectively.

It may be helpful to write down the current reality first, and then describe what it will be like when it is fixed. Use this as the basis to write your affirmations. Transfer your completed affirmations to 3 x 5 cards and place them in your Affirmation Folder.

### My Affirmations

**Read**
▼
**Picture**
▼
**Feel**

### Assimilation

Refer to the Affirmation Imprinting Reminders on page 240 as you go through your affirmations.

*I get a clear and vivid picture in my mind and I feel the wonderful emotion and mood of already achieving my goal. I dwell on this feeling of achievement, which gives life to my affirmations. I do this for each affirmation. I set aside time at least twice daily to imprint them.*

## Journal

# DAY 8
# Comfort Zones

## Audio Summary

In order for us to really accomplish, we're talking about change inside of ourselves. Changing what? Changing habits? Changing attitudes, routines, and ways of doing things. What many of you are going to need to do, in order to really accomplish more, is to get people to help you. How do you feel about that? How do you feel about having somebody to help with the house, if you need more time? How do you feel about someone helping you with the garden, if you need that? How do you feel about somebody doing some of the things that you're presently doing, like driving your children to school, if you need to? How are you feeling about whatever? Some of those things really need to be examined in your reflective thinking to release this potential. The affirmation process will change the habit. It will change the attitude. And as you put this goal in, you're trying to do things on the conscious level, but you have these old patterns holding you back.

Years ago, when I was teaching high school, we were always looking for ways to raise money for certain projects. It could have been for new equipment or new something to do. So, when I had a lot of these young people around me, I would come up with ideas about what could we do to raise money. We could sell cupcakes, you can hold a bake sale, you can wash cars. I mean there are all kinds of ways of raising money for what projects they wanted, which are fun things to do. I remember one time, when I was looking for a way for them to make money, I said, "Here's an idea." When we have these parades and carnivals and events going on during the summertime in the community where we were living, which was Seattle, there are a lot of opportunities for you. If you will go out and invest in a container of helium gas and get some penny balloons and some string, and then you just fill the balloons full of helium, tie some string around them, and go to the parade. If somebody is selling them for a dollar, sell them for 75 cents. If somebody is selling for 75, sell them for 50 cents. If somebody is selling for 50, sell them for a quarter.

Have you ever been around people when you offer opportunities there's always this "yes, but?" Yes, but, and they try to tell you why it won't work. Yes, that's a good idea, but. Have you run into those lately? Well, here I was giving them these ideas about selling balloons, and this one kid raised his hand, and he said, "Yes, but what if we're selling these balloons and the police come and we don't have a license?" Holy cow! I looked at this kid, and I said to him, "Well, you have two handfuls of balloons. If the police come and you don't have a license, all you do is go, 'What balloons?' And open your hands and let go of the string."

Now, I only use that to illustrate how many of you, should I make a lot of suggestions about what is possible and what you could be doing with your future, you keep going "Yes, but; yes, but; yes, but. The "Yes" is to shut me up and the "but" is to change the subject. It's an interesting thing that sometimes you need to let go of what you're holding onto. You need to let go of all the reasons why something won't work.

# DAY 8
# Comfort Zones

I used the story from a lady that used to work for us. When she was being raised as a child in one of the New England states of the United States, coming from a Catholic family, she was the only girl. When she was about 19 years old, her mother was always fussing over her, worried and concerned, she said, "Mother, I'm going out tonight," and mother said, "Well, where are you going?" "Well, I'm going to the dance." "What time are you going to be home?" "Well, I'll be home at 12 o'clock or 1 o'clock." "How are you going to get there?" "Oh, I'm going to drive the car." And mother says, "What if you're driving the car and you get a flat fire and it's 12 o'clock?" Something to be concerned about, really, and she replied, "Well, I'll stop and get the spare tire out and fix the tire." Mother said, "But if you're by yourself and somebody comes, what are you going to do? What if you're changing the tire and somebody comes and attacks you?" She said, "I'll hit them with the jack handle." Mother said, "But what if he's bigger than you?" And she said, "Then I'll run." "What if he's faster than you?" She said, "You're right, I shouldn't go."

How many of you "what if" yourself or someone else to death, or allow somebody else to "what if" you to death and you get caught up in it? Let go of the balloons. Option think. Let go. What do you need to let go of? Not just now, but this must be a way of your life. This needs to be second nature. What are you hanging onto that's holding you back?

Remember the story about the farmer who brought a pumpkin, like a squash, to a county fair. And it was unusual because it was the exact size and shape of a two gallon jug – the same shape as a jug with a handle and kind of a mouth to it. He won some blue ribbons, and people would go by and "ooh" and "ah" about the pumpkin. They'd say, "How in the dickens did you ever grow a pumpkin like a two gallon jug?" The farmer said, "Well, it's easy. As soon as the plant started to blossom, I just stuck it inside of a two gallon jug. Then it just grew to be the exact size and shape of the two gallon jug. As soon as it was grown, I broke the glass, and here it is."

Ah, I thought, that's what we do with our creativity, with our ideas, with our lives. We build a container of "can'ts," "they won't let me's," and "it's not possible." We build the container within which we build our business future, our life. Some of us build a container the size of an aspirin bottle, and we put our whole life into a small container. Now, what is the container? It's our imagination. It is that imagination that is allowing your mind to wonder, allowing your mind to expand, to explore. It's an aspiration. It's an ideal. It's an vision. It's a, "I wonder what I could be. I wonder what I could do. I wonder where I could go." I wonder. I wonder. And watch out for the "what ifs." Watch out for the "shoulds" and "hold onto all the balloons" and "what if the police come."

Many of you talk yourself out of things. Now, why do we do that? Ah, you remember. When you look forward out of your comfort zone and you see something that is dangerous that might oc-cur, your subconscious, without asking it, stimulates negative creativity. Most of these people are out of their comfort zone. And when you're out of your comfort zone, you don't ask for it, but your subconscious gives you three reasons why it won't work; or 30 reasons why it won't work; or 300 reasons why it won't work. First of all, if you're going to do something, you need to ask

# DAY 8
# Comfort Zones

yourself, "Do I want to?" If you don't want to, forget about it, because you're going to come up with why it won't work. You'll talk yourself out of it. Quit talking yourself out of your future and your potential. The first thing you need to do is decide, "Why do I want it? Why would it be personally profitable to me? Why would it be beneficial?" Think about why you do want it, because if you don't want it, your whole creativity will talk you out of it. Just the opposite, if you do want it and you do see you want it, your subconscious stimulates positive ideas about how to get it, how to do it. See how important it is to control your forethought? See how important it is to allow yourself to think expansively, creatively?

So as you keep growing on the inside with your affirmations, and building your strength, with your flick-back and flick-up, and with all the things that you've done well and all the resiliency that we've talked about, what it does is it seems to put the lid on that negative creativity and get you to start thinking about constructively how to do it and why to do it. See you soon.

## DAY 9
# Attitudes

## Key Concepts

Affirmation; Attitude; Comfort Zone; Creative Subconscious; Goal; Potential; Reflective Thinking; Self-Talk; Visualization.

*Attitude awareness through reflective thinking.*

## Main Concepts

**The most important ideas and insights I have gained from this session are:**

## Choice Of Activities

**My attitude about being a "morning" or "evening" person is:**

How does this attitude of mine affect my day and the accomplishment of my goals?

# DAY 9
# Attitudes

**As I prioritize my day, my goals (in order of importance) are:**

The goals that are easy for me to accomplish are:

The goals I creatively avoid are:

My attitude is:

**An individual with whom I have trouble working is:**

What is my attitude?

This week I will change my attitude and look for positive things that he or she does.

## DAY 9
# Attitudes

## Affirmations

Write your own Attitudes Affirmations using your ideas gained from this session, your review of related information and notes, as well as affirmation ideas from your Participant Manual.

- Refer to the Action/Emotion Word List on pages 215 through 217 for appropriate words.

- Review the Affirmation Checklist on page 213 to be sure you are writing them effectively.

It may be helpful to write down the current reality first, and then describe what it will be like when it is fixed. Use this as the basis to write your affirmations. Transfer your completed affirmations to 3 x 5 cards and place them in your Affirmation Folder.

### My Affirmations

**Read**
▼
**Picture**
▼
**Feel**

### Assimilation

Refer to the Affirmation Imprinting Reminders on page 240 as you go through your affirmations.

*I get a clear and vivid picture in my mind and I feel the wonderful emotion and mood of already achieving my goal. I dwell on this feeling of achievement, which gives life to my affirmations. I do this for each affirmation. I set aside time at least twice daily to imprint them.*

## Journal

# DAY 9
# Attitudes

## Audio Summary

I wonder where this negative self-talk comes from. Are you hanging around people who are telling you why things won't work? And even within yourself, where does your negative self-talk originate? How does it get there? Well, it could be habitual, but it could be because you're forcing yourself out of your comfort zone. It could be because, as you take yourself out of your social comfort zone, your subconscious is telling you why you shouldn't go. Your children need you or you have too many other things to do. "I've got some work to do."

You see, negative creativity is best stimulated when you drop yourself into a situation where you're intimidated by it. And when you're intimidated by the situation or the event or the investment or the work, your subconscious starts figuring out avoidant behaviors. Now, that's something to be guarded against; that's what you use your reflective thinking for, to capture that. Now, I don't want you to bully yourself into it. I don't want you to force yourself into it. What I want you to do is use your affirmation process to stretch your comfort zone, to visualize yourself into the next plateau safely. "Next plateau" meaning into that social situation or into that business situation; into that trip or into that world where it's so different – that different restaurant, that different store, that new process at work.

You look at what is it that is intimidating, and you need to be subtle about this, not to make yourself look weak or cowardly. When I'm talking about intimidating, you know what I'm talking about. It gets inside you. You can see yourself or hear yourself in your own mind come up with reasons why you ought to avoid. That's why you use your reflective thinking, because I want you to go back each day and see what it is you're avoiding. How come you can't get yourself started? How come you get started, but you get diverted? How come you're getting off track? How come you can't stay focused? How come you can't concentrate? "I think what I need is to work on my day planner more." "I think what I ought to do is really lock into this." "I've got to get my routine down." What you need to do is to get your attitude right. You need to get your mind right about what you're going after. That's where your negative creativity is being stimulated; your negative self-talk is coming from; and you also become very susceptible to other people. It doesn't take much for them to talk you out of going.

What if you have a whole group around you that needs to move forward at work and you're all talking yourself out of it because you're all frightened of the future? Now, have a good talk. You need to take care of your own mind, your own thinking, your own future. So this negative self-talk, coupled with old negative attitudes, wow. Remember, attitudes are not positive or negative until you set a new goal, and let's go back to the definition of positive and negative. Positive means moving towards. Negative means moving away, or avoidant.

So here we are, sometimes talking about we're going to go after this, going to go after that, and I'm going to do this and I'm going to be that. You really mean it while you're sitting here and it's safe. But as you start pursuing the outcome or the goal, you just can't get yourself to do it. Now, you don't necessarily tell yourself not to do it. You engage in avoidant behavior or avoidant activities. You find yourself getting off the path, off the track. Instead of going directly – forcefully, creatively, assertively – towards the outcome, you find yourself filling your day or your week with things that don't need to be done.

I would guess that many of you are so busy not because you are so busy, but I would guess that many of you are busy avoiding what it is that you don't want to do. So much of what you're doing isn't because you need to do it. Much of what you're doing, I would guess, is to keep you from doing what you don't want to do. Think about that and write that down. Now, what are you going to do? Give up on your goal or change your attitude? Change your attitude. This is a lifetime process, particularly if you're going to keep growing, continually setting new goals. Many of the old attitudes were absolutely fine for the old goals or the way we're doing life now. But as I set new aspirations and new goals, my old attitudes jump right out.

How do you recognize an attitude? That is what you need to do with your reflective thinking. You need to look and see, "Today, how come I didn't do what I set out to do?" "Well, the reason is," go ahead and believe it, if you want; it may be true, may be an accident and something did interrupt, and that could very well be. But day after day? Is this just bad luck, or do you really need to examine the attitudes you have? I've needed to examine attitudes all the time on myself in order to let myself grow.

Now, hear what I'm saying? Letting myself grow. I needed to change attitudes. I always need to change attitudes. I don't know when I got some of them. I know when I get them now. When I use the affirmation process, I assimilate new attitudes in me. So many of the attitudes I had, I just picked up sloppily, casually, kind of by osmosis – hanging around the people I'm hanging around, reading what I'm reading, doing what I'm doing, listening to what I'm listening to. These attitudes were just picked up. I didn't really set out to get many of them. It wasn't like I decided, "This is the one I want and this is the one I want," until I knew this information.

Going forward, there's more to it than like this ad that we see by this sporting shoe manufacturer, "just do it." "Just do it" isn't that easy, because you can't override and overpower that subconscious will to avoid danger, fear, or unpleasantness. You're too inventive and too creative. Your subconscious will work to get you out of it and hold you back from being what you're capable of being.

It's very important that once you discover the attitude, that's where you're going to use the affirmation process. Get to work on the attitude, and then release the potential that's inside of you and make some wonderful changes that you're capable of making. Otherwise, forget your goal. You're not going to do it. You just might as well forget it. You're not going to do it.

# DAY 9
# Attitudes

Willpower cannot override that subconscious power of avoidance and creativity. You're not tough enough to overcome that subconscious trying to get you out of something that's unpleasant trying to use willpower and discipline. All it's going to do is put you into a double bind. You're going to be working back out of it, stronger than you're going forward. You just keep saying, "I've got to get tougher." No, no, no. You need to change the attitude, change the routines. Don't give up on your goals. Give up on outdated attitudes. See you soon.

# DAY 9
# Attitudes

## DAY 10
# Self-Esteem

## Key Concepts

Attitudinal Balance Scale; Assimilation; Credibility; Sanction; Self-Esteem; Self-Talk; Subconscious; Truth.

*The word "esteem" comes from the verb "to estimate."*

## Main Concepts

**The most important ideas and insights I have gained from this session are:**

## Choice Of Activities

**Some of the negative or limiting estimations I, and others (parents, teachers, managers, colleagues), have made about me are:**

Which are true?

What have I done about the ones that were true?

I am going to get rid of the false ones that I have accepted up until now by:

# DAY 10
# Self-Esteem

**People whose judgment of me I respect are:**

What can I do to make their wisdom more available to me?

**A list of my achievements of which I am proud is:**

# DAY 10
## Self-Esteem

## Affirmations

Write your own Self-Esteem Affirmations using your ideas gained from this session, your review of related information and notes, as well as affirmation ideas from your Participant Manual.

- Refer to the Action/Emotion Word List on pages 215 through 217 for appropriate words.

- Review the Affirmation Checklist on page 213 to be sure you are writing them effectively.

It may be helpful to write down the current reality first, and then describe what it will be like when it is fixed. Use this as the basis to write your affirmations. Transfer your completed affirmations to 3 x 5 cards and place them in your Affirmation Folder.

### My Affirmations

**Read**
▼
**Picture**
▼
**Feel**

### Assimilation

Refer to the Affirmation Imprinting Reminders on page 240 as you go through your affirmations.

*I get a clear and vivid picture in my mind and I feel the wonderful emotion and mood of already achieving my goal. I dwell on this feeling of achievement, which gives life to my affirmations. I do this for each affirmation. I set aside time at least twice daily to imprint them.*

## Journal

# DAY 10
# Self-Esteem

## Audio Summary

Let's talk about self-esteem in this segment. First of all, a really interesting way of thinking about self-esteem, very simply, is what is your estimation of your own worth? If we were going to sell a piece of property – let's say you had a house or a vacant piece of property someplace and you were going to sell that vacant piece of property – would you go to your best friend and say, "Tell me what it's worth?" Or would you go to, say, just a neighbor and say, "Tell me what it's worth?" Would you get somebody off the street and say, "Please, just tell me what it's worth, because I'm going to sell my piece of property?" Would you perhaps at work say to somebody you know well at work, and you like what they do, and say, "Tell me, what's this piece of property worth?" Well, there might be a better way. As you ask what it's worth, are they a credible expert in evaluating this piece of property? They may be a good doctor, they may be the best that you have on the job. It may be your best friend, but do they really know the value of property?

So an estimator is someone who needs to have some background or credibility in what they're estimating. What we do if we're not careful, though, is go around and we ask people what they think of us, or what do you think of my chances in this career or in this job? Please give me an estimation of my worth; my worth personally now, my worth in the future, and so on. And I don't think that you would be well advised in the first place, if we were talking about a piece of property, to go to your neighbor or your friend. But how many times do we allow other people to give us an estimation of our own worth? Stop it.

Really ask the question. They may be wonderful people, but do they really know me? Do they really know what I want to be? Do they really know this information? Do they know what I know presently, now that I've gone through this curriculum? Do I really know that I need to be careful how I even evaluate myself? Am I qualified to estimate my own worth? Well, I'm probably as well qualified as a lot of them, but not if, in fact, I don't think well of myself.

See, one of the things we find in estimating our own worth, is we don't respect our own opinion enough. Let's be silly and you might say as you go out – because you're not so sure, not confident about how you look, you're a little unsure of yourself – you're going to go someplace for an interview or you're going to go someplace that's special or you're going to give a talk someplace or you're going to some special occasion. So you say to your friend or your spouse or somebody, "Well, tell me, how do I look?" Well, why would you ask them? You want their estimate of how you look. "Do I look all right?" Oh, no, you look a mess. You look terrible. Why your hair is – oh, no. "Well, I'm sure glad I asked you, because I almost went out looking like this."

See, what we're doing constantly is asking others' opinions of ourselves and what they think. Why? Because we're not sure of our own worth appraisal. It seems when you gain in self-esteem or feeling of self-worth, you no longer need to be constantly eliciting the approval or the esti-

# DAY 10
# Self-Esteem

mate of another person. That's where I want to get you. It doesn't mean that we don't ask for advice or ask for some mentoring or criticism. But we stop being vulnerable to the opinions, the comments, the estimates, if you will, of just anybody off the street, or anybody at work.

Now, one of the challenges seems to be – and when I say this, I want you to take it the way it's meant – be most careful about the people who you respect the most around you, and be most careful about the people that you are closest to, because I think those are the ones you will give sanction, more than likely, to their opinions than you would a stranger. And they can be the ones that would be the most damaging, because you really do value what they think. Keep in mind now, it doesn't make any difference what comes your direction. It's only when you give sanction or approval or agree with them.

We can become so vulnerable, can't we? Particularly when things aren't going right for us, or something is not going well at work, or something's not going well at home. We become more susceptible and unsure of ourselves. So you need to watch those vulnerable moments when you're more susceptible to the approval or the comment of another. Remember now what you're doing is building your own self-esteem with your own appraisal or your own self-talk. You don't need to be harsh and critical and negative towards the other person. One of the things that you must learn is to really become a good appraiser of the comments that are being directed your way. Watch for all the negative weights that people are trying to put on your attitudinal balance scale. They don't mean to, it's almost thoughtless or careless. It's almost like it's freely given. It's almost like they really don't know what they're doing. But you know what effect it will have on your own sense of value, your own sense of worth, if you give sanction to it.

Now, as you start building your self-esteem, your performance seems to follow. The stronger the self-worth, then what do you do? Well, you draw people to you, business opportunity to you, friendships to you, that you feel worthy of receiving. And if, in fact, you've spent a good week or two, or a month or two, or a year or two of lowering your own self-esteem, you can see it by the kind of opportunity, the kind of friends, the kind of relationships and so on that are coming your way. Now, do you sit and wait for the outside to change, or do we change the inside? Try it. Change the inside. Speak well of yourself. Think well of yourself. Tell yourself, "Yes, that's like me. Yes, I am good at that. Yes, I am a person of high value." See you soon.

## DAY 11
# Changing Habit Patterns

## Key Concepts

Affirmation; Attitude; Belief; Fear; Forethought; Habit; Internal Standard; Potential; Second Nature.

*We rarely exceed our inner standards.*

## Main Concepts

The most important ideas and insights I have gained from this session are:

## Choice Of Activities

Three habits, routines or internal standards I admire in others, which I think would help me in the achievement of those goals that I have chosen to pursue, are:

# DAY 11
# Changing Habit Patterns

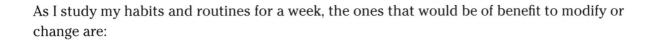

As I study my habits and routines for a week, the ones that would be of benefit to modify or change are:

My habits and routines that I have kept out of fear are:

# DAY 11
# Changing Habit Patterns

## Affirmations

Write your own Changing Habit Patterns Affirmations using your ideas gained from this session, your review of related information and notes, as well as affirmation ideas from your Participant Manual.

- Refer to the Action/Emotion Word List on pages 215 through 217 for appropriate words.

- Review the Affirmation Checklist on page 213 to be sure you are writing them effectively.

It may be helpful to write down the current reality first, and then describe what it will be like when it is fixed. Use this as the basis to write your affirmations. Transfer your completed affirmations to 3 x 5 cards and place them in your Affirmation Folder.

### My Affirmations

**Read**
▼
**Picture**
▼
**Feel**

### Assimilation

Refer to the Affirmation Imprinting Reminders on page 240 as you go through your affirmations.

*I get a clear and vivid picture in my mind and I feel the wonderful emotion and mood of already achieving my goal. I dwell on this feeling of achievement, which gives life to my affirmations. I do this for each affirmation. I set aside time at least twice daily to imprint them.*

# DAY 11
# Changing Habit Patterns

## Journal

# DAY 11
# Changing Habit Patterns

## Audio Summary

Let's take the issue of working harder, trying to get more done; getting more done with less help or less resources; or getting things done in what seems to be a shorter day. People are demanding more of us in some way. Oh, dear, how are we going to do it? Well, again, is it a matter of using more discipline on yourself? Or is it a matter of working harder on yourself, or maybe changing some attitudes? Is it a matter of changing some of the patterns that we call habits? Is it a matter of really changing inside myself some beliefs that become an internal standard, of which I can't seem to get past?

Well, I don't know if you have any potential inside yourself, because that's up to you. I would suggest that you say you do and that it is possible to be much more effective. To get 10 times more done than you're presently getting done, or even a hundred times more or 500 times more, how in the dickens could we do that? Well, it isn't going to be by staying up later or getting up earlier, although that might help. It's really going to be to take a look at some of the patterns – where I'm spending my time – and then to observe how others, who are doing those kinds of things that I admire or would like to be doing. Then, to use the affirmation process to change my pattern of what I do with my time or my work or my day.

It's a matter of observing another who seems to be successful in the work that you would like to do, and then you write out that pattern in affirmation form. In the comfort of your own living room or a chair, wherever you seem to be comfortable, take yourself through the new routine. In your mind, just go through it. Change the pattern.

See, until you can get yourself into a new groove and let yourself flow, you might only do this one time on this day. Tomorrow you'll be right back where you were. It's a matter of reprogramming the way you work, what you do with your morning, what you do with your evening; what you do on a Wednesday, what you do on a Friday; what you do each month. Observe the pattern you're doing now and say, "Well, that was all right, but now that I have new goals or I have new objectives. I'm not getting it done with the old pattern. What new pattern do I need?" And that's where you use the affirmation process to groove in a new routine.

When you groove in the new routine, you cannot use fear. Don't bully yourself. Don't use fear. If you use fear to pattern yourself, then it's hard to change in the future. So, it needs to be constructive input. It needs to be one that will allow you to let go of this pattern, because in several months, you're going to groove a new one. In areas where you have difficulty grooving new habit patterns, it could be that those were put in with a fear feedback loop.

That's the way we used to coach when I was coaching football. You would punish people or you would yell at them or you would scream at them. If they didn't do things right or step correctly, you would make them do push ups or run a lap or get angry with them, or embarrass them or ridicule them. So they get grooved in their pattern very well, and they function with that tech-

# DAY 11
# Changing Habit Patterns

nique or that offensive pattern or that movement very well. But the problem is, when you try to bring in a new pattern or change them, they'll fight you to the death. It isn't because they are too stubborn, it is that to deviate from a fear imprinted habit pattern takes a lot of courage.

Some of you are so grooved out of a fear feedback process that you won't allow yourself to undo the habit pattern you're caught up in. You want to look: were you frightened, or were you around a manager who was angry, or who would perhaps withhold your future if you made a mistake? You did get the pattern down so well, but now you're so grooved with that fear feedback, you won't allow yourself to deviate from it. It's almost as if it's sinful. It's almost like it's immoral. But it really isn't; it's just the patterns you've been grooved with.

Examine why you won't let yourself into new routine, into new habits, into new patterns, then use the affirmation process – once you decide the new pattern that would be beneficial – use the affirmation process in a constructive way to groove it so that you flow as it is needed. When it isn't needed, discard it and move on. As we set new goals, as we grow and change our career path, as we change the size of our business and change what we want to do during the week, the month or the year, we can't do it the same old way. So, you need to use this process every time you want a new second nature, a new free flowing of the way you want your week, your day, your month, and then be willing to let it go. The other issue, of course, was the attitudes. We'll pick up attitudes in the next segment. So see you soon.

# DAY 12
# Attitudes Review

## Key Concepts

Affirmation; Attitude; Creativity; Emotion; Energy; Flick-Back/Flick-Up; Forethought; GI/GO; Goal; Habit; Visualization.

*Attitudes can help us reach our goals, or they can block us.*

## Main Concepts

**The most important ideas and insights I have gained from this session are:**

## Choice Of Activities

**Which current attitudes do I have that will hinder the achievement of the goals that I have chosen?**

Which attitudes would it benefit me to modify and which should I get rid of?

# DAY 12
# Attitudes Review

Some people I know to be highly effective are:

The attitudes that they possess that contribute greatly to their achievements are:

My library of positive emotions, to flick-back to, includes:

## DAY 12
# Attitudes Review

## Affirmations

Write your own Attitudes Review Affirmations using your ideas gained from this session, your review of related information and notes, as well as affirmation ideas from your Participant Manual.

- Refer to the Action/Emotion Word List on pages 215 through 217 for appropriate words.

- Review the Affirmation Checklist on page 213 to be sure you are writing them effectively.

It may be helpful to write down the current reality first, and then describe what it will be like when it is fixed. Use this as the basis to write your affirmations. Transfer your completed affirmations to 3 x 5 cards and place them in your Affirmation Folder.

### My Affirmations

**Read**
▼
**Picture**
▼
**Feel**

### Assimilation

Refer to the Affirmation Imprinting Reminders on page 240 as you go through your affirmations.

*I get a clear and vivid picture in my mind and I feel the wonderful emotion and mood of already achieving my goal. I dwell on this feeling of achievement, which gives life to my affirmations. I do this for each affirmation. I set aside time at least twice daily to imprint them.*

# DAY 12
# Attitudes Review

## Journal

# DAY 12
# Attitudes Review

## Audio Summary

Can we discuss the necessity of changing habit patterns? So few people really do that and then the stress occurs of trying to jam more into their day, or take a conscious control over their pattern at the present moment. Like somebody who uses martial arts or an astronaut or someone who would be an elite strike force person, what they do is they build simulations, sometimes in simulators, and they take themselves through in their mind. They groove their pattern over and over, with the proper emotion, until it flows smoothly.

Remember the example I where we talked about an airliner that I was on? When the tires blew out, the pilot put the nose back down and kept us on the runway without killing anybody. You see, what happened is he had grooved that pattern, that habit pattern of what to do when this emergency exists. You don't look it up. It's already grooved. It's habitual.

So, you look forward and see the patterns you need three months from now, seven months from now. When this occurs, "This is the way I'll behave." When this occurs, "This is what I'll do." Now, that's not enough, because we also need to know that we have attitudes or emotional patterns that are grooved. Those are habits of emotion, if you will. Some of those are very constructive and they save our lives, and they cause our lives to go well. But some of those attitudes interfere with allowing ourselves to use the potential, or seek out new opportunity or new goals. They help us engage in creative, avoidant behavior, as opposed to behavior that would cause us and stimulate us to move forward.

Let's take a look and review what attitude is. It's just the direction in which you lean. In aeronautical terminology, if you remember, an attitude was the wings of the airplane in relationship to a fixed point like the horizon. What you say is, does it lean? In a sense, the way that it leans is what they call the attitude of the airplane, the direction in which it is leaning. A positive attitude then, if we're going to use that, means that you're leaning toward the goal, toward the social situation, toward the financial situation, toward what it is that you see would bring you some value. That's a positive attitude, and you feel good about it. It brings up a positive emotion that's attractive. It causes you to be drawn toward it, and it stimulates subconsciously the creativity that gives you the ideas of how to possess it.

What if, in your forethought, you perceive something that would be uncomfortable. It might be something embarrassing, something that would be painful, something that would be awful; and you have that grooved. Not necessarily because of what this new situation might be, but because of something in your history – your individual personal history – your image of reality keeps throwing that emotional, negative feeling back at you every time your eyes or sense of smell or other senses detect an opportunity or a situation. You say to yourself, "What is this leading me toward?" And you say, "Nothing good." Now, remember, negative doesn't mean bad. It means

# DAY 12
# Attitudes Review

avoidant. It means moving away. It stimulates your creativity to move back, to move away from that which you perceive as being unpleasant.

I want to encourage you that, as you set all these new goals for yourself – whether it be career or social, financial, all the things that you want – when you set a new goal, some of the old attitudes that served you well in your old comfort zone will no longer serve you well. As you try to pursue a new career, a new occupation, or a new education or new social strata – whatever it might be that you're going after – your old attitudes will jump out at you. You need to be consciously aware of them. Are they leading me towards what I want or are they causing me to engage in avoidant behavior? And if I'm engaging in avoidant behavior, do I give up on my goal or do I change my attitude? It's your choice. I have my own choices to make, and if I'm smart about it, I want to change my attitude. I don't want to change what I've said would be of value for me or my family or my career or my business. See? But, how many people do you know that just give up on their goal? Changing an attitude is the affirmation process.

You must get rid of the old garbage-in, no longer valuable, negative, upheaval emotion that comes to you. You do so not by just willing it, but by taking the affirmation process; writing an affirmation, and visualizing the positive response that you want when the situation occurs. If you need to, use the flick-back/flick-up technique to find a positive emotion in something similar. Then, you visualize the something similar, let the emotion build up in you, and then drop it into what you are currently avoiding or whatever is causing you to move away from it. You don't just do it once; you may need to do it a hundred times. It may need to be 200 times. I don't know how many times. Nobody does. It has a lot to do with the vividness with which you're doing it.

Build up from your history a library of very successful, positive emotion that you can borrow from. Then, just drop that into whatever is causing you to avoid, causing you to not be or to have that which you really deserve. Very important, you won't get this feedback of negative attitudes while you're sitting here listening to me; and you won't get it even while you're in a safe environment. It's when you put yourself out into the business community, or the social community that you've been avoiding all this time, that you're going to start becoming aware of the attitudes that are holding you back. That's why you need to do that reflective thinking that we keep insisting on. Capture those attitudes. Examine, then make the affirmations to release the wonderful potential and achieve those goals that you're capable of achieving.

## DAY 13
# Invest In Yourself

## Key Concepts

Affirmation; Current Reality; Goal.

*Balance keeps our wheels running smoothly.*

## Main Concepts

**The most important ideas and insights I have gained from this session are:**

## Choice Of Activities

**Where am I in relation to my potential in each aspect of my life?**

Is my life balanced?

# DAY 13
# Invest In Yourself

Where do I need to improve?

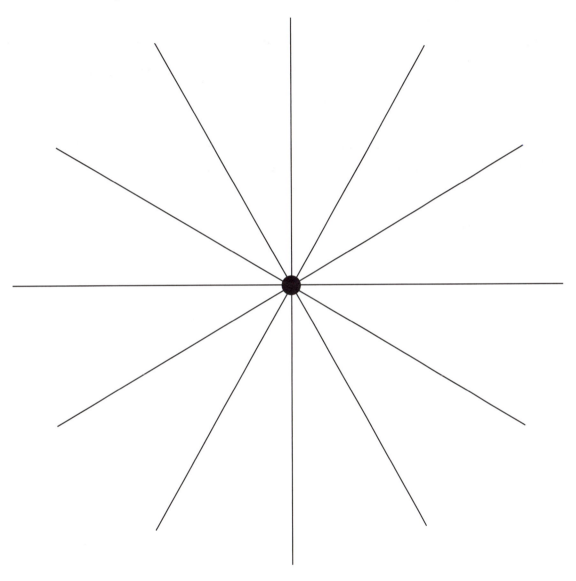

- Family
- Personal
- Community Service
- Education
- Health/Physical

- Health/Mental
- Recreation/Leisure
- Spiritual
- Relationship/Friends

- CareerJob/Vocation
- Sports
- Social
- Other

## DAY 13
# Invest In Yourself

## Affirmations

Write your own Invest in Yourself Affirmations using your ideas gained from this session, your review of related information and notes, as well as affirmation ideas from your Participant Manual.

- Refer to the Action/Emotion Word List on pages 215 through 217 for appropriate words.

- Review the Affirmation Checklist on page 213 to be sure you are writing them effectively.

It may be helpful to write down the current reality first, and then describe what it will be like when it is fixed. Use this as the basis to write your affirmations. Transfer your completed affirmations to 3 x 5 cards and place them in your Affirmation Folder.

### My Affirmations

**Read**
▼
**Picture**
▼
**Feel**

### Assimilation

Refer to the Affirmation Imprinting Reminders on page 240 as you go through your affirmations.

*I get a clear and vivid picture in my mind and I feel the wonderful emotion and mood of already achieving my goal. I dwell on this feeling of achievement, which gives life to my affirmations. I do this for each affirmation. I set aside time at least twice daily to imprint them.*

# DAY 13
# Invest In Yourself

## Journal

# DAY 13
# Invest In Yourself

## Audio Summary

This time let's take a look at another principle, the principle of we move toward and we become like that which we think about. Now, let's add another one, that our present thoughts determine our future. Okay. The basis of this is that you're teleological in nature. What that means is that as a human being, you're goal oriented. You need an idea. You need something focused in your mind, like a target or an object to achieve. Then physiologically, psychologically, and emotionally, you're drawn towards what you concentrate on or what you focus on or what you have your mind on.

Remember, you think in pictures. The language that you use triggers the picture. You'll hear people say, "Oh, I have an idea. I have an idea of what I want to do with my life." Hmm, well, that's beneficial. Some people don't have that, of course. They haven't taken the time to think it out or they haven't quite made up their mind yet, which is all right. Some people say, "Well, I have an idea what I want to do for my weekend." Some people, though, can't think that far ahead, because it's only Wednesday. Some people say, "Well, no, I have an idea what I want to do when I get home," and they can think that far ahead. Some people don't even know what they want to do when they get home until they get home. Can we take this whole process of what we're talking about and see what is the furthest out that we can extend what we want to move toward? What is the biggest object or ideal that we can think of right now, of what it is that we want to have happen in our life?

We move toward and we become like that which we think about. Our present thoughts determine our future. See, if we get caught in current reality, talking about how things actually are around us – on the job financially, socially, in our marriage, spiritually, health wise – and we think that we're really realists, then remember that tomorrow looks like today. If that holds true, that we move toward and become like what we think about, our thinking is pretty well dominated by our sensory perception around us. We're dominated by who we listen to, who is in our environment, the quality or quantity of the environment at the present moment. You're not deliberately causing yourself to think forward out of your comfort zone or out of your current reality, so change doesn't happen very fast for you, or doesn't happen in any great amount. You're not allowing yourself to think past your sensory current reality, what you're reading in the newspaper, the reality of your present financial situation.

If we're moving toward and becoming like that which we think about, and if our present thoughts determine our future, it is the affirmation process that helps you deliberately project into your future. It's not me to decide for you. It's you to decide for you. If you only do it twice a day, dog-gone it, that's good enough. That's better than what you were doing it. But what if you do it three times, five times, seven times a day? Of course, if you make too many affirmations and you can't repeat them, you really don't have enough time. You have other things to do. But yet, again, we need to have balance in our life, as we set our affirmations and goals. If we don't and we're just

# DAY 13
# Invest In Yourself

using our affirmations for our income increase or our vocational increase, and we just really spend our focused time on, say, that issue, that area, your subconscious will steal time from your family or from your social life. You'll become so narrow and so obsessed about this one thing that you're going to leave the other parts of your life behind.

Does that make sense when you understand the gestalt inside yourself? When you throw your system out of order, you're going to re-create the order, and you're re-creating order in only one direction, in one area on one issue. But if, in fact, you can set goals with some balance, which we're encouraging you to do, then you're creative enough to achieve it all and not become obsessive or narrow in your life or your thinking.

Maybe you want to select five or seven or eight areas of your life, and don't try to make too many affirmations in each one, because then you won't give it the focused time. I don't know how long it takes each one of you to make an affirmation, but let's say each affirmation takes a minute, and you've got 10, that's 10 minutes, and if you've got 20, that's 20 minutes. Well, if you're ever going to invest, invest the 20 minutes, invest the 30 minutes. 30 minutes in the morning, and the 30 minutes in the evening, and it doesn't need to be 30. If you don't have 30, then make it 10, make it 15 minutes, but do it five or ten times a day. Couldn't be a better investment than the investment in yourself through this affirmation process.

You move toward and become like what you've deliberately decided that you've chosen to become. You've written them properly, so it affects the neuron of your brain correctly. See, you're thinking future in the present tense. So the reason you write it out is so it becomes accurate, so it becomes focused, so it becomes detailed, so it becomes clear. It's something that you have deliberately and intentionally decided. It's premeditated. (You know, if you were committing a murder and somebody said, "Well, was it accidental or was it premeditated?") Well, why would you get more of a punishment if it was premeditated? Because you did it deliberately, that's why. And that's what I'm telling you, do it deliberately, premeditated. Think about it. Does that make sense?

## DAY 14
# Go After What You Really Want

## Key Concepts

Adventure; Affirmation; Creativity; Current Reality; Efficacy; Emotion; Energy; Forethought; Goal; RAS; Resilience; Subconscious; Visualization.

*We get what we expect, not what we want.*

## Main Concepts

**The most important ideas and insights I have gained from this session are:**

## Choice Of Activities

A dream I have decided to go for is:

My dream, in the present tense, is:

## DAY 14
# Go After What You Really Want

Putting the details of "how-to" aside, what three things would I really like to have, do or be?

1.

2.

3.

Visualizing these as if they have already been achieved makes me feel:

## DAY 14
# Go After What You Really Want

## Affirmations

Write your own What I Really Want Affirmations using your ideas gained from this session, your review of related information and notes, as well as affirmation ideas from your Participant Manual.

- Refer to the Action/Emotion Word List on pages 215 through 217 for appropriate words.

- Review the Affirmation Checklist on page 213 to be sure you are writing them effectively.

It may be helpful to write down the current reality first, and then describe what it will be like when it is fixed. Use this as the basis to write your affirmations. Transfer your completed affirmations to 3 x 5 cards and place them in your Affirmation Folder.

### My Affirmations

**Read**
▼
**Picture**
▼
**Feel**

### Assimilation

Refer to the Affirmation Imprinting Reminders on page 240 as you go through your affirmations.

*I get a clear and vivid picture in my mind and I feel the wonderful emotion and mood of already achieving my goal. I dwell on this feeling of achievement, which gives life to my affirmations. I do this for each affirmation. I set aside time at least twice daily to imprint them.*

## DAY 14
# Go After What You Really Want

## Journal

## DAY 14
# Go After What You Really Want

## Audio Summary

Let's take a look at what happens when our expectations aren't met. A lot of things happen. One of the things that happens is you're disappointed. You had an appointment with your future, and you are disappointed, it didn't happen. Now, what happens if you really wanted it and really committed to it, it's like the death of a loved one. So what you do is you may safeguard yourself from feeling this way by not setting a high expectation for yourself or going after what you really want. You go after something you settle for.

What kind of car would you really like to have? What would be the ideal car for you? Hmm, think about that. Well, maybe you ought to settle for something just about half as good. What kind of a career would really be ideal for you? Well, don't expect that much. You'd only be disappointed. Maybe we should settle for something about half as good. What kind of a family would you really want? Well, let's not be thinking about that. Let's just settle for something about half as good.

"Be happy with what you have, my dear." You've heard that from a lot of people, haven't you? "Because if you get your hopes up and it doesn't happen, you'll be dashed, you'll be so sad. And it's because I love you that I'm really talking to you this way; because I don't want you to start thinking big ideas and then having these big ideas not materialize." Good words from parents who love their children. "Oh, don't run for president. Why don't you just run for secretary? Nobody else wants the job, and you'll get is easily." I don't want to be secretary. I want to be president. "Well, don't get your hopes up." See, constantly settling for second best because you're using your forethought to anticipate forward and seeing the loss, you're cushioning yourself from the loss of what you really want. You don't go after it with the fervor and the drive. If you wanted to be president, why not go after president? If you wanted to go after secretary, go after secretary. But if you wanted to be president and you're settling for secretary, watch. When you were in high school or grade school, you didn't even make a poster. You didn't even campaign. How come? "I don't even want the job. What I really wanted was president."

Go after what you really want. You're more likely to get what you really want than settling for something that you only half want. Build up your resiliency inside yourself, that tenacity and drive inside yourself, knowing that if you aren't successful and you do get knocked down, you'll feel like anybody who wanted something greatly and you didn't get it. It just knocks the wind right out of your sails. It makes you sick at your stomach. It drops you to your knees. But know you can recover from it. Also know that if you don't expect it, you won't get it. It will only be luck, it will only be circumstance outside yourself. So it's all right to expect. In fact, you get what you expect. You don't get what you want.

Everybody wants to live well. Some of them don't expect it. Everybody wants to have a wonderful job and a wonderful marriage and a wonderful life around them. They just don't expect it, and they've learned not to expect. Shoot for the stars. No. People say, "Why don't you just aim for an

# DAY 14
# Go After What You Really Want

eagle and maybe you'll hit a pigeon. Don't think too big, you know. Why don't we just settle for . . ." Maybe a lot of times they fool themselves and they say, "Well, I'm going to really think big, because I know I won't get it. I'm going to get something a little less, but if I don't think really big, then I probably won't get this little piece." Why don't you just think big?

Now, remember, big for you is relevant. Just design the life you want, design the career you want. But, hey, current reality denies that it's possible right now. Just remember the power of the subconscious. Remember to develop your efficacy. You're not qualified now for what you really want. In fact, if you know how to get what you really want, you're not stretching enough. You already know the process. You already know the way. If you already know how you're going to do it, you probably aren't stretching yourself enough. Why don't you put a dream out there you don't even know how to get right now. See if you can't use your reticular activating system to discover knowledge, to discover information and resources and people that can get you there. Why don't you do that so you stimulate that creativity inside yourself that comes up with the ideas. Why don't you make life an adventure and a surprise to yourself and have it unfold with wonderful surprises. You're causing it with your intent, you're causing it with your awareness, you're causing it with your readiness to seize opportunity.

So you set a goal far beyond, based upon what it is that you want with your life. It's a dream. Dare yourself to dream. Allow yourself to dream. Allow yourself to know the difference between a declaration of possibility and a promise. You're not promising right now. You're only envisioning. Just get yourself to envision, to envision, to dream. Don't hold yourself to it right now. Don't set the dream and then force yourself to do it. Here comes the "have to" again. Set the dream and allow it to happen. Set the dream and relax. Set the dream, and then just flow. Set the dream. Go after it. Go after it. Don't force it. Visualize it. Create the drive. Create the excitement; create the want. Allow yourself to get inventive and creative, and it may come as an entirely different surprise for you.

For instance, I always wanted to be a football coach. I always wanted to coach. But as I didn't play college football, I only coached when I was in college. I coached at a very good high school and so on, and I still wanted to be a football coach. I became a football coach in high school, and then I became a head coach. I probably would never be able to coach in the pros because you would have to have played at that higher level and so on, or you wouldn't get the opportunity.

Well, still wanting to be a football coach, I came to the realization that I coach the best coaches in the world, and I didn't go through the ordinary way. I didn't go through working my way up through high school coach and then on up into a college coach and then on up into maybe the pros and then on up. No, but I still have what I want. I still coach. I coach people who are the best coaches, in hockey, basketball, football – and I don't even need to go to practice. I don't need to do all that stuff. I'm just coaching the guys that coach. And I enjoy and live vicariously through their success. See how it comes out?

## DAY 14
# Go After What You Really Want

Sometimes it comes out different. I wanted to be a teacher. I am not a teacher in the classroom, but my classroom is all over the world. So envisioning what I really wanted, my subconscious invented things that are much better – and not the ordinary, not the routine, not the way that you presently see it. Not the way that I presently planned it. But it comes out even much better oftentimes. So allow yourself to dream. Don't get all caught up in whether you're qualified right now, and don't get all caught up in whether you know the process. The important thing is to dream as though you have it. Dream in the present tense. Dream you in it, not someone else in it. Dream correctly. And to control your dreams, write your affirmations. Don't just write them; use your affirmations to control the dream.

# DAY 14
# Go After What You Really Want

## DAY 15
# I Have a Positive Expectancy Of

## Key Concepts

Affirmation; Goal; LO/LO; Pygmalion; Resilience; Self-Esteem; Self-Talk; Subconscious.

*Setbacks are temporary.*

## Main Concepts

**The most important ideas and insights I have gained from this session are:**

## Choice Of Activities

**Today I will add this affirmation to my affirmations:**

"I have a positive expectancy of _____ and I take every setback as temporary."

**DAY 15**
# I Have a Positive Expectancy Of

Three events from my past where I overcame setbacks and achieved my goals were:

I overcame them by:

# DAY 15
# I Have a Positive Expectancy Of

## Affirmations

Write your own Positive Expectancy Affirmations using your ideas gained from this session, your review of related information and notes, as well as affirmation ideas from your Participant Manual.

- Refer to the Action/Emotion Word List on pages 215 through 217 for appropriate words.

- Review the Affirmation Checklist on page 213 to be sure you are writing them effectively.

It may be helpful to write down the current reality first, and then describe what it will be like when it is fixed. Use this as the basis to write your affirmations. Transfer your completed affirmations to 3 x 5 cards and place them in your Affirmation Folder.

### My Affirmations

**Read**
▼
**Picture**
▼
**Feel**

### Assimilation

Refer to the Affirmation Imprinting Reminders on page 240 as you go through your affirmations.

*I get a clear and vivid picture in my mind and I feel the wonderful emotion and mood of already achieving my goal. I dwell on this feeling of achievement, which gives life to my affirmations. I do this for each affirmation. I set aside time at least twice daily to imprint them.*

**DAY 15**
# I Have a Positive Expectancy Of

## Journal

# DAY 15
# I Have a Positive Expectancy Of

## Audio Summary

A quality that I would like to encourage all of us to develop more is the quality of resiliency; a characteristic of tenacity within us. I guess what we're talking about is being tough, but too often we've made the mistake of thinking tough might be beating up on somebody with a chain or pushing somebody around or whatever. Really that's not necessarily what toughness is. Toughness seems to be the quality of being able to lock onto a goal or an end result of a project or a task, and to be able to take disappointment, to be able to take setbacks and blocks as only temporary and not as final. It seems that we lose when we give up on the picture. So the only time you become a loser is when you say," The heck with it" and give up on it.

Well, my question to you might be: Are you using your potential or do you have any of your potential you're not utilizing? Would it be personally profitable for you to grow or expand in that characteristic or quality? Well, let's examine some people. You take a person like Edison, who invented the filament for the lights that we're using. If you go back and see, he was a very, very creative, a very natural kind of a person. You know, he had over 3,000 temporary setbacks before he got the project completed; over 3,000 failures before he got the task done. See, he was able to lock on to an end result and take all setbacks as temporary. There was a guy by the name of Lou Brock who, awhile back, broke a world's record for stealing bases. In the same doggone year, he set another record. Do you know what that was? Being thrown out for trying to steal bases the most times. You see, he also set a record for failure at the same time.

So we look at being tough, and it doesn't mean that everything is going to go well for you. Hey, if it was easy, what you're doing, everybody would be doing it, okay? So somewhere you have a tremendous quality already of tenacity. Let's talk about building it up. Let's talk about being tough a little bit.

I think if I was to use a person who we would all be familiar with, who has that quality or characteristic, I would think it would be somebody like Rose Kennedy. I understand that as she first started out raising her family that she had a child who died, and then she had another child who was born retarded, and she bounces right back. She has another child who was killed in the war, and she bounces right back. She has a son who is assassinated, and she bounces right back. And she has another son assassinated, and she bounces right back. She has a husband die, and she bounces right back. She has another son scandalized, and she bounces right back. She has a grandson with a leg amputated, and she bounces right back. Some people would say, "Ah, the heck with it, I quit." The message is, that's okay. You see, she had a positive expectancy of winning, and she takes every setback as temporary.

That's a quality you want to develop within yourself. How many no's can you take? How easily are you intimidated? How easily are you intimidated by others around you, or by failure or by blocks when things don't go right? Intimidation is in your own mind, Pygmalion. You mustn't al-

# DAY 15
# I Have a Positive Expectancy Of

low other people to intimidate. You mustn't allow other circumstances to intimidate you. But you can build that quality of tenacity within you. It doesn't make any difference whether we're white or black or red or yellow, male or female, whether we're big or little. That is the quality that I find most people who are super at winning have.

Now, how do we go about developing that quality of tenacity within us? You can use imagery to do so. Remember your subconscious doesn't know the difference between vividly imagining experiences or whether you're actually experiencing it, having handled it successfully. Then, as you accumulate, over and over and over, experiences in your mind, you build that opinion that this is like you.

What I would recommend is that you design an affirmation, and use something quite similar like this: You could visualize yourself, perhaps, in a well, and it's very dark in there. You reach to get out and somebody strikes your hand and you pull your hand back in because it's painful. You put your hand out, and somebody strikes you, and you pull it back in because it's painful. You keep putting your hands out and pulling them back in, and as you pull them out, that person who is striking your hands – the setback, so to speak – gets more tired and the striking becomes further and further apart. Pretty soon, you feel that one more time and you're out. You just come right out of that hole a winner, and you build that quality that nothing can keep you in — nothing.

You see, it doesn't need to be coming out of a well. You can be going after a job or going after a sale or raising a child or holding your marriage together. I will work with young athletes. As we would work with football players, I would ask them to visualize themselves running through the woods at night and it's dark. There are a tremendous amount of trees, and as you run, you strike a tree, and it's painful. But instead of just sitting down and crying and whimpering and making excuses, just slide to the side and work toward the next on. You hit the next one, you bounce back; and you strike another one, you bounce back. You strike another one, you bounce back. Nothing is going to keep you from the end result.

As you build that quality of tenacity within you, you walk around like you're a pretty tough person, knowing that you can keep your marriage together, that nothing will cause it to be destroyed.  You know that when you go after a task in your corporation or your company, that nothing can keep you down. You know that you are such a winner that nothing – nothing – will keep you from achieving the goal that you want. I would recommend that you take and build that tremendous quality of tenacity and resiliency within you to where you can go after the goals that are vitally important for you in your marriage and in your company and in your life.

# DAY 16
# Goal-Setting/Life Style I

## Key Concepts

Belief; Comfort Zone; Efficacy; Environmental; Goal-Set; Magis; Philosophy of Life; Potential.

*Who am I? Why am I? Where am I going?*

## Main Concepts

**The most important ideas and insights I have gained from this session are:**

## Choice Of Activities

Who am I?

Why am I?

Where am I going?

# DAY 16
# Goal-Setting/Life Style I

The best ideal Sunday would be:

Five things that make me happy are:

## DAY 16
# Goal-Setting/Life Style I

## Affirmations

Write your own Goal-Setting Affirmations using your ideas gained from this session, your review of related information and notes, as well as affirmation ideas from your Participant Manual.

*   Refer to the Action/Emotion Word List on pages 215 through 217 for appropriate words.

*   Review the Affirmation Checklist on page 213 to be sure you are writing them effectively.

It may be helpful to write down the current reality first, and then describe what it will be like when it is fixed. Use this as the basis to write your affirmations. Transfer your completed affirmations to 3 x 5 cards and place them in your Affirmation Folder.

### My Affirmations

**Read**
▼
**Picture**
▼
**Feel**

## Assimilation

Refer to the Affirmation Imprinting Reminders on page 240 as you go through your affirmations.

*I get a clear and vivid picture in my mind and I feel the wonderful emotion and mood of already achieving my goal. I dwell on this feeling of achievement, which gives life to my affirmations. I do this for each affirmation. I set aside time at least twice daily to imprint them.*

# DAY 16
# Goal-Setting/Life Style I

## Journal

# DAY 16
# Goal-Setting/Life Style I

## Audio Summary

Up until now, we've spent most of the time working on growing on the inside, and you never want to let that go. That's not ever to be let go. You always want to hold onto the development on the inside. One reason why, is there's a direct relationship between the way you think on the inside and the way your world looks on the outside. How many people, though, sit around waiting for the world on the outside to change, and then they're going to improve or get better? Most people. If what we're saying is true, then we need to, inside of ourselves, develop our efficacy, which you already know about. You need to then work on those core beliefs that maybe hold you back, and releasing those. This is always ongoing.

Now, let's talk about the physical – the environmental comfort zone, or the environmental reality. Some of you may think, of course, it's money, and in most cases much of it is. Some of you may think in terms of, "Well, there's a lot of other things," other resources and so on that are necessary in order to achieve the goals that we want – relationships and teamwork and technology and all kinds of things, and all that is true.

But let's just talk about how can we get past this week, this month, the next five months, and really start goal setting to alter – dramatically alter – the physical world around us, if that's what we desire. Here's one way that's essential: Again, I want you to develop for yourself, if you will, a philosophy of where you're going and why you're going there. "Going." What does that mean? Well, what are you doing with your life's energy? What are you alive for? Why don't you just pack it in right now? Why don't you just finish it off? What are you doing hanging around on earth for? Those are interesting questions. What do you really want to be when you grow up? What are you doing and what is your purpose? Those kind of questions need to be asked.

The questions, "Who am I? Why am I? Where am I going?" seem never to get past just asking. You must answer them. Who am I? Why am I? Where am I going? Okay. Now, when you develop a philosophy about what you want to be doing with your life's energy and what you're trying to create, I think then what we want to do is to design for ourselves a style of life. Start looking at, "What is my style?" Is it going to be working with people or is it going to be working by myself? Is it going to be involved travel, or is it going to involve pretty much staying at home? Is it going to involve both? Is it going to involve working for myself or working for another? Is it going to involve no work at all? Is it going to be working to maybe do something very spectacular with my life, or is it just being a good person, hanging around my family and my friends and so on, is that enough?

So what are all these things? What do I want to do? Now, it seems very difficult to do unless . . . For me, it was, unless I just broke it down into something ordinary like a day. What do I want to do if I was going to design the best Sunday? Okay. What would be the best Sunday in the winter? What would be the best Sunday in the summer? What would be the best Sunday in the spring?

# DAY 16
# Goal-Setting/Life Style I

What would be best Sunday in the fall? Because, they might be different. So you just start with a Sunday, and allow yourself to dream and think about Sunday. Then what you want to do from there is to say to yourself, "Am I talking about Sunday morning or Sunday afternoon or Sunday evening?" Would I be doing the same thing all day? Who would I have around me? Where would I be placing myself? What would lunch look like? What would dinner look like? What would it be like after dinner? What about a Monday, what would a Monday look like?

Well, as we were messing around with this one time, Diane and I, a Sunday we had was on a ranch. But, we lived in the city, so we had to figure out a ranch. I was working in the city, so how am I going to get to work? Maybe I don't go to work. No, you go to work. Well, how you going to get there? I guess I need to fly. Well, I don't fly. Well, do you want to fly? No, I don't want to learn to fly. Okay, then what you need to do is hire somebody or hire an airplane to take you back to the city, don't you? Hmm. Yes, but that gets expensive. I guess you better earn more money, hadn't you?

Then, what do you say to yourself? "Well, I'm not worth that much." Well, that's true. So what you need to do now is you develop yourself. If we're going to design this, don't worry about whether you're presently qualified, because once we design it, then we're going to get presently qualified. Then we're going to get qualified.

So I designed the best Monday in the fall, the best Monday in the summer, the best Monday in the winter. Then take a Wednesday, take a Saturday, take a Friday. Then take the best week in the spring, the best week in the summer, the best week in the winter. What would it look like? What would be ideal? And you just allow yourself to start designing the ideal of where you want to be, how you want to travel, who you want around you, the kinds of people. As you do that, you write all these weird ideas down, and you do it over and over, and you do it with the people you really care about. If it's your spouse or your family or if it's people at work, you start designing the ideal. What would be the ideal way?

And then, remember, you're presently not qualified, more than likely presently not qualified. In fact, if you are presently qualified, I doubt if you're stretching yourself, because you are already pretty closely doing what it was that you're describing. Ah, that's too close. Diane and I, one time, decided we wanted a ranch, but we didn't want to live on the ranch all the time. We just started designing a ranch. We didn't really have any financial resources to bring it about at the time, but you start designing it anyway. Even the home that we presently live in, we've lived in it for 20 some years. When we decided that, we were just out of high school teaching, and we had many children to take care of.

One time, going from the Oregon coast up to Seattle we had the kids design – and these were little kids, some of them were five, some of them were nine, some of them were twelve – what you do want in a home. No restrictions, just tell us what you want. Oh, gee whiz, they wrote 170 some things down that they wanted, and among them were sunken garbage cans, because the dogs kept knocking them over and their job was to pick up the garbage. The other things they wanted were, oh, swimming pools, and they wanted eagles and they went on and on and on – jukeboxes, and they wanted pool tables – they just kept going. They wanted to be on a lake and they wanted a boat. Keep in mind, we did this, and we didn't have the money. But we found a home with at least half of what they asked for, including the jukebox, and the pool table, and many of the other things were in the home that we found.

Now, several years later, I don't know how many, let's just say almost 10 years later, Diane found the list. It was a list with misspelling, you know, it was 160, 170 some things, whatever it was. We came to the realization, "I think we have them all now," and we weren't consciously going after it. It was something that just happened. Now we do have a ranch, and with that ranch we have eagles; we do have barns; we do have horses; we do have all the other things that they put on their list; but we didn't get it in one place. We got it in two, and we had no conscious level intent to do so. But we were so dead serious about the style in which we wanted to live, the environments that we wanted to create, and we allowed our imagination to invent it before we ever had the resources. And, sure enough, there it is.

Now, we haven't done that again like that, although we do when we build our office or we build other things. We do allow ourselves to think outrageously, or magis. You just let yourself think it. You don't know how you're going to do it. Keep in mind, again, you're not presently qualified. That's why you keep working on the inside. You get qualified. Now, in the next audio, what we're going to do is talk more about goal setting and how you get that inside change so the outside occurs.

# DAY 16
# Goal-Setting/Life Style I

## DAY 17
# Life Style II

## Key Concepts

Affirmation; Comfort Zone; Creative Subconscious; Creativity; Future as Now; Reality; Servo-Mechanism; Subconscious; Visualization.

*Deliberately designed for fulfillment.*

## Main Concepts

**The most important ideas and insights I have gained from this session are:**

## Choice Of Activities

**The lifestyle I would like to create is:**

# DAY 17
# Life Style II

What additional resources would I need to make this level of achievement normal?

What do I expect right now?

## DAY 17
# Life Style II

# Affirmations

Write your own Life Style Affirmations using your ideas gained from this session, your review of related information and notes, as well as affirmation ideas from your Participant Manual.

- Refer to the Action/Emotion Word List on pages 215 through 217 for appropriate words.

- Review the Affirmation Checklist on page 213 to be sure you are writing them effectively.

It may be helpful to write down the current reality first, and then describe what it will be like when it is fixed. Use this as the basis to write your affirmations. Transfer your completed affirmations to 3 x 5 cards and place them in your Affirmation Folder.

## My Affirmations

**Read**
▼
**Picture**
▼
**Feel**

## Assimilation

Refer to the Affirmation Imprinting Reminders on page 240 as you go through your affirmations.

*I get a clear and vivid picture in my mind and I feel the wonderful emotion and mood of already achieving my goal. I dwell on this feeling of achievement, which gives life to my affirmations. I do this for each affirmation. I set aside time at least twice daily to imprint them.*

## Journal

## DAY 17
# Life Style II

## Audio Summary

I have a lot of goods friends who, I think I mentioned before, were generals in the Army. They retired in their early 50s, and when they retire, they usually go and look for a job where there's a defense contract. This isn't out of the ordinary, because they get hired by the firms that manufacture a lot of the supplies that the military would use. I was talking to this one lovely couple; they were in their late 40s and looking forward to retiring in about a year and a half. And I said, "Well, what are you going to do?" They were going to go to Dallas to go to work – I think it was for Ross Perot in one of the companies he had there – and she was saying, "I really don't like Dallas, but we're going." And I said, "Holy cow! Why don't you just stop for a moment, and instead of finding a job and building your life around the job, why don't you design your life and then find the job?" Oh, never thought of that.

That's really what I'm encouraging you to do. Now, I don't encourage you now to leave what you're doing at all, because what you're doing may be exactly what you want to do. But how many people place themselves into a neighborhood or into a job or some kind of a business and they really don't like it? "It isn't what I want to do, but it is the way I make a living." Then what you do is you design your life around the way you make your living. And I would say, let's just play with this. Why don't you just see if you can design your life and then find some way to make enough money to support the way you want to live?

Really, that's about the way Diane and I did it. We knew what we wanted to be doing. We wanted to be teaching, and we wanted to teach this kind of information, but nobody would hire us. I wouldn't have hired myself. With the style of life I was designing, nobody could hire me and pay me that much money to be able to support that life style. So what I needed to do was create the life style and then to develop myself and develop a business and develop income that would support the life style. So that's really what I'm encouraging you to do: design the style and then develop the income stream.

Let's go back to how the subconscious works and how the creative subconscious works, and let's talk a little bit about tithing. Tithing is an interesting concept. You give perhaps 10% to charity or 10% to the church. But in tithing, it's the first 10%, and not the last 10%. That's an interesting concept, because if you waited to give what you had left over, it would be like some of you who save what you have left after you pay your bills, or you invest what you have left after you've paid your bills. Quite frankly, you're living right now to the max, and so you don't have enough to save. You don't have enough to give to the church, you don't have enough to give to charity. Oh, but some day, you're going to.

Keep in mind, I think your subconscious is a lot like your children. If you told them to wash the dishes, they would, but not the pots and pans and not the silverware, not the cups and saucers. They do exactly what they're told. So the creative subconscious does exactly what it's told.

# DAY 17
# Life Style II

And it will create enough income to support not what you wish for, but what you've come to expect. Inside your expectation level of what you know your life style is, "I don't expect to give any money to the church right now. I want to some day." So your subconscious says, "Well, okay, we'll figure out enough ideas. We'll develop you sufficiently to create the income, not for what you want in the future, but for what you expect right now – what you expect right now, what you expect right now, what you expect right now.

That's why the affirmation process is so essential. You must change what you expect right now, then you get creative to earn the income. It's not extra money that's necessary. Your creative subconscious does what's necessary. So you need to, in your mind, create the environment, create the life style, and live it in your mind over and over. Give yourself feedback through your senses to the contrary. "Hey, we're not living that way." Your creative subconscious now will correct for the mistake. It solves the problem. It creates the energy. It may cause you to increase your business. It may cause you now to get out of the location you are and become worldly, because there's not enough income where you're sitting. You may need to expand your product. You may need to create a new one. What it will do, it will give you enough creativity and drive to consistently earn the income that you've come to expect or that you need, not what you want.

What if we create the need first, but not by going out and buying something you can't afford, not by placing yourself in debt. There's an interesting saying by a lot of car salespeople that we hang around, if you don't have a wolf at your door, maybe it would pay you to go out and hire one. It's like you ought to put yourself in debt, buy something big so now you have to sell something. No, no, no, that's not what I'm talking about. I'm talking about really visualizing the style of the home and create in your mind first the necessity. It isn't a want. It isn't a wish. It isn't what I hope to be. It is really "I expect to do this."

So let's go back to tithing. If you expect to give 10% of your income to the church, you say, "Well, wait a minute. I wouldn't have enough money to pay the electricity bill." Well, "then earn more," your subconscious says. It isn't just "give them if we've got it." You give it, and then you get it. So, if you're going to save, you need to expect to save. And if you're going to invest, you must expect to invest. And as you start increasing the expectation of the style of life, there is no pressure. It isn't now a matter of being uptight about earning the money. It becomes automatic. It just comes to you. It isn't just like, "Oh, I just sit and it comes to me." It means I study, I develop, I create the work, I create the business, I create the income. I create the income stream to support my life style. I always have. Now, saving is a part of it. Investing is a part of it. Living and traveling the way I travel is a part of it.

What I need to do then is to somehow create the business around me, and sometimes I can't find it in Seattle. Sometimes I need to go to Guatemala or I need to go to Europe or I need to go to Asia, so that becomes a part of it. I just get inventive. You become inventive to support the life style. Create the life style. That's what you visualize, not the process, not the method, and

# DAY 17
# Life Style II

you don't worry about the money to start with. You create the ranch. You create the home. You create the style of travel, the vacations, the security financially, whatever it is that you want. You create that in your mind, not just by thinking about it once, but actually living in it in a first person present tense, living as though the future is right there now. You place yourself in it and you have a good time in it.

And what you're going to find is, "I'll be darned, I seem to be expanding my business. I'll be darned, my income is really increasing, isn't it?" Remember now, your subconscious has an idea of how much money you need to support your life style. Not what you wish for, not what you want. Your creative subconscious stimulates enough drive and energy to earn the money to support your internal reality. Change your internal reality, and you'll earn more money.

# DAY 17
# Life Style II

# DAY 18
# What's Good Enough?

## Key Concepts

Aspiration; Creative Subconscious; Creativity; Energy; Goal; Potential; Self-Talk.

*Goal-set up to, and through.*

## Main Concepts

**The most important ideas and insights I have gained from this session are:**

## Choice Of Activities

**An example of where, in the past, I have Goal-Set To but not Through is:**

# DAY 18
# What's Good Enough?

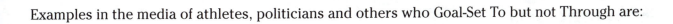

Examples in the media of athletes, politicians and others who Goal-Set To but not Through are:

One goal I have set now that I need to Goal-Set Through and beyond is:

## DAY 18
# What's Good Enough?

## Affirmations

Write your own What's Good Enough Affirmations using your ideas gained from this session, your review of related information and notes, as well as affirmation ideas from your Participant Manual.

- Refer to the Action/Emotion Word List on pages 215 through 217 for appropriate words.

- Review the Affirmation Checklist on page 213 to be sure you are writing them effectively.

It may be helpful to write down the current reality first, and then describe what it will be like when it is fixed. Use this as the basis to write your affirmations. Transfer your completed affirmations to 3 x 5 cards and place them in your Affirmation Folder.

### My Affirmations

**Read**
▼
**Picture**
▼
**Feel**

### Assimilation

Refer to the Affirmation Imprinting Reminders on page 240 as you go through your affirmations.

*I get a clear and vivid picture in my mind and I feel the wonderful emotion and mood of already achieving my goal. I dwell on this feeling of achievement, which gives life to my affirmations. I do this for each affirmation. I set aside time at least twice daily to imprint them.*

# What's Good Enough?

## Journal

## DAY 18
# What's Good Enough?

## Audio Summary

One of the things that I think stops you or me the most isn't that we don't have the resources, it's that we don't have the idea. We don't have the dream. We don't have the aspiration. One of the things I think that stops us is that we've arrived at something that we felt was as much as we ever deserved or as much as we would want. You know, when we've done so, we've hit against that concept that I've shared with you. Once you arrive at a goal that you set, remember what happens? You lose your drive, you lose what we call energy, and you lose your creativity.

Now, you don't lose it, you keep enough energy to sustain the status quo. In other words, you work hard enough to keep it as it is. You get enough ideas to keep it looking about the way that you see it, but no more. Now, how much potential do you have? Who knows? That creative subconscious is a genius. But remember, the creative subconscious only does enough to sustain the picture that you hold in your mind of what is good enough. Remember the example I said, if you told your kids (and your kids would be like the creative subconscious) to wash the dishes, they would, but not the pots and pans, because you didn't say pots and pans. You didn't say silverware. It does what it's told to do. It has potential to do the pots and pans, but not if you don't ask, not if it doesn't become expected. So once you arrive at a goal that you set, you exert only enough energy to sustain that status quo, to sustain that level of performance.

I've seen so many people whose goals might have been to, say, as a doctor or as a dentist, open a practice. Now, look at the fallacy. If you listen to them, open a practice they did. Go out of business quick they did also. They only opened the practice, they didn't grow the practice. Now, can you see so many examples of where your business has flattened out? You must take this concept and see inside, in listening to your people or listening to your own self-talk and going back and reflecting. Where have you stopped you? Where have you arrived at, as far as your career, as far as your income, as far as your environment, as far as where you allow yourself to take vacations? What have you come to expect? That's what you get.

So once you arrive at the goal that you've set, your energy and your drive doesn't take you past that. I think there was a saying in the old days that was called the Peter Principle. It was a psychological phenomenon where people said they reached the level of their incompetence. Well, that's probably true. But, you see, is it because they don't have the potential? Oh, yes, because in many of those days, could you believe they thought people were born with only a certain capacity? Well, they may be. But that was a good excuse for not setting a new goal and growing beyond it, wasn't it? Because if you're born that way, or if you really viewed your own people and your own organization as not really having the capacity to go beyond or grow, well, of course, now I don't need to mentor or coach or manage you past that expectation. Okay, so it's very important that Peter Principle is true, but it doesn't need to be.

# DAY 18
# What's Good Enough?

I would think in most cases there was still more to develop, but the problem was they didn't see past that horizon. They didn't see past that fixed point. So, do you wait until you achieve that fixed point before you set a new horizon? A lot of people do. But if you want sustained momentum and sustained growth, then you set the aspiration out about as far as you can see yourself having the refrigerator, and then you don't wait until it's completed. What you do is, as you approach that aspiration or goal, wouldn't you think that that would be the time to start projecting into the future?

Now, goal-setting isn't a once in a year kind of a process. It maybe once a year in some areas of your life, but it might be every three months in some others. What you need to do is really have some good talks with yourself. What is it that I really want? How far do I want to go? And then you need to set your aspirations past that fixed point of setting up a practice or a business. "No, that's not what I really wanted."

I remember when I first started many years ago, I didn't know anything about selling. So what I'd do is I would set goals to go call on important people, and I would. But I didn't have any business from it. I remember walking down Fourth Avenue in downtown Seattle by the Olympic Hotel, and I said, "My goodness, I know what I was doing." My goal was to call on them, and I was. I didn't at all tell myself the goal really was to get them engaged in our curriculum and have them pay for it and then have them grow from it and have them refer new business. All I was doing was setting a goal to call on important people. I changed my mind, and it changed my business. Isn't that amazing? Now, how many times have you done the same thing? I don't know. But I would guess that you stop you more than anybody else or any other circumstances. That is the one concept that stops most companies and most organizations, most people, most armies.

If you go back and study in the Revolutionary War, there was a great study done about somebody whose goal it was to take a bridge. They got to that point, and they stopped. If they had only marched further, they could have perhaps won the war, but they didn't. They achieved the objective and quit, and got clobbered.

You can look at this all over, especially little kids. Listening to them, what is their aspiration, what is their goal? As a mentor, as a coach, knowing this principle, you just talk them past their stopping point. "Oh, I want to make the team." Does that mean you just want to be on the team, or do you want to start on the team? And do you want to then win or just make the team and start? Do you want to go past winning and do you want? Really, it's just a matter of listening carefully, knowing these objectives. You can do it with a little kid or you do it with big kids in your business. This is a liberating principle. It liberates within you that prison that you put yourself in by reaching the objective that you set and not setting another one. Turn yourself loose.

## DAY 19
# Visualize the New

## Key Concepts

Current Reality; Creativity; Energy; Goal; Goal-Setting; Potential; Visualization.

*Small beginnings.*

## Main Concepts

**The most important ideas and insights I have gained from this session are:**

## Choice Of Activities

**My current top three small goals are:**

If I imagined I was asked to share my goals with a group of fifty people, using as few words as possible, what words would I choose?

# DAY 19
# Visualize the New

Where do I feel dissatisfaction because I visualize my goals vividly and emotionally?

What new small or medium-sized goals could I set for myself now to practice?

## DAY 19
# Visualize the New

## Affirmations

Write your own Visualization Affirmations using your ideas gained from this session, your review of related information and notes, as well as affirmation ideas from your Participant Manual.

*   Refer to the Action/Emotion Word List on pages 215 through 217 for appropriate words.

*   Review the Affirmation Checklist on page 213 to be sure you are writing them effectively.

It may be helpful to write down the current reality first, and then describe what it will be like when it is fixed. Use this as the basis to write your affirmations. Transfer your completed affirmations to 3 x 5 cards and place them in your Affirmation Folder.

### My Affirmations

**Read**
▼
**Picture**
▼
**Feel**

### Assimilation

Refer to the Affirmation Imprinting Reminders on page 240 as you go through your affirmations.

*I get a clear and vivid picture in my mind and I feel the wonderful emotion and mood of already achieving my goal. I dwell on this feeling of achievement, which gives life to my affirmations. I do this for each affirmation. I set aside time at least twice daily to imprint them.*

# DAY 19
# Visualize the New

## Journal

## DAY 19
# Visualize the New

## Audio Summary

Okay, in this goal-setting process, we must make the new image – the new vision, the new idea, or generally in the style of life that you want – so dominant in our mind. We want to live in it so dominant in our mind that the environment in which you are presently placed becomes irritating in a sense, almost irritating. It almost catapults you out of the environment. "I'm out of here," you've probably heard people say; that freedom from, which we've discussed a little bit already.

When I left high school teaching, you need to understand that this was where I wanted to be, from the time I was nine. Leaving something that I had set so seriously in my mind and prepared everything for, it was almost unthinkable in my mind to allow myself to even dwell on being outside of that structure of teaching in a high school. But I started to visualize a different style of life, of being still a teacher, but teaching in a much different way and in a different environment. As I started letting my mind see the freedom, the income, the results that I was accomplishing, only in my mind instead of with kids, it would be with business leaders or government leaders or community and so on.

As I would do that over and over, it got to the point where I could not stand to go to another faculty meeting. It drove me nuts. I hated the bells. When the bells rang, every 45 minutes or every hour, you'd have the first bell and the second bell, the bells were literally driving me irritably nuts. And the kids that I cared about, that I was there for, if they knocked on the door and wanted to see me, I would go, "What do you want?" I was so irritated in that environment that I couldn't wait to get out. I found every reason.  It was just, "When am I going to be out of here?" Had I not visualized the new and made myself feel – I know the principle, but I was really experiencing – so uncomfortable, I would never have left. It would have been too scary. I would have stayed right where I was.

So remember the principle. As you visualize the new, you become dissatisfied with the old. That could be a car, or it could be a career. It could be the next level of development for yourself. As you visualize the new, you become unhappy or dissatisfied with the old. Don't burn the bridge behind you though. Don't go out, you know, complaining about everybody. Don't think that all of a sudden everybody just kind of fell apart and it got ugly around you. No, it was always that way.

That environment, that school environment, didn't change. I changed. As I visualized myself into a better environment for me – not better environment but better environment for me – I started noticing blemishes all over the place. If I hadn't noticed the blemishes, I would have been too comfortable there. I would have allowed myself to stay right there with another excuse not for leaving. So allow yourself. See how this process works. It takes some time. You must visualize yourself into that new level of environment, the new level of performance, the new level socially or whatever it might be, and then you'll notice you become inside yourself dissatisfied with your present job or your present income status. I mean, you become almost stagnant in your social

# DAY 19
# Visualize the New

life. I mean, these are the same people we've seen over and over. I mean, they're nice people. "I don't want to see them." Was there something wrong with them? No. It's a sign of growth. It's a sign of growth, if, in fact, you're visualizing a better way.

Start causing that inside yourself through the visualizing of a better level of quality in whatever area you're trying to improve – a better area of quality of home environment, business environment, and pretty soon you get dissatisfied with the size of your company. But if you're not dissatisfied with the size of your company, you won't cause the growth in it. If you're not dissatisfied with the product that you're delivering, you'll keep delivering the same product.

You need to feel toward the product or toward the size of your company, or whatever you're doing, the same way I felt about being in Kennedy High School. And Kennedy High School is Kennedy High School. It didn't fall apart. It's been going pretty good since I left it. But I needed to cause myself to leave it; and I did, and I was happy to get out. But you know what was going through my mind? "Well, in case this business doesn't work out, I could always go back to my old job." This was in February, and the year wasn't going to be complete until June. But when I left, they immediately hired a new coach and a new teacher. "Oh, no. Now I can't go back." That seemed sad, but that was great. I had no option to return, no option. Now, the only thing I could do was make it.

I didn't have a lot of money either, which, when I look back, wasn't so bad. Because if I had had a lot of money, I would have probably used the money before I became effective. But I needed the urgency of making it happen now. That urgency inside oneself is not a badness that you feel. See, it is that drive that causes you to take the right kind of action. Don't leave where you are in what you're doing until you've created enough dissatisfaction – with where you presently are or what you're presently doing – that will drive you with enough drive and creativity to go forward. It isn't just jump from where you are into the new, because I think you'll find yourself not knowing if you want to go back, go forward, go back.

So somehow use this process, not in something so huge for you or something that's the greatest challenge of your life, but use it with your lawn mower. Get unhappy with your lawn mower, pushing it, and find one you can ride. I mean just something simple, something dumb. Pretty soon this lawn mower, you might even make it fall apart, if you don't like it. You could ruin it. Do the same with your car. You'll find your car will fall apart on you. You want to just find some things, and then say, "Now, what could I do with other parts of my life?" See how you do that?

## DAY 20
# Power of Your Word

## Key Concepts

Affirmation; Integrity; Magis; Spirit of Intent; Trust.

*Trust is reliance on the integrity of others.*

## Main Concepts

**The most important ideas and insights I have gained from this session are:**

## Choice Of Activities

**Recent promises I have made to myself, both big and small, are:**

How many have I kept?

What does this tell me about my word?

What does this tell me about my spirit of intent?

# DAY 20
# Power of Your Word

**Promises I have made, and not kept, to others are:**

How does this make me feel?

My plan to improve my keeping of promises, to myself and others, is:

## DAY 20
# Power of Your Word

## Affirmations

Write your own Power of Your Word Affirmations using your ideas gained from this session, your review of related information and notes, as well as affirmation ideas from your Participant Manual.

- Refer to the Action/Emotion Word List on pages 215 through 217 for appropriate words.

- Review the Affirmation Checklist on page 213 to be sure you are writing them effectively.

It may be helpful to write down the current reality first, and then describe what it will be like when it is fixed. Use this as the basis to write your affirmations. Transfer your completed affirmations to 3 x 5 cards and place them in your Affirmation Folder.

### My Affirmations

**Read**
▼
**Picture**
▼
**Feel**

### Assimilation

Refer to the Affirmation Imprinting Reminders on page 240 as you go through your affirmations.

*I get a clear and vivid picture in my mind and I feel the wonderful emotion and mood of already achieving my goal. I dwell on this feeling of achievement, which gives life to my affirmations. I do this for each affirmation. I set aside time at least twice daily to imprint them.*

## DAY 20
# Power of Your Word

## Journal

## DAY 20
# Power of Your Word

## Audio Summary

In order for you to really get the value of your affirmations, I want to share with you something I think is very important, and that is to improve the power of your word to yourself. You could hear people give promises like "the check is in the mail," but the spirit behind it wasn't there. Or, "let's get together for lunch some day." That is just a nice thing to say, but you don't really mean it. You hope they don't call.

Sometimes what we do is we say something, "Have a nice day," but we don't really care if you do or not. It's our word that we're giving or the words that we use that have the power. Now, it's very important, I think, that if I would ask you if you gave your word to another person, would you keep it? You would probably say, in most cases, "yes." And I would say, yes, that's true. But now the next statement that I'd like to have you reflect on would be, "Is your word to yourself as good as your word to another?" That's the key. If you tell yourself you're going to do something, do you do it?

I think for me, I am not nearly as strong at my word to myself as I am my word to another. That's really where some affirmations or some work could take place. If you could really get to the ultimate, where you would say, if you were a smoker, "I'm no longer a smoker. I quit," and your word to yourself would be that powerful, so be it. I mean you need a one-time affirmation, and just zap, and you're it. But, for the most part, that's not probable. I really want to encourage you to work towards making your word to yourself as strong, if you can, as your word to another. That's where your power comes from. One time, when we were first in our business with Australia, we promised we would send something to them, and we didn't send it. It got delayed or something. So, I think for $2,500, Diane delivered it in person. She flew over, handed it to them, and flew back. If we tell you it's coming, count on it. Well, that's a nice way to run your business. That's a nice way to run your life. And, again, that's pretty well the way Diane and I are. If we're going to tell you we're going to do something, you can pretty well count on it.

The other thing, though, is I don't know that I'm that strong with myself. See, some days I'll say to myself, "I think I'll lose weight today. Yep, today's the day," I'll tell myself. I'm in the shower, and today's the day. Then what goes through my mind is, "If nothing else gets in the way," and what gets in the way is lunch. I'll get about that far. But the next day with great resolve, I'll say, "Today's the day, if nothing else gets in my way." And what gets in my way is guests and a good bottle of wine. Ah, but the next day with great resolve, "Today's the day." And what happens then . . . One time, I remember Diane saying, you're losing your power if you keep doing things like that. See you're losing your power, because your word to yourself isn't any good.

So you either don't make yourself a promise, or keep it, one of the two. Otherwise, you lose that inner power, that inner strength that I want you to develop. So let's work on that word to oneself, that real intent. It isn't in every part of my life, because in some parts of my life I have fierce

# DAY 20
# Power of Your Word

resolve, but in some parts of my life I'm weak as the dickens. So it isn't like it's an either/or that this is the way it is. Does that make sense? It isn't like I'm weak in everything at all. You want to keep working in those areas where you are really letting yourself down and watch your inner power come, watch your strength come. Your affirmations works better, your self-talk works better, your life goes better. Your word is just strong that way.

Then there's another problem that we talked about. You won't let yourself think outrageously. You won't let yourself think in magis terms. You won't let yourself think in like declarations of possibility, because if you start thinking in declarations of possibility, you confuse that with a promise. So, if you confuse that with a promise, then you keep your aspirations and your goals pretty close to what you're already doing because you can deliver. Maybe have a good talk with yourself, and say, "Hey, this is a declaration of possibility. It's possible I can lose weight. I don't know if I want it right now. It's possible I could do it, yep." That's a declaration option. It's a possibility, it ain't no promise. Okay, when I make a promise, I'll make a promise.

Now, same with stretching your business, stretching your life. Allow yourself to think that horizon beyond the horizon. Know the difference between a promise and the difference between when you're really exploring with your thinking and you're going to think outrageous. Let yourself think outrageous, but there's a time when you need to make a promise. Then make that promise and keep it inside yourself – yes, it's done.

Now, one of the things that Dr. Matthew Budd has taught me over the last few years is this idea about requests and promises. That idea, very simply, is when you are making a promise to another in an agreement and so on, what you're really doing is you're agreeing to build a future together. See, what you're doing is you're saying, "Let's get together for lunch," and what you need to do then is to set a time frame; put some conditions on it like, "Let's get together for lunch at noon on Tuesday." And that's not enough. Now we need to become more specific in order for it to be become just something that will never occur by saying "where."

Now, to all this, force yourself for clarity in this goal-setting process, because that's goal-setting. That goal-setting to "get together for lunch" was your understanding that the other person is building their future on your promise. They're building their future on your word. They're going to show up. Your reliability of keeping that promise becomes essential. People build the business on promises. That's all. They build a marriage on the promise. They build future on promise. It's a matter now of knowing that there are those specifics that we're talking about that need to be put into it so that you have a greater likelihood of the promise coming to a reality.

So force clarity on this. When people make a statement and you make a statement, force clarity. "Well, what time are we going to gather for lunch?" See the difference? "Let's get together for lunch some day." It ain't gonna happen. But it will happen if you say, "Let's get together for lunch on Tuesday at 12 o'clock at Rosselini's. I'll be there." Now you must show up, because if you

## DAY 20
# Power of Your Word

don't show up, you make a promise the next time, people won't necessarily want to build their future with you.

So that's what business is like. It's a matter of requests and promises and keeping promises and building your competency, building your strength inside yourself, building inside so that you can deliver the promise. Some of you, you may want to keep the promise, but you're not competent. You may care, you may be sincere, but you just don't know how to do it. So it's not only a matter of giving your word, but you need to be able to be competent. Learn the skills, start growing, really develop yourself so that you can deliver on your promise. When you do that, then your promises will get bigger. Does that make sense?

# Relevant Biographies

*Programs of The Pacific Institute are based on current, highly credible education verified by the most valid, reliable research available.*

The Pacific Institute maintains continuing relationships with a number of distinguished human development and social learning theory researchers. We do this to ensure that we are current on important findings related to thought patterns and belief systems – findings that are crucial to our clients. Prominent among these widely respected researchers are the following:

## Dr. Albert Bandura

Dr. Bandura is the David Starr Jordan Professor of Social Science in Psychology at Stanford University and one of the most frequently cited psychologists in the world. In a recent ranking of the 100 most eminent psychologists of the 20th Century, Dr. Bandura came in fourth, behind B. F. Skinner, Jean Piaget and Sigmund Freud. He is author of countless articles on a wide range of issues in psychology, as well as seven books, including *Principles of Behavior Modification, Social Learning Theory, Social Foundations of Thought and Action,* and *Self-Efficacy: The Exercise of Control.*

Dr. Bandura has been a keynote speaker at The Pacific Institute's International Conference on several occasions. He has also spent many hours with Lou Tice and key Pacific Institute staff informally discussing the relevance of his work on individual and collective efficacy to our education. These discussions have focused on how efficacy is developed, and how perceived high efficacy changes behavior, concepts central to all programs of The Pacific Institute, including *Thought Patterns for a Successful Career*™.

## Dr. Martin E.P. Seligman

Dr. Seligman is Professor of Psychology and Director of Clinical Training at the University of Pennsylvania, where he holds the Kogod Term Professor chair. He is a prolific writer and internationally recognized scholar and researcher. Throughout his career, he has conducted extensive research with grants from the National Institute of Mental Health, the National Institute on Aging, the National Science Foundation, the Guggenheim Foundation, and the MacArthur Foundation. His book, *Learned Optimism: How to Change Your Mind and Your Life,* and his latest work, *What You Can Change and What You Can't,* have received rave reviews. Dr. Seligman has also served as President of the American Psychological Association.

Dr. Seligman's theories of learned helplessness and learned optimism have contributed a great deal to our understanding of human thought and behavior. The Seligman Attributional Style Questionnaire (SASQ) is a widely used tool that measures levels of optimism/pessimism. Dr. Seligman's visits to The Pacific Institute, his keynote presentation at our International Conference, and the time he has spent with Lou Tice at the Tice Ranch, have served to verify and strengthen the conceptual foundation of our curriculum.

# Relevant Biographies

## Dr. Gary Latham

Dr. Latham holds the Secretary of State Chair, Faculty of Management, at the University of Toronto. His expertise is in personal and organizational goal-setting and performance appraisal/compensation systems and is well acquainted with The Pacific Institute's curriculum. His latest book, coauthored with Kenneth N. Wexley and published in 1994, is entitled *Increasing Productivity Through Performance Appraisal,* a recent edition of an earlier book of the same title. Dr. Latham was elected President of the Canadian Psychological Association in 1999.

Dr. Latham has consulted with Lou Tice and has addressed The Pacific Institute's staff and clients on numerous occasions, primarily concerning practical applications of the scientific principles of goal-setting, feedback, and performance improvement. He is an outspoken and enthusiastic advocate of our educational processes, and has been a speaker at several International Conferences.

## Dr. David Matsumoto

Dr. Matsumoto is currently an associate professor in the Department of Psychology and Director of the Intercultural and Emotion Research Laboratory at San Francisco State University. His books and monographs include *Culture and Diversity: A World of Differences* (in preparation) and *People: Psychology from a Cultural Perspective.* He is also preparing a video presentation entitled *Culture and Diversity: A World of Differences.* He is the author of more than 50 articles and related symposia presentations throughout the world. As a prior keynote speaker at our International Conference, Dr. Matsumoto consults with The Pacific Institute on matters of cultural diversity – with particular focus on how culture influences behavior and how to manage cultural diversity within organizations.

## Leon Festinger

In 1954, Leon Festinger developed a concept he called "Cognitive Dissonance." He used it to explain the discomfort he observed in human test subjects when they held two conflicting thoughts at the same time. This discomfort was observed to cause some action: the subject either moved toward one thought or the other. Both thoughts could not be held at the same time.

Rather than see this as a negative situation, Lou takes the idea of cognitive dissonance and uses it as a springboard to create positive change and growth. Since change requires some form of movement, we intentionally create cognitive dissonance in an area where we wish to grow. We make the picture of where we want to be so bright and vivid, that we move toward it, thereby returning harmony.

# Relevant Biographies

## Dr. Viktor Frankl

Distinguished philosopher and author of several books on purpose in life, including *Man's Search for Meaning*. In this book, Dr. Frankl, a concentration camp survivor, relates that the men and women who were best able to survive the terrible physical and psychological deprivation were those who were determined to stay alive because of some reason bigger than themselves. In some cases it was their families. In other cases, it was important work they wanted to continue. And in some instances, it was the services and support they were providing for fellow prisoners.

## Richard Gregory

Distinguished psychologist and author of numerous publications. His area of expertise is the cognitive process, especially the relationship between perception and intelligence.

According to the dictionary, intelligence is the capacity for learning and understanding.

Gregory once told Lou that intelligence is simply the "art of guessing correctly." Anything we can do to improve our guesswork is going to make us more intelligent.

## Dr. Wilder Penfield

A cognitive scientist, and author of *Speech and Brain Mechanisms*. During exploratory surgery on a conscious epilepsy patient, with a portion of the skull removed, Dr. Penfield noticed that as he touched the temporal cortex of the patient's brain, the patient relived an experience that had happened years before. As they did further experiments, Dr. Penfield discovered that the information, the individual's version of the experience, was stored in the temporal cortex – never to be lost, never to be forgotten.

## Norbert Wiener

"Founding Father" of the computer, and co-author of the book, *Differential Space, Quantum Systems and Prediction*. Wiener coined the phrase, "Garbage in – Garbage out," in relation to data entered into the computer "brain." Simply put, if you put wrong information into a computer, you cannot get anything but wrong information out of it.

The same thing applies to the human mind. If we accept incorrect information about ourselves into our minds, then we are operating, and making decisions, with incorrect information. We must be careful to accept only correct information, and disregard the incorrect.

# Relevant Biographies

## Dr. Glenn Terrell

Dr. Glenn Terrell serves as academic advisor to The Pacific Institute in curriculum creations, as well as research into the effectiveness of The Institute's programs. Dr. Terrell earned his B.A. in Political Science from Davidson College, his M.S. in Psychology from Florida State University, and a Ph.D. from the University of Iowa.

Dr. Terrell served as Chairman of the Department of Psychology, University of Colorado, Dean of the College of Liberal Arts and Sciences and as Dean of Faculties at the University of Illinois in Chicago before an 18-year tenure as President of Washington State University. He also served as President of the National Association of State Universities and Colleges, Commissioner for the State of Washington on the Western Interstate Commission for Higher Education, served on the Board for General Telephone Northwest and West for 23 years, was a Fellow for the Society for Research in Child Development, and a Fellow for the American Psychological Association.

Dr. Terrell has received numerous honorary degrees and awards, among them a listing in Who's Who in America: American Men of Science, and Distinguished Graduate of the Department of Psychology, University of Iowa. He has managed multimillion dollar technology transfers and faculty and student exchange programs throughout the world. Dr. Terrell's publication, The LETTER, is published quarterly by The Pacific Institute.

# A Brief Bibliography

*On Cognitive Theory and Research applicable to The Pacific Institute's services*

## General

Ashton & Webb (1986) *Making a Difference: Teacher Efficacy and Student Achievement.* Monogram. White Plains, NY: Longman.

Bandura, A. (1986) *Social Foundations of Thought and Action: A Social Cognitive Theory.* Englewood Cliffs, NJ: Prentice Hall.

Bandura, A. (1988, Dec) "Organizational Applications of Social Cognitive Theory." *Australian Journal of Management Review,* (Vol. 13, 2, 275-302). The University of New South Wales.

Bandura, A. (1989) "Human Agency in Social Cognitive Theory." *American Psychologist,* (Vol. 44, No. 9, 1175-1184). The American Psychological Association, Inc.

Bandura, A. (1991) "Self Efficacy Mechanism in Psychological Activation and Health Promoting Behavior." *Neurology of Learning Emotion and Affect.* (J. Madden, IV, Ed. 229-270) New York: Raven Press.

Bandura, A. (1991) "Self-Regulation of Motivation through Anticipatory and Self-Regulatory Mechanisms." In R.A. Dienstbiere (Ed.), *Perspectives on Motivation: Nebraska Symposium on Motivation* (Vol. 38, 69-164). Lincoln: University of Nebraska Press.

Bandura, A. (1994) "Self-Efficacy." *Encyclopedia of Human Behavior.* (Vol. 4) Academic Press.

Bandura, A. (1997) *Self-Efficacy. The Exercise of Control,* Freeman, New York, N.Y.

Bandura, A. (2001) "Special Cognitive Theory: An Agentic Perspective." *Annual Review of Psychology.* (52: 1 to 26)

Bandura, A., Barbaranelli, C., Caprara, V., and Pastorelli, C. (2001) "Self-Efficacy Beliefs as Shapers of Children's Aspirations and Career Trajectories." *Child Development,* January/February (Vol. 12, 187-206)

Bandura, A., Caprara, V. and Zsolnai, L. (2001) "Corporate Transgressions Through Moral Disengagement." *Journal of Human Values,* 6.1

Bandura, A. (2004) "Health Promotion by Social-Cognitive Theory." *Health Education and Behavior.* (Vol. 31, 143-164)

Barling, J. & Abel, M. (1983) "Self-Efficacy Beliefs and Performance." *Cognitive Theory and Research.* (Vol 7, 265-272).

Barling, J. & Beattie, R. (1983) "Self-Efficacy Beliefs and Sales Performance." *Journal of Organizational Behavior Management.* (Vol. 5, 41-51).

Dembo & Gibson (1984) "Teacher Efficacy." *Journal of Educational Psychology.* (Vol. 76, 569-582).

# A Brief Bibliography

Gardner, H. (1985) "The Mind's New Science." *In A History of The Cognitive Revolution.* New York: Basic Books.

Goldman, D. (1995) *"Emotional Intelligence."* New York, N.Y., Bantam Books

Mahoney, M. (1978) *Cognition and Behavior Modification.* Cambridge: Ballinger.

## Clinical Applications

Beck, A. (1979) *Cognitive Therapy and Emotional Disorders.* New York: New York Anniversary Library.

Beck, A. (1991) "Cognitive Therapy: A Thirty Years Retrospective." *American Psychologist.* (Vol. 46, No. 4, 368-375).

Beck, A., Emery, G., & Greenberg, R. *Anxiety Disorders and Phobias: A Cognitive Perspective.* New York: Basic Books.

Beck, A., Rush, J., Shaw, B., & Emery, G. (1979) *Cognitive Therapy of Depression.* New York: Guilford Press.

Ellis, H. (1975) *A New Guide to Rational Living.* North Hollywood, CA: Wilshire Books.

Niemark, J. (1987) "The Power of Positive Thinkers." Reprinted from *Success Magazine,* September 1987.

Rush, J., Beck, A., eds. (1988) "Cognitive Therapy." in Francis, A and Hales, R., eds. *Review of Psychiatry.* (Vol. 7). Washington, DC: American Psychiatric Press.

Seligman, Martin, E.P. (1990) *Learned Optimism.* New York: Pocket Books (Simon & Schuster).

## Goal-Setting – Performance Evaluation

Latham, G.P. & Wexley, K.N. (1994) *Increasing Productivity Through Performance Appraisal,* 2nd Edition. Reading, Massachusetts: Addison- Wesley Publishing Company.

Locke, E.A., & Latham, G.P. (1984) *Goal Setting: A Motivational Technique that Works.* Englewood Cliffs, NJ: Prentice-Hall.

# A Brief Bibliography

## Publications Which Are of Significant Value to The Pacific Institute

Bennis, Warren. (1994) *On Becoming A Leader,* Perseus Publication. Greenwald, Tony. (1995) *Implicit Social Cognition: Attitudes, Self Esteem and Stereotypes Through Social Support Training.* Psychological Review (102) 4-27.

Levin, Henry (1995) "Accomplishments of Accelerated Schools." National Center for Accelerated Schools Project, Stanford.

Marlatt. (1992) "Substance Abuse: Implications of a Biopsychosocial Model for Prevention Treatment and Relapse Prevention." Psychopharmacology. Smoll, Frank (1993) "Enhancement of Children's Self Esteem." *Journal of Applied Psychology.*

Zigler, E. (1993) "Using Research and Theory to Justify and Inform Head Start Expansion." *Social Policy Report, S.R.C.D.* (Vol. VII #2).

# A Brief Bibliography

# Key Concept Glossary

**Achieve** – To accomplish goals.

**Accepting Credit** – To agree that one has done something well.

**Accountable/Accountability** – Responsible; answerable for an outcome.

**Accurate Thinker** – One whose thoughts are accurate.

**Actualize** – To make happen.

**Adventure** – When one deliberately takes oneself out of one's old comfort zone, safely imprinting the new into one's subconscious, life becomes an adventure.

**Affirm/Affirmation/Affirmation Process** – A statement of fact; an internal, cognitive act that establishes a specific course, direction, outcome, or state of being for the future; a confirmation or ratification of a truth.

**Aggressive-Aggressive** – A personality trait; extraordinary ascendant.

**Ah-ha** – An insight; sudden realization of new information.

**Alpha State** – A state of physical and mental relaxation, while still being aware of what is going on around us. An ideal state for synthetic thought and creativity.

**Anxiety/Tension** – An unpleasant emotional state of apprehension, dread, or distress that exists oftentimes with no objective.

**Appetite For Growth** – Desire for improvement and self-development.

**Appraisal** – Analysis of the worth of self, others or other events.

**Aspiration** – Desire, hope, goal toward which one strives.

**Assimilate/Assimilation** – The incorporating of an idea or thought into the subconscious; the absorption or process of incorporating something external into one's body or cognitive processes; making new visions a part of our lives; e.g., one learns and can behaviorally manifest mastery of fundamental mathematical processes.

**Associate/Association** – Any learned, functional connection between two or more elements; a particular psychological experience evoked by a stimulus or event.

**Attitude(s)** – A consciously held belief or opinion; easiest to visualize if we picture ourselves leaning toward those things we like (positive) and away from those things we dislike (negative).

**Attitudinal Balance Scale** – A cognitive means of assessing one's positive or negative acts; e.g., positive self-talk (I am a capable person and people like me.).

**Authentic** – Genuine.

# Key Concept Glossary

**Autopilot** – An instrument that guides a ship or airplane, without active participation of a human pilot.

**Avoidant/Avoidant Behavior** – Response of moving away from undesirable events.

**Awareness** – An internal, subjective state of being cognizant or conscious of something; alertness; consciousness.

**Balance** – Appropriate attention to desirable values in one's life.

**Behavior(s)** – In terms of human activity, any measurable response of a person.

**Belief(s)** – An emotional acceptance of a proposition, statement, or doctrine.

**Belief Without Evidence** – Conviction; confidence in a truth; a faith in the ability to establish a goal without first considering the means whereby it will be achieved. (The means to an end follows the establishment of the end.) Once a goal is set, the RAS will actively seek opportunities/means to reach the goal.

**Beta State** – A state of being consciously alert; a general state of consciousness.

**Blind Spot** – see Scotoma.

**Capable** – mentally, emotionally and physically able to succeed at a task or challenge.

**Captain of the World** – An obsessive, compulsive behavior displaying a pervasive pattern of perfectionism and inflexibility; preoccupation with rules, details, lists, and schedules to the extent that the major point of the activity is lost.

**Causative/Causative Power** – A person's ability to make happen, which can influence or determine behavior.

**Central Cortex** – That portion of the brain associated with intellect, rather than emotion.

**Change Beyond Pretense** – Change driven by genuine desire only.

**Check and Balance System** – A distribution of power or influence, where each part keeps all other parts in check.

**Choose-To** – A voluntary act as opposed to a required act.

**Coaching/Managing Backwards** – A system of beginning with a behavior of those being managed.

**Co-Creativity** – Mutual or joint activity that transcends the ordinary and brings into being original ideas or outcomes.

**Coercive Motivation** – A drive based on fear and/or authority; a have-to.

# Key Concept Glossary

**Cognitive Dissonance** – An emotional state where two simultaneously held attitudes or cognitions are inconsistent, or there is a conflict between belief and overt behavior; thought conflict; the uncomfortable psychological condition created when a person experiences contradictory or conflicting opinions, beliefs, or attitudes at the same time. The resolution of this conflict is assumed to serve as the basis for attitude change, in that belief patterns are generally modified to be consistent with behavior. We can hold different attitudes without emotional disharmony as long as a situation does not occur where these attitudes are brought into direct confrontation with one another.

**Collective Truth** – ideas or beliefs held to be true by a group, team, or organization.

**Comfort Zone** – A limited area of perception and association wherein the individual/group can function effectively without experiencing uneasiness or fear; a limited, defined physical or psychological area in which a person feels at ease; self-regulating mechanism; anxiety arousal control.

**Compliant** – the state of bending one's own will to the wishes of another; going along with or agreeing with.

**Compulsive** – Super conscientious.

**Condition/Conditioning** – A predisposition to a mode of behavior given the appropriate stimulus.

**Confidential** – (Lat. confidere: to trust) A matter not to be divulged.

**Conflict** – (Lat. conflictus: to strike together) Incompatibility arising from opposing demands or impulses.

**Conscience** – One's inner beliefs of right and wrong.

**Conscious** – The aspect of mind that encompasses all that one is momentarily aware of; that is, those aspects of mental life that one is attending to.

**Constructive Motivation** – A positive and free-flowing drive on a want-to basis.

**Co-Responsibility** – Mutual or joint accountability; an obligation to act responsibly; shared responsibility for the outcomes of an act.

**Create/Creativity** – The quality of being creative; the ability to create.

**Creative Avoidance** – A movement away from an object or goal by means of the imagination with the intent of anxiety reduction. Procrastination is one way to creatively avoid a situation.

**Creative Energy** – The drive or associated stimulus to change, originating in the creative subconscious.

**Creative Genius** – The inherent ability to find solutions, theories, and ideas.

# Key Concept Glossary

**Creative Implementation** – The act of implementing solutions to a challenge or problem; vital step in the creative process.

**Creative Subconscious** – The source of mental processes that leads to solutions, ideas, conceptualizations, artistic forms, theories, or products that are unique and novel.

**Credibility** – Worthy of belief; sufficiently good to bring esteem or praise.

**Critical Listening** – Careful observation; hearing.

**Culture** – An organization's cumulative values, attitudes and beliefs.

**Current Reality** – All that which forms an integral part of what an individual believes to be real at the moment.

**Decision-Making** – The act of arriving at a course of action.

**Dignity and Respect** – Highly valued descriptions of a person.

**Discrepancy Production (Out of Order)** – To increase differences or inconsistencies; to deliberately attempt to create conflict.

**Discrepancy Reduction (Into Order)** – To decrease differences or inconsistencies; to increase levels of agreement; to move toward consistency.

**Dispute** – Disagreement, conflict

**Dissonance** – A state produced by two opposing views; see Cognitive Dissonance.

**Diversity** – Variety; not the same.

**Dominant Idea** – The prevailing view; the strongest picture; a ruling view or belief that is primary.

**Downward Spiral** – A pattern of belief in which one feels life is hostile, hopeless, and worthless.

**Drive** – A motivational state learned through association and directed toward a particular goal or objective; an inner urge that stimulates activity or inhibition.

**Effective/Effectiveness** – The ability to cause a result or outcome.

**Effectiveness Zone** – An area of thought or life where one feels confident, or at home.

**Efficacious** – Result producing behavior, able to gain ends through efficient means.

**Efficacy** – The power to produce results; a generative capability in which cognitive, social, and behavioral sub-skills are organized into integrated courses of action to secure innumerable purposes.

**Emotion** – An experience of feeling as opposed to thinking.

**End-Result Thinking** – End-result oriented, without knowing the "how" at the present moment.

# Key Concept Glossary

**Energy** – A force that drives one to a goal.

**Environment** – The combination of external physical surroundings that affect and influence the growth of organisms; the social and cultural conditions that affect the nature of an individual and community. May be a positive or negative environment.

**Environmental Comfort Zone** – The kind of environmental conditions to which we have been accustomed; e.g., the kind of clothes we wear, the car we drive, the home we live in.

**Environmental Self-Image** – A self-image relating to the current environment. This self-image may change with differing environments.

**Escalate** – To raise higher.

**Evaluate/Evaluation** – The determining of the value or worth of something; generally measured against a previous experience.

**Expectation** – The prospect of a future embodiment of an abstract idea; an anticipation.

**Experiential** – A state or activity through which one has learned and gained knowledge. Some (experientialists) argue that experience is the only or principal basis for knowledge.

**Familiarization Process** – A procedure designed to learn something.

**Fascination** – A strong feeling about something.

**Fear** – An emotional state in the presence or anticipation of a dangerous or noxious stimulus; an internal subjective experience that is often physically manifested.

**Feedback** – Psychological or sensory information about an event that modifies or reinforces future behavior; a reaction from the environment (including people) that serves as a basis for future action; generally, the functioning of one or more components of a system. A smile is an example of positive feedback; a frown, an example of negative feedback.

**Feedback Loop** – An operational mode/system that provides information about an ongoing operation or the state of the system at a point in time that may serve as a basis for future action or modification.

**Feel** – Sense of touch; an emotional awareness.

**First Nature** – Genetically inherited tendencies and traits.

**First Person** – A grammatical state in which a speaker (writer) refers to himself or herself or to a group including himself or herself.

**Flatten Out** – Behavior, performance or a view related to life that seems to be constant, continuing, and unchanging.

**Flexibility** – Pliable, a willingness to change.

# Key Concept Glossary

**Flick Back/Flick Up** – To borrow from a past, positive experience and bring the feeling into your present visualization of your affirmation; systematic desensitization.

**Forecast** – To predict.

**Forethought** – Thinking ahead.

**Four Levels of Happiness** – Activities, in ascending order, of joy: H1 – self; H2 – competition; H3 – the good of all; H4 – the ultimate.

**Four Levels of Self-Talk** – 1) Negative resignation; 2) "I should . . ."; 3) "I quit . . ."; 4) "I intend to . . ."

**Freedom For** – Choosing to do something, or make decisions, without fear of possible outcomes.

**Freedom From** – Choosing to do something, or make decisions, based on fear of possible outcomes.

**Free-Flow** – Unimpeded flow of thought and action coming from the subconscious.

**Free Will** – A state wherein one can make choices.

**Fulfillment** – The state of mind following the achievement of goals.

**Future as Now** – Seeing the future end-result as already having happened.

**Generativity** – Giving of oneself unselfishly, without needing to control; guiding and directing the next generation toward the fulfillment of sound goals.

**Gestalt** – Human beings are always working to complete the incomplete, working for closure; discrepancy production, discrepancy reduction; a view that psychological phenomena could only be understood if viewed as organized, structured wholes (Gestalten). The Gestalt point of view challenged the idea that phenomena could be introspectively broken down into primitive perceptual elements, for such analysis left out the notion of the whole unitary essence of the phenomena.

**Getting Used To** – Satisfied with the current state of affairs.

**GI/GO (Garbage In/Garbage Out)** – Meaningless or unwanted data. In the world of computers, if one puts misinformation into a computer, the only thing that can come out is the wrong answer. The subconscious mind functions in the same way. It does not make value judgments about what the programmer (or conscious mind) wants to put in.

**Goal(s)** – A sought end that may be actual and objective, or internal, subjective and operational; conceived future; distal goals are end-results, targets; proximal goals are near-term means to the end-result.

**Goal-Seeking Mechanism** – The process of setting goals. As humans, we are goal-seeking by design.

# Key Concept Glossary

**Goal-Setting** – The act of establishing what we want.

**Goal-Set Through** – Goal-setting beyond more proximal goals.

**Grooved Behavior** – Actions that become automatic; patterned.

**Growth Change** – The result of a process whereby development or progression has occurred; e.g., increased understanding.

**Habit(s)** – A learned act; a pattern of activity that has, through repetition, become automatic, fixed, and easily and effortlessly carried out.

**Half-Step Method** – Achieving a goal by two stages.

**Happiness** – The possession or attainment of what one considers to be good.

**Have-To** – Motivation by threat, fear or coercion.

**Hesitation/Doubt** – A state brought about by indecision.

**High-Performance People** – Individuals who are analytical and skeptical of information (truth) that comes their way, accept accountability for their own thinking and what goes on around them, and really feel they can make a difference in the world; scotoma busters.

**Hopeless** – Having no hope; refer to Downward Spiral.

**Hostility** – Anger, expressed or released.

**Humility** – A trait characterized by lack of pretense.

**I x V=R** – Imagination times vividness equals reality (in the subconscious).

**Idea(s)** – A product of thought.

**Ideal(s)** – Values about a perfect world.

**Image of Reality** – A cognitive process that operates as if one had a mental picture that was a representation of a real world scene; a construction; a picture in the mind.

**Imagery** – The formation of mental pictures through the use of the imaginative faculty.

**Imagination** – The ability to envision creative solutions.

**Imprint(ing)** – To establish firmly or impress on the mind or memory; a kind of restricted learning that takes place within a relatively compressed time span, generally is exceedingly resistant to extinction and reversal, and has a profound and lasting effect on later social behavior with respect to the stimulus objects for the behavior; an acquired behavioral response that is difficult to reverse and is normally released by a certain triggering stimulus or situation.

# Key Concept Glossary

**Incubation** – A period of time during which no conscious effort is made to solve problems, but which terminates with a solution for the subconscious.

**Inefficacious** - Behavior that does not produce results.

**Inhibitive Motivation** – A kind of restrictive motivation; a habit of acting on an, "I have to...or else something awful will happen to me," fear-pattern basis.

**Inner Concept/Construct** – Self-image; ideas or beliefs that come from within.

**Inner Strength** – A trait that comes with resilience.

**Insight** – Sudden comprehension, an "ah-ha."

**Integrity** – Adherence to moral and ethical principles; whole; sound; unimpaired.

**Internal (inner) Standard** – Your internal idea of who you are; that point at which you self-regulate your behavior, actions and performance. That which is "good enough" for you.

**Invent the Future** – To determine one's own desires for what lies ahead.

**Invent the "How"** – To determine how one's desires are to be achieved.

**Isolation** – A separateness, a feeling apart from others and events.

**Level of Expectation** – Our view of what we are capable of accomplishing.

**Literal Mechanism** – Actual meaning of words; not figurative.

**Logo Psychology** – A distinctive trademark of psychology.

**LO/LO (Lock-On/Lock-Out)** – An act whereby one has a limited perception of possibilities, problems, or solutions; a restricted, narrow, or singular view of alternatives. When we lock-on to an opinion, belief, or attitude as being the truth about something, we build scotomas to, or lock-out, contrary or different information. This is a defense mechanism that helps us to survive and provides security, but it also works against us when change and flexibility are needed.

**Locus of Control** – The degree to which an individual feels that he/she has control over the events that impact his/her life. A person who believes in self-reliance and self-centered accountability is said to have an internal locus of control. Conversely, one who feels victimized or not accountable for events professes an external locus of control.

**Magis** – Outrageous, forward thinking.

**Maintain Reality** – Being aware of the current state of affairs, and working to keep this current state the same.

**Mental Discipline** – Ability to think straight under all conditions.

# Key Concept Glossary

**Mentor** – Someone who advises and supports another to assist in their development.

**Mindset** – A pattern of thought.

**Motivation** – A need or drive to action based on incentive value of the goal or the expectation of reward or punishment. Emotional states have motivational properties.

**Necessity** – An imperative or indispensable requirement; an unavoidable need.

**Negative Attitude** – A pessimistic view; leaning away from something.

**Negative Creativity** – Ideas that come from your creative subconscious when you want to avoid something.

**Negative Forethought** – Pessimistic thinking ahead

**Negative Ideas** – Prone to pessimistic thoughts.

**Negative Picture** – A view of oneself that is reinforced by negative self-talk, resulting in a diminished self-image.

**Negative Self-Talk** – Conversation with one's self that is self-criticizing.

**Negative Wizard** – One who claims authority in making pessimistic pronouncements.

**Neuron** – A nerve cell.

**Newtonian Point of View** – Sir Isaac Newton, an English physicist and mathematician, was a key figure in the scientific revolution of the 17th century. Often called the father of modern physical optics, he also originated the three laws of motion and devised calculus. His view of creation is that all matter in the universe is subject to unchanging laws. When applied to the human condition, the conclusion is that man's destiny is limited. Newtonian leadership is a style that suggests that God created a perfect world with the exception of human beings.

**Normal/New Normal** - The way things usually are. A "new" normal is the new way things are.

**Option Thinking** – Thought which includes two or more interpretations.

**Order and Consistency of Goals** – The stability of life's goals; prioritizing what is important.

**Or Else** – Implicit threat for failure to act according to dictates.

**Out of Order/Into Order** – Discrepancy production/Discrepancy reduction.

**Override** – To establish one dominant belief in place of another.

**Paralysis of Will** – A state brought about by inability to act.

**Passive-Aggressive** – Aggressive behavior that appears to be benign.

# Key Concept Glossary

**Past/Present/Future Time Frame** – The three areas of time in which humans can choose from to create their realities.

**Perceive** – An awareness that comes about through sensory or extrasensory processes.

**Perception** – Those mental processes that give coherence and unity to sensory input; a conscious event initiated by some external or internal event; an organized complex dependent on a host of other factors (attention, constancy, motivation, illusion, etc.).

**Performance** – An act or behavior of any kind.

**Performance Reality** – How one acts and performs based on one's currently dominant self-image.

**Philosophy of Life** – A set of assumptions about one's purpose in life.

**Picture(s)** – A detailed vision of current affairs or the future.

**Positive Attitude** – An optimistic view; leaning toward something.

**Positive Motivation** – Moved to action by an optimistic view of life.

**Positive Self-Talk** – Conversation with one's self that stresses good qualities, characteristics, and achievements.

**Positive Wizard** – A "who-said of the greatest magnitude" who supports and encourages.

**Possibility Thinking** – A cognitive, reflective, and creative process by which one considers all alternatives of a given situation. This process may also include an assessment of the reality, veracity, impact, and relative weight of all elements that compose a situation or condition.

**Post-Dissonance** – An emotional state of uncertainty as to the merit of an act following its completion; sometimes referred to as buyer's remorse.

**Potential** – Having the strong possibility for development into a state of actuality; possible or in the making; latent.

**Pre-Dissonance** – An emotional state whereby one is disposed to act; however, movement toward, or the completion of, the act is dissuaded by uncertainty as to the merit therein or the benefit thereof. Generally, constant overriding reassurance from an external source is required to complete the act.

**Present Reality** – The way things are perceived to be in the current time frame.

**Present Tense** – Current state of being or existence, usually expressed in grammar by the use of a verb ("I am a considerate, loving person."). Stating the future as now.

**Pressure** – see Anxiety; Tension.

# Key Concept Glossary

**Problem** – A challenge, difficulty needing a solution.

**Process of Thought** – The interaction of the conscious, subconscious, and creative subconscious.

**Procrastination** – To defer action or delay; prolong; postpone; a type of creative avoidance.

**Progressive** – Actions generated by new and better ideas.

**Psycholinguistics** – A study of the relationship between language and the cognitive or behavioral characteristics of those who use it; the power that words have on our behavior.

**Purpose In Life** – Reason for existing.

**Push-Push Back** – When one is pushed, one unconsciously pushes back.

**Pygmalion Effect** – The effect by which people come to behave in ways that correspond to others' expectations concerning them.

**Quality** – An attribute; a degree of excellence.

**Read-Picture-Feel** – Three concepts important to effective affirmations; critical components to effective imprinting of affirmations or ideas.

**Realistic** – Conforming to a common-sense notion of what is possible.

**Reality** – All that forms an integral part of what an individual believes to be real; the perception and assessment of the environment in ways that coordinate with one's social and cultural schemes and values; an awareness of the environment and the need to accommodate to the demands thereof.

**Reflective Thinking** – A casting back or returning to a thing; an introspection; a reflection on a previous experience or event and its significance.

**Reiterate(ing)** – To repeat; the action of repeating.

**Resilience** – Ability to bounce back in the face of adversity.

**Respect** – See Dignity

**Restrictive** – Whatever blocks the ability to see beyond current reality

**Restrictive Motivation** – Motivation by threats, fear, or coercion; have-to or else.

**Restrictive Zones** – Subjective areas of thought processes that interfere with and limit rational thought or action.

**Reticular Activating System (RAS)** – A network of neurons in the brainstem involved in consciousness, regulation of breathing; the transmission of sensory stimuli to higher brain centers; a primary alert to awareness network that may function differently in varying degrees of consciousness.

# Key Concept Glossary

**Risk Avoidant** – A trait of a person or group to steer clear of risk.

**Rite of Passage** – An event or ceremony with significant internal meaning and associated belief. A one-time affirmation.

**Root Cause** – Primary cause, or causes, of a specific behavior patterns that are reflected in performance.

**Routinize(d)** – To make a course of action habitual.

**Sanction** – To give approval to; to agree with.

**Sanity** – A mental state whereby one is capable of adequate, adaptive functioning on a day-to-day basis; soundness of mind and judgment.

**Sarcasm** – A caustic remark.

**Scotoma** – An expression to indicate that one fails to see or is blind to alternatives and therefore can see only limited possibilities; a sensory locking out of information from our environment. We develop scotomas to the truth about our world and ourselves because of our preconceived ideas, other people's preconceived ideas (flat worlds or cultural trances), and conditioning. We do not see or are blind to certain things.

**Second Nature** – Acquired habit or tendency, so deeply ingrained as to appear automatic.

**Selective Information Gathering** – A process involved in situations whereby attention is focused on positive or negative stimulus input; assumes a predisposition toward the stimulus based on preconceived value judgments.

**Selective Perceiver** – Someone whose perception of an event or person is governed by personal attitudes.

**Self-Actualize** – Resorting to initiative.

**Self-Concept** – One's opinion of self-worth.

**Self-Correct** – To adjust one's own behavior.

**Self-Determined** – To decide, take control, of one's own being and actions. To make one's own decisions about the future.

**Self-Efficacy** – One's appraisal of one's own ability to cause, to bring about, make happen; one's own power or capacity to produce the desired effect; a combination of one's self-esteem, skills, and resources; task specific.

**Self-Esteem** – The degree to which one values oneself; the worth/value of the picture.

**Self-Examination** – The process one uses in arriving at one's worth or one's opinion.

# Key Concept Glossary

**Self-Fulfilling Prophecy** – A phenomenon wherein one's prediction about the future may come to pass, because of the belief that underlies the prediction.

**Self-Image** – The accumulation of all the attitudes and opinions one has perceived about oneself that form a subconscious picture of oneself; the imagined self; the self that one supposes oneself to be; the picture; self-regulation.

**Self-Motivation** – Energy for action comes from within.

**Self-Regulation** – Adhering to and following an internal standard.

**Self-Sabotage** – To contribute to one's own downfall.

**Self-Talk** – An act whereby one evaluates or assesses one's behavior; how one talks or reaffirms to oneself when one reacts to one's own evaluation, or others' evaluations of one's performance. Self-talk may have an affirming influence in establishing self-image.

**Sense(s)** – To become aware of something. In humans, to perceive through sight, sound, smell, touch and taste.

**Serendipitous** – Come upon by accident rather than by design.

**Servomechanism** – An ability to evaluate behavior in order to make adjustments designed to exercise desired control.

**Setting Priorities** – To develop a plan of attaching relative importance to actions to be taken.

**Significant** – To make a difference; may be positive or negative.

**Skeptical** – Being wary of something done or said. Discriminating, as in "skeptical listener."

**Smart** – Possessing intelligence; ability to think and learn.

**Solve Conflict** – To eliminate or resolve; completing goals.

**Spirit of Intent** – The intent or motivating force behind one's acts, words, or deeds.

**Stability** – A steady, predictable state of affairs.

**Standards** – A degree or level of requirement, excellence or attainment; what you perceive the level of quality or excellence to be. It is critical for organizations to clearly articulate and define their expectations or standards, because not everyone will operate from the same level if their picture is not clearly defined.

**Stress/Tension** – A state of psychological tension produced by physical, and social forces and pressures.

**Structured Affirmation Process** – A well-ordered plan for one's goal-setting and goal achievement.

# Key Concept Glossary

**Structured Process** – A system for accomplishing one's activities.

**Stuck / Unstuck** – To be imprisoned, resulting in inaction followed by thoughts or actions that move one forward.

**Subconscious** – The level of mind through which material passes on the way toward full consciousness; an information store containing memories that are momentarily outside of awareness but that can easily be brought into consciousness.

**Subconscious Reality** – Real circumstances of which we are unaware.

**Sub-Goals** – Goals of current, lesser, immediate importance whose accomplishment is required for main goals to be achieved.

**Success/Successful** – The state of reaching goals; goal achievement.

**Superstition** – Belief in something that has no basis in fact.

**"Sure Enough" Principle** – By believing something will happen, it will. "You expect a bad day and, sure enough, you get a bad day."

**Systematic Desensitization** – A technique used to reduce fear (or other maladaptive response) by frequent and organized exposure to the feared object.

**Teleological** – A doctrine or belief that a final cause exists, that there is a purpose to being, that all move toward a goal or final destination, and that order in the universe is not random.

**Tension** – An emotional state characterized by restlessness and anxiety; a mental state where one is thwarted from achieving an end.

**The next time . . .** – A vow to better performance at the next opportunity.

**Third-Party Affirmation** – To verbalize good opinions about a person, in the presence of another person.

**Thought Patterns** – Organization of thoughts, reflected in actions and performance.

**Threat** – Words or actions that frighten or imperil.

**Three Dimensions of Thought** – Human beings think in three dimensions: words, triggering pictures, which cause emotions.

**True (Truth)** – A characteristic of a proposition, statement, or belief that corresponds with reality, as it is known, possibly based on an earlier evaluative process.

**Trust** – Belief in the honesty and good intentions of others.

**Under-Living** – Not living up to one's potential.

**Unwarranted Self-Esteem** – Self-esteem not based on the actual value of the self.

# Key Concept Glossary

**Value(s)** – Quality of worth, merit; custom or ideal that people desire as an end or means of itself; something of excellence or importance.

**Vision** – A dream, aspiration, goal, or aim relating to the future.

**Visualize (Visualization)** – To recall or form mental images from the imagination; to make perceptive to the mind; forethought; mental stimulation. Creative visualization is often a means of unblocking or dissolving barriers that we ourselves have created.

**Vivid** – Bright; intense; living; lifelike.

**Vow** – A solemn pledge, promise, or commitment of oneself to an act, service, or condition.

**Want To** – To desire to do something.

**Warranted Self-Esteem** – Self-esteem based on the actual value of the self.

**Whiteheadian Point of View** – Alfred North Whitehead, an English philosopher and mathematician, taught philosophy at Harvard in the 1920s and established a reputation as a critic of scientific materialism that he retained until his death. His approach to human behavior suggests that man is not locked in to a condition, but can co-create, with God, a better life through the exercise of free choice. Whiteheadian leadership is based on this belief that creation is ongoing.

**Who-Said** – An authority figure to whose word you give sanction.

**Words-Pictures-Emotions** – Three critical components to the affirmation process.

**Worthless** – Having no worth; being worth "less" than before.

**Zone of Proximity** – Nearness in time or distance (with reference to goals).

# Key Concept Glossary